Dr. Patricia Carrington is a clinical psychologist, researcher and psychotherapist specializing in the use of stress management techniques. Formerly a Lecturer in the Department of Psychology at Princeton University, she is presently Associate Clinical Professor of Psychiatry at UMDNJ-Robert Wood Johnson Medical School in New Jersey, where she instructs medical students in how to relate to patients in a manner that honors their dignity as human beings.

Her widely acclaimed, medically approved method of meditation, known as Clinically Standardized Meditation (CSM), is used by numerous organizations throughout the world, and individuals from all walks of life have found that CSM and the technique of Releasing described in this book can greatly reduce stress and improve the quality of their lives.

At present Dr. Carrington divides her professional time between work with patients, teaching, research and writing. She is the author of *The Book of Meditation* and the *Learn to Meditate Kit*, also published by Element Books.

Also available by Patricia Carrington

Learn to Meditate kit
The Book of Meditation

The Power of Letting Go

A Practical Approach to
Releasing the Pressures in Your Life

Patricia Carrington, Ph.D.

ELEMENT
Shaftesbury, Dorset • Boston, Massachusetts • Melbourne, Victoria

This new, revised edition first published in the UK in 1999 by
Element Books Limited
Shaftesbury, Dorset SP7 8BP

Published in the USA in 1999 by
Element Books, Inc.
160 North Washington Street, Boston MA 02114

Published in Australia in 1999 by
Element Books and distributed
by Penguin Australia Ltd
487 Maroondah Highway, Ringwood,
Victoria 3134

Cover design by Slatter-Anderson
Design by Roger Lightfoot
Typeset by Bournemouth Colour Press, Parkstone
Printed and bound in Great Britain by JW Arrowsmith Ltd, Bristol, Avon

British Library Cataloguing in Publication
data available

Library of Congress Cataloging in Publication
data available

ISBN 1 86204 329 9

To the memory of
my very dear
friend-brother

Brad Wilson

CONTENTS

INTRODUCTION

Throughout history sages have advised us to go with the flow of life, to accept "what is" even as we work diligently to improve our lives.

On some levels we may recognize the truth in this advice, and at times we may even notice the ironic fact that when we no longer need something desperately, when we stop demanding it from life and striving for it urgently, then this same thing may be handed us by fate. When we have made peace with the ways of the universe, whatever these may be, then fortune may suddenly smile on us and graciously bestow what we had been struggling so futilely to achieve. It is as though a divine force takes care of us when we are in harmony with its ways. This does not happen with the same ease when we are fighting against the tide.

Over the years that I have been working as a psychotherapist I have encountered many clients who understood the wisdom of the "letting go" principle and who have sincerely tried to relinquish their need to control the uncontrollable. Those few who have succeeded in doing this have found their lives far more serene and enriching. Unfortunately, however, for most of us letting go of the sense of urgency that pervades our lives remains an ideal to be pursued rather than an everyday reality.

For a long time I couldn't understand why it was so difficult to put the principle of "letting go" into practice, but gradually the answer came to me. The great religious and philosophical traditions which have advocated letting go of our overattachment to outcomes have almost universally failed to give us clear instructions on exactly how to do this. They have provided us with a meaningful ideal, but without the practical tools to make it work.

For a number of years I sought a technique which would put this philosophy into action and then I found the answer in the "Releasing" method which I teach in this book. This method not only provides the "how to" of letting go but serves to correct a common misconception about the meaning of "acceptance." In my practice I have watched numerous clients mistakenly try to live a life of "acceptance" as though "acceptance" were the same thing as "resignation." This is far from the case, but because they did not understand this fact, instead of going with the flow of life as the philosophy of "letting go" advocates, these people determinedly resigned themselves to an undesirable fate, protested little if at all (trying to be stoic and keep a stiff upper lip no matter what), and denied their wish for adventure, their normal drive to accomplish, and their eagerness for life. An attitude of resignation effectively deadens enthusiasm, excitement and other life-enhancing feelings. It can create a deep underlying resentment which leads to depression. Far from the gracious and loving handing over of those life events which we cannot control to a higher power or to life as it is, resignation is the reverse of true letting go.

The Releasing method was designed to bring about true letting go. It works to bring inner peace to those who use it by freeing them to deal effectively with life's challenges—not by asking them to resign themselves to defeat. Releasing is remarkably compatible with the oriental notion of yielding in order to achieve a goal. The idea of winning by moving with a force exerted against one rather than opposing it with counter force is implicit in such martial arts as aikido, judo, karate, and the original form of tai chi.

For students of Eastern philosophies, the paradoxical or "opposite" nature of Releasing also appears intriguingly similar to the principles of the traditional Zen koans, or riddles. The koan poses an unanswerable question—one which startles the person to whom it is addressed into letting go of his or her usual ways of thinking or acting. The surprised student is then said to achieve a new perspective, or "enlightenment." In Releasing there is also a strong element of surprise as the person using it startles herself by her own self-questions. The unique method of mental questioning employed in Releasing can instantly switch the mind so that a radically different, more objective view of any situation emerges.

I found it easy and natural to translate the letting go principle into a workable, step-by-step method because I had for so many years worked to make meditation training simple and practical for the average person. Some powerful modern forms of meditation are now available to the public that are effective for almost everyone and I am pleased that I have been instrumental in developing one of these new forms, Clinically Standardized Meditation (CSM). CSM has been successfully used for over twenty years in medical settings and corporations worldwide and for individuals in all walks of life. It is presently available as a home-study course in the *Learn to Meditate Kit*, and in my book, *The Book of Meditation*, I describe the astonishing ability of modern meditation to transform the lives of those who use it. This ability has particular relevance to the Releasing method too.

Because of my extensive experience with meditation it was exciting for me to discover that the sense of flowing with the tide fostered by the Releasing technique has much in common with the open, accepting attitude created by meditation. Both of these techniques have been profoundly effective for me as well as for those I work with. Although the means used in Releasing to achieve a state of open acceptance is very different from that used in meditation, the two techniques share the same goal and when they are used to complement each other this combination can bring about a profound shift in one's entire outlook on life. While either Releasing or meditation can be used alone effectively, and often are, when combined their positive effects may even be multiplied. Appendix E presents this combination.

As I proceeded to explore various uses of the Releasing technique, I discovered that the strategic self-questioning device used to help people "release" lent itself to variations along lines that at first I had scarcely suspected. Using my background as a therapist I was able to devise a number of special strategies which I call the "unlocking tactics." These are to use when the going gets tough, when it is extremely difficult to let go of what

I call an "overpush" to achieve goals or to let go of strong negative feelings. The unlocking tactics can instantly free the mind so that it achieves a radical shift in perspective. I teach these strategies in this book, as well as a new and effective method for dealing with unwanted emotions. I also teach a technique for holding on to one's constructive goals while simultaneously letting go of any self-defeating over-involvement with those goals. These methods are all presented in the following pages, ready for you to put to use immediately.

When I was developing the Releasing method, my late husband, Harmon S. Ephron, M.D., a distinguished professor of psychiatry at UMDNJ-Robert Wood Johnson Medical School, used Releasing extensively in his clinical work and was a great advocate of the method. He found it remarkably useful for his patients, and he and I together soon began to amass information on the clinical applications of Releasing. We then shared this information with other therapists who in turn used the technique with their patients. Releasing workshops for the general public became a regular part of my work in the stress reduction field. As I conducted them I became increasingly aware of the many implications of the technique.

As well as being related to many different spiritual traditions, the self-questioning device used for Releasing also has origins in contemporary scientific work. Psychologists, psychiatrists, and other specialists in human behavior have frequently observed that in order to influence someone to do a specific thing, it is sometimes useful to ask that person to do exactly the *opposite*. Others have noticed that the human mind occasionally needs to be distracted in order to relinquish its bulldog grip on an unproductive solution to a problem. No existing technique used by those in the psychological field is identical to the Releasing method, however. Releasing gives us a much-needed device for putting into practice inherently sensible principles which have previously been impossible for many people to translate into action.

This book draws heavily on the experience of participants in my Releasing workshops and on that of those patients in psychotherapy to whom I have taught this method. Because the technique is strongly influenced by my background as a clinical psychologist, my own approach differs from other methods, such as spiritually oriented approaches, for helping people let go of their emotional overpush or overattachment. These other methods, however, when sensitively applied, very valuable. As I often point out with respect to meditation, there is no one way to teach a method designed to foster human development. The innovations I have introduced into the instruction of Releasing I find very useful indeed but, like meditation, the basic act of releasing can be taught in a number of different ways. Some ways will be more suitable for a given individual than others; all of them can contribute to our ultimate mastery of this vital principle.

As I have been gathering material for these pages, the Releasing technique has continued to expand as newcomers have lent their enthusiasm and talents to the work at hand, and new variations on the basic unlocking tactics have been developed, tested, and put to use. I include some of these in Appendix D and invite you to use them as valuable additions to your collection of "unlocking tactics."

I hope that the spirit of inquiry that has marked the initial era of the Releasing method will continue, and that this book will introduce many new and innovative users to the exciting possibilities of this method and allow them to experience the power of letting go.

Patricia Carrington, Ph.D.
Kendall Park, New Jersey, USA

HOW TO GET STARTED WITH YOUR "RELEASING" PRACTICE

What You Can Expect

Welcome to a new way of looking at life—your life!

You may already recognize the value of "acceptance." At the least you have heard a great deal about it. This philosophy underlies many successful self-development programs and is the cornerstone of the Twelve Step program used by Alcoholics Anonymous and its "relatives," those groups successfully addressing various other forms of addiction. It has also been a primary teaching of the great spiritual traditions throughout recorded history.

People are often advised, and wisely so, to LET GO of their need to change what cannot be changed and to concentrate on those things that they can control in their lives. This advice has saved countless people from self-recrimination and self-forcing that leads to depression, stress-related illnesses and addictive behavior, among other serious problems. It has also helped many to face with equanimity the difficulties and frustrations of everyday life.

Probably all of us know in our hearts that "letting go" of our insistence on controlling what is beyond our reach at any given moment is a key to peace of mind. How to go about achieving this desirable state is another matter, however. Letting go (acceptance) is certainly easier said than done!

Answering the "how" of acceptance is what Releasing is all about. This technique is a down-to-earth, practical tool for achieving the state of inner peace that we all desire.

Suggestions for Beginners

When you first learn the Releasing technique you will be asked to select some simple everyday situations to "release" on. These will be your first steps, like getting your toes wet when you enter the water before plunging in for a full swim. Later on you will learn to release successfully on the major problems in your life, but first things come first.

To assist you in getting started, I have assembled the following list of common problems that people face. Because these frustrating situations respond readily to the Releasing technique, I suggest that you read over this list before learning the method. It will help you get in the mood to "release," and will give you many ideas to work with as you begin reading this book.

List of Common Frustrations to Release on:

copier is out of paper
waiting in line
short of cash
machine you need displays "out of order" sign
ripped garment at last minute
bad investment
luggage damaged
can't find the tickets
taxes due tomorrow
speeding ticket
loud neighbors
unexpectedly expired service contract
new car's fender is scraped

didn't get that raise
constant busy signal
can't find contact lens or eyeglasses
overdue bills are piling up
lost important message
teller's window closed
red lights at every corner
deadline looms
one more parking ticket
unreasonable co-workers
in-laws
computer down for rest of day
awful haircut
expired driver's license
out of toothpaste this morning
airport fogged in
check bounced
highway construction en route
inconsiderate smokers
can't untangle knot
spilled coffee
missed last bus

Surprising as it may seem, once you have learned to "release" you will easily be able to let go of the distress associated with such situations as the above. This will allow you to handle them much more effectively. All you need do to achieve this desirable state is follow the instructions in this book. I wish you an enjoyable experience with this new way of looking at things!

Part 1

LEARNING TO RELEASE

When you have finished reading part 1 of this book, you will know how to "release"—but only if you recognize an essential point.

Releasing is an experience, *not a theory. You won't know what it is unless you go through the process yourself in a step-by-step fashion. To try to understand Releasing by reading a description of it is the same as trying to find out what the experience of jogging is (or playing the piano, or singing, or meditating, or whatever) by reading a book that tells you about these things. That simply doesn't work.*

This book is not about *Releasing—it offers you the opportunity to experience this method firsthand. It must therefore be read in a special way. You will need to become a participant and give yourself the chance to try the exercises in order to discover how it feels to release. After that, you can decide how you may want to use it. You will have tried it on for size.*

Chapter 1

WHAT IS RELEASING?

A Zen tale tells of two pious monks who were on their yearly pilgrimage through the mountains when they caught sight of a young woman by the edge of a brook. She had fallen from her horse and injured her foot. In the meantime her animal had wandered off, crossed the brook by itself, and stood grazing indifferently on the far bank.

Spying the two monks, the young woman hastily signaled to them and begged them to carry her across the steam, which she could not cross alone because of her injury. She was anxious to remount her horse and ride to safety before dark.

Despite the young woman's pleas, the younger of the two monks declined to assist her because of his vow of chastity which forbade him ever touching a woman. The elder monk reacted differently. Realizing how few travelers ever came this way and aware of the dangers that might beset the young woman at nightfall, he swiftly carried her across the brook, placed her on her horse, and made sure that she started safely on her journey home.

The two monks then resumed their pilgrimage. When they had traveled down the road a way, the younger one, becoming more upset each moment by what he had seen, was finally unable to contain himself any longer and cried out to his companion, "I cannot believe what I saw! You broke your vow of chastity by carrying a woman in your arms!"

The elder monk turned to him and with a quiet smile replied, "But, little brother, I let go of her ten miles back!"

This, in a sense, is the story of the human race. Like the older monk, we can sometimes respond to a problem by shedding our rigid ways of behaving so that we can handle the matter and go on from there. All too often, however, we behave like the younger monk—trapped in inflexible notions and overwhelmed by distress. This reaction can destroy our peace of mind and undermine our effectiveness. How to rid ourselves of negative feelings that hang on and incapacitate us is the subject of this book.

At times you may drop such burdensome feelings because of a change of circumstances. Suppose you know your day is going to be particularly difficult. Someone who works with you is irritable and heavy demands are being made on you—many things have gone wrong and no one else is able to deal with them. Although you may have been in a good mood before, you now find yourself upset. You feel angry, anxious, depressed, or tense.

Then comes an unexpected event. In the middle of this harassing day you receive a phone call which brings some good news. You discover that something that you really wanted has occurred. For a few minutes you take time out to enjoy this pleasant announcement; then you calm down and return to the job at hand.

The situation and the people around you are unchanged. You face the same frustrating circumstances and excessive demands as you did before. But now problems which ten minutes earlier were overwhelming have suddenly become manageable. Other people's bad tempers don't get to you anymore, and as those around you see you acting differently, they begin to modify their behavior and become easier to deal with.

This change in the tone of the day is due to only one thing. You now see, hear, and experience your surroundings differently. Your perception is *all* that had to change for you to become more effective.

While a pleasant surprise like this will help you shift gears, it is obviously not practical to wait around for a piece of good news to help you solve your problems. What you need is something—some device—that can do this for you exactly when you need it most. You want a method you can depend on to lift you out of a vicious circle and start a constructive one.

It is exactly for this purpose that the releasing technique has been developed. Releasing is a method for rapid, on-the-spot change. It is simple, takes seconds to do, and can defuse problems in your life as they arise.

The technique works in this manner because it corrects a common distortion of thinking. When confronted by frustration, we often feel driven to do battle—to solve a problem quickly and at all costs. If the problem fails to yield to this initial pushing, we then assume that the answer lies in pushing *that much harder*.

Unfortunately, pushing harder can be self-defeating. In fact, it almost invariably makes matters worse. When we overpush this way, we find ourselves caught in a desperate effort to mend with a sledge-hammer something that the gentle touch of a little finger could handle far more effectively.

Surprisingly enough, when we *stop* our overpush, new options open up and the situation becomes manageable. The procedure is similar to the method an experienced automobile driver uses to pull a car out of a skid. The most effective way to do this is to turn the wheels *with the skid*—not to fight against it. In the same way, a bicycle rider learns almost instinctively that when balance begins to go and the bike tilts dangerously, if the wheel is turned in the direction in which the bike is leaning, the vehicle immediately rights itself. As with the driver and bike rider, Releasing encourages us to *go with* the problem to regain our emotional balance.

This is, of course, exactly the reverse of what we've been taught to do when faced with difficulties. You will understand it fully only after reading the following chapters and learning to release—but the approach can be likened to the strategies of the oriental martial arts. By employing Releasing you are able to sidestep an opposing force without having to waste energy applying unnecessary counterforce. As a result, those who have mastered the art of Releasing and use it during an argument find themselves quietly in control. This is similar to the effectiveness seen in the martial arts of aikido, judo, karate, and the original form of Tai Chi. Such methods teach how to counter physical force directed against a person by a maneuver that at first seems like yielding, but which is actually a disarming protective device. When you learn the releasing method, it is as though you had acquired a mental judo, leaving you steady and balanced in the face of confrontation.

The following examples will give you an idea of how this works.

Example 1

You have missed your plane and have to rearrange your plans at great inconvenience. Instead of becoming angry or frustrated, you immediately make use of the new technique you have learned—Releasing. As soon as you stop struggling mentally against the inconvenience involved, you are able to handle the matter easily and efficiently.

What has happened is similar to what sometimes occurs when people feel they are drowning. If they thrash about, their very struggle can cause them to drown. But if they stop trying so desperately to save themselves, they may float to safety or may even discover that all the time they have been swimming in shallow enough water to touch bottom.

Example 2

You return home in a great mood because you have had an unusually pleasant day. You then discover that a member of your household is annoyed at you for something that happened previously. That bad mood could spoil your day.

You don't want this to happen, so you use the Releasing technique to "defuse" the incident. The minute you let go of your intensity, your mind clears. You no longer feel like a robot forced to respond automatically to someone who is pushing your anger button. Now, free to consider the situation objectively, you can see that the other person himself is under pressure. You decide to ask a few questions about *his* day. Because you ask in an easy, nonpushing manner, the air begins to clear. Having released, you are able to wait out the situation instead of letting it get you down. You have not surrendered to the other person, nor have you been hostile—but you have gained his cooperation.

Example 3

You are working to get a particularly "important" project done in a way you consider really worthy of yourself. Whether you are preparing for a dinner party, finishing a creative piece of work, helping someone solve her problems, or engaged in another task with special meaning for you, you are aiming so high that you find yourself tensing up.

As soon as you release on the situation, you let go of this overpush. When you do this, your perspective changes. You now find yourself zeroing in on the task with a concentration that was notably absent just a few minutes ago. Before, your attention was deflected by thoughts about possible negative consequences. Now you are no longer distracted by these thoughts, and your ability to handle the task takes a qualitative leap. You find yourself at your very best.

When under pressure, people frequently occupy themselves with anxious thoughts about what may happen to them if the situation turns out badly. These thoughts distract from the task at hand. The reason they can focus on tasks more efficiently after releasing is because, having let go of these negative thoughts, their minds are free to concentrate on what to *do*, rather than what can go wrong. Paradoxically, removing excess pressure to accomplish can result in greater accomplishment!

Example 4

Someone close to you is taken ill on a weekend when medical assistance is hard to find. You are frightened about his undiagnosed condition. To cope with your anxiety, you release on your *overpush* to be of help. This allows you to perceive the reality of his condition more clearly. Now you recognize more alternatives. There are ways to find help which had not occurred to you before when you were overwhelmed by your feelings. You are now able to assist the ill person more effectively, and your newfound calm is conveyed to him. He, too, benefits from your releasing.

Your Releasing Ability

Before you start learning the Releasing strategy, you may be interested to know that you probably have already had Releasing experiences at some time in your life. Perhaps you recall being in the middle of an argument when you suddenly stopped and thought, "Wait a minute. *What am I doing?* This isn't that important!"

If you've ever done this, you know that your perspective then took a 180-degree turn. It was like getting a breath of fresh air. You could now view the incident clearheadedly. As a result, you were better able to cope with your adversary. *You had released.*

Or you may recall a time when you had to meet a tough deadline. The closer the deadline approached, the more upset you got and the less efficient you became. Then perhaps you made an about-face. "Hey, what's going on here?" you said to yourself. "Why am I getting so worked up?" If you did that, you will remember that your sense of urgency dropped away. You were then able to mobilize your energies more effectively. You had released.

At one time or another, many of us have devised ways of letting go of our overpush when faced with difficulties. As soon as we were able to do this, we felt better and functioned better.

There is a drawback to such self-devised methods of releasing, however. Like all other intuitive reactions, they are not under our own control, so we don't know how to create these spontaneous releases when we need them. Also, when an event is emotionally charged for us, spontaneous releasing is least apt to occur. At such times we can be so upset we don't think of letting go.

Releasing and Clarity

Releasing permits us to reach clarity of thinking that is new to some people. As we use this technique, a balanced viewpoint emerges as naturally as the reflection of trees in the still waters of a mountain lake. When we are emotionally upset, it is as though the waters of such a lake were stirred up by a storm.

Lashed by the storm, the images of the trees break into a thousand fragments. Flashes of color dart across the water and if we catch sight of a leaf here, a branch there, or even the shadow of a tree, we are fortunate, for these are soon dissolved into chaos. But when the storm is over and the rain no longer churns up the lake, then a clear and unmistakable picture emerges. The trees and the immensity of the sky are now depicted *in absolute clarity* before us.

This is precisely what happens when the turbulence of our emotions is removed by the simple expedient of releasing. The act of releasing leaves our minds clear, balanced, immensely wide in scope, and highly effective. We now see the nature of the problem before us and are free to take suitable action.

In summary, we release to achieve greater pleasure and increased effectiveness in the things we do.

A Twofold Process

The method you are about to learn has two aspects to it. First, Releasing is a specific technique to use when you choose to handle a problem or improve the quality of a life experience. Second, it is a means of creating a change in your habitual long-term response to stressful situations.

Once learned, Releasing can exert a strong influence on your life apart from whether or not you consciously choose to release. The practice retrains your reflexes so that you can now respond to stress in a different way than you did formerly. For many people who have learned to release, things simply go more smoothly than they did before.

An example of how these two aspects of Releasing can operate is illustrated by the experience of an executive of a large communications corporation who had taken an early plane to get to an important 11.00 A.M. meeting in another city. The airport had fogged over and his plane had landed in a different city instead. There was no way he could make the meeting.

This executive reports that if the incident had happened before he had learned Releasing, he would have been beside himself with agitation. Now he calmly made a phone-call, rescheduled the meeting with his colleague, and turned his mind to other matters. He was impressed by the fact that even before he started to release consciously, he was already much less upset by the incident than he would have been before he had learned the Releasing technique. When he did consciously let go of wanting to change the fact that he had missed his appointment, the problem no longer bothered him.

You can therefore look forward to some fundamental changes in your habitual reactions to stress as you go along. A Releasing attitude will become a regular part of your life.

The Next Step

We have now talked about Releasing; the next step is to learn how to do it.

Part 1 of this book will teach you how to release and presents the special tactics you will need for difficult situations. You don't need to remember these strategies as you come to them, for they are summarized in the Table of Tactics in the back of the book. This table will help you locate a suitable strategy for any problem you face at a moment's notice.

Part 2 will describe people who have used Releasing to cope with many different types of life problems. Their widely varying experiences will give you a clear idea of the Releasing process in action and provide you with many opportunities to practice releasing.

Part 3 will offer practical suggestions. This is the basic application section of the book. Here you will learn how to use Releasing both for solving problems and for personal growth.

Now you are ready to learn to release. . . .

Chapter 2

HOW TO RELEASE

Releasing is easily learned, so that many people release the first time they try the technique. Others take longer, but eventually everyone learns.

In the beginning, you will use the Releasing technique for very simple situations. These are your first steps, like learning to crawl before you walk. As you go along, you will be using the method for more complex problems.

Now let's look at two important words. The Releasing technique relies on the use of mental questions that you will be asking yourself. Before we get to the questions, we will consider these special words.

Could

Like most other words, *could* can be used in a number of different ways. Here are some examples:

- A boss hands a disc with dictation to his secretary and says, "Could you get this out by three this afternoon." Notice that there is no question mark in this sentence. He is *not* asking a question. What he is saying, "Get this out by three this afternoon." The word *could* here is a polite way of giving a command. In this instance, *could* is used to control another person.

- A parent asks a child entering the house, "Could you just once hang up your coat in the closet where it belongs instead of throwing it on the floor?" This isn't a question either. It's a form of sarcasm. This *could* may be the opening thrust in an ensuing battle.
- A man attempting to lift an unmanageable piece of furniture turns to a friend who is standing nearby and asks, "Could you give me a hand with this?" His *could* means *please*. He is asking his friend for help. Depending on his tone of voice, his statement might either be controlling in nature (in this case, the man's tone would be somewhat abrupt and peremptory), or it might be only mildly controlling (an attempt to gently convince his friend to help)—or it might not have any element of control in it at all but be a genuine inquiry, the man trying to find out whether his friend is available.
- A couple are considering installing a water-filtering system in their home. They ask the salesman, "Could this system process all the water we use in a day?" Here the *could* is used for a true question. The couple is asking if it is *possible* for the filtering system to handle the necessary amount of water. There is no intention to control here; the questioners simply want more information.

You've probably heard *could* used in all of the above ways and some others as well, so the word will have many different associations for you. This is why it's doubly important for you to know the exact meaning of the *could* used in the Releasing method.

In the Releasing technique, *could* is used in the fourth and last sense described—to pose a simple question. When releasing, you will be asking yourself whether something is possible for you to do—that is, whether you would *be able to do it* if you wanted to. It's important to remember that this *could* introduces a simple question to yourself about a possibility—that is all.

Intentions vs. Wanting

The word *want* is the second special word used in the Releasing method. This word, too, is generally used to mean more than one thing, so we need to be clear about its meaning here. In everyday speech we often use the words *want* and *intend* to mean roughly the same thing. In the Releasing technique we make a sharp distinction between them.

An *intention* is an idea that serves to guide our actions. Having an intention makes it possible to organize our behavior effectively so that we can move toward our goals. Intentions are usually kept in the back of our minds, since once we've settled on them we no longer need to pay attention to them.

Wanting, on the other hand (in the sense we will be using this word when releasing), is an emotional reaction. When we *want* something, we long for it, crave it, or desire it. This kind of *wanting* has little to do with the reasonable kinds of wishes that shape our intentions. While being guided by an intention can be an easy, efficient process, *wanting* involves struggle and emotion and can produce much stress. Ironically, *wanting* may actually block our attainment of the very goals we strive for.

Here is an example:

Imagine yourself about to take an automobile trip. You are driving to a city some miles distant (let's say to Albany). You get into your car and start towards your destination. The car is in good working condition and the road is smooth, although traffic is fairly heavy—a business day.

Because you have a reasonable intention in mind (going to Albany), you don't have to think much about where you are heading. You certainly don't think repeatedly as you drive along, "I'm going to Albany . . . I'm going to Albany! . . ." It's simply your intention to get there. As a result, you feel free to watch the road, other motorists, or the scenery; or occupy your mind with interesting thoughts. The kind of wanting involved here is so reasonable that you're not even aware of it. It merely serves to guide you.

Now imagine a different scene. Instead of having a simple intention to drive to Albany, you feel a push, a strong urge to get there. Now you really *want* to get to Albany. This time, as you drive along, you think to yourself, "I *want* to get to Albany. I *have* to get to Albany!..." (Perhaps you don't put it in these words to yourself, but there are your feelings.) Unlike simply intending, the *wanting* occupies your mind fully. It takes over the stage. It stirs you up and won't let you put your destination in the back of your mind.

All your actions and reactions are now determined by the *wanting*. Every car on the road has become a potential obstacle barring the way to your goal. You swear (inwardly and outwardly) at the other drivers who are not moving along fast enough, and you try to maneuver your car past theirs. You are outraged by the pedestrians who thoughtlessly insist on crossing the street at intersections. You feel despair when you have to wait for a red light or arrive at a crossroads that demands slowing down. You incessantly glance at your watch, as though attention to it will speed up your progress.

As a result of *wanting*, you are now driving less safely than you could because you are focusing on only a small segment of reality—those things directly concerned with your getting to (or not getting to) Albany. Your awareness of the world and of the road is narrowed down to tunnel vision. Productive thinking about any other matters in your life grinds to a halt.

Soon you lose sight of how many delays it is reasonable to expect on the road at this time of day, or how much outmaneuvering of other drivers is safe. You even begin to imagine exaggerated consequences of being a few minutes late (losing that important account or losing your job or having your date walk out on you).

Finally you get to Albany. You may actually have gained a few minutes by your maneuvering, or your impaired judgment may have cost you time on the road. Either way, the price you pay for your *wanting* is high. Physical distress (muscle tension, elevated blood pressure, speeded-up heart rate) leaves you breathless. Emotional distress has drained you so that by now it scarcely matters to you any longer whether you arrived on time or not. On top of this, you may be in poor shape for anything that happens in Albany (including your important business of the day).

All this adds up. We might say that *wanting* to get to Albany had made getting to Albany somewhat of a bust. In the meantime, while driving, you lost the opportunity to use your driving time for productive planning or pleasant thoughts. In this case, *wanting* has led to inefficiency as well as distress.

Another example. Imagine yourself *wanting* to get to sleep at night and thinking to yourself, "I've *got* to get a good night's sleep!" If your desire to get to sleep is strong enough, it can effectively block going to sleep, as many a restless person on the eve of an important event has discovered. Having an *intention* to go to sleep is another matter. The intention can lead to practical steps, such as getting into bed, turning off the lights, shutting your eyes, and relaxing. These steps (if not interfered with by an internal *overpush*) can bring about the desired goal—falling asleep.

This difference between intentions and unproductive *wanting* is useful to keep in mind because when I suggest (and I'll do so shortly) that you ask yourself whether you could let go of wanting to change something, I will not be suggesting that you let go of your *intention* to accomplish your original goal. As you release on wanting to change the matter in question, you can (if you wish) hold on firmly to your goal. Letting go of *wanting* (the overpush) will clear your mind so that you can view the matter objectively and decide how best to achieve the goal. If, after you have released, you still desire your original goal (sometimes you may not), you will then be able to move toward it more effectively.

It is easiest to begin releasing by using the method with on an inanimate object rather than a person. To do this, look around and find something in your immediate surroundings that you would like to change—but not too strongly. Maybe you'd like some object in the room to be in a different place, or something to be rearranged or straightened up. Maybe you'd like to get rid of a stain, or have some object repaired, or have one color be a different one. Or perhaps you'd like the weather to be warmer or cooler, your shoes more comfortable, or your chair fit your back better. Or maybe you'd like the dog next door to stop barking; or a neighbor's radio to be turned off; or a lawnmower, air conditioner, or furnace to be shut down.

Try to choose something which you will want to change *somewhat* but not too urgently, an object or a situation that's not a central issue in your life. If your neighbor has been annoying you for months by playing a stereo at top volume when you're trying to sleep and you happen to hear it playing now, don't try to release on *that*—it will be far too loaded! For now, you want to pick something that is really not too important to you (we will be dealing with more important issues later on).

Most people readily find something they'd like to change in their environment, but if you can't, have some fun and create something you'd like to change. Tear up a sheet of paper and scatter the scraps. Dump a chair on its side. Remove a lamp shade so that the bulb shines into your eyes. Assume a twisted sitting position. Turn on a dishwasher, electric fan, or some other machine that makes an annoying noise. *Make* something happen that you will want to change—but not too urgently. Then proceed with the following steps.

Now that you have selected it, jot down what it is you would like to change:

I would like to change_____

Then think to yourself, or say out loud (off handedly):

"Could I let go of wanting to change that?"

Answer:_____
(Ask this question as though you were thinking to yourself, "I wonder if it's *possible* for me to let go of wanting to change it?")

Then, without thinking further about the matter, just let go—as easily as you would allow an object to drop from your hands.

Many people find this easy. An occasional person finds that he/she can't let go when he or she first tries. An excellent way to demonstrate the Releasing process to yourself is the following.

Select a small object that you can easily hold in your hand; it should have enough weight so that it will fall to the floor rapidly when let go. A tennis ball or other common object will do, or you can make a beanbag for yourself by putting a handful of beans (or salt, sand, etc.) into a plastic sandwich bag and sealing it in. The point is that you will want to be able to *feel* this object drop away from your hand when you release it.

Now hold the object in your *dominant* hand (right hand if you're right-handed, left if not), with your *other* hand you will establish the Releasing signal. You do this by touching together your thumb and little finger (or pinkie) of your non-dominant hand, so that the soft pads of these two fingers meet. Since this is an unusual gesture, it's a useful way to remind yourself of the special feeling of Releasing.

Now practice your thumb-to-pinkie touch several times. Then let your fingers relax and remain open in the readiness to make this signal.

Next, squeeze with your dominant hand the object you have selected *while at the same time* thinking to yourself (or saying out loud) the phrase "Could I *let go*?" At the exact moment when you use the words *let go*, *physically* let go of the object so that it drops to the floor, while you simultaneously make the thumb-pinkie signal with your *other* hand.

Let's review this procedure:

> *Step 1:* Squeeze the object in your dominant hand (other hand remains relaxed).
> *Step 2:* Say to yourself, "Could I *let go*?"
> *Step 3:* At the exact moment you say the words *let go*, *physically* let go of the object, allowing it to drop to the floor.
> *Step 4:* Along with the words *let go*, *and* the dropping of the object, use your thumb-pinkie releasing signal.

You will probably need to do this exercise at least ten times or so to establish your Releasing signal, and then you will be ready to test the signal. Do this by simply bringing your thumb and pinkie together in the Releasing signal (no holding the object or dropping it this time). Now the contact of the two fingers should automatically bring back the easy letting-go feeling. If it doesn't do this, continue to practice the exercise and let go of wanting to hurry the learning process.

When this simple thumb-pinkie contact gives you the letting-go feeling, you are ready to use your newly created signal to help you release. At this point you will go back to your original question and ask yourself **"Could I let go of wanting to change (whatever it was you wanted to change)?"**

But this time as you think the words *let go*, use your thumb-pinkie signal *at the same time*. You will be surprised to find how effective this signal can be in giving you a feeling of releasing exactly when you want to. Later on, as you become more familiar with the process of Releasing, just thinking the words *let go* will probably do the trick for you without your having to touch thumb to pinkie. You may always want to use your Releasing signal under stressful circumstances, however, particularly if releasing becomes difficult. We will discuss this possibility later on.

It at this point you are still having some difficulty with Releasing, it may simply mean that you have chosen for your first release a situation that is too vital to you. If so, choose a less loaded one instead and go over these same steps again. If you still don't find it easy to let go after that, don't force it. You'll catch on to the process soon enough. For now you can simply relax, read further, and absorb the idea of Releasing as you go along.

If when you asked yourself the Releasing question you answered that you *could* let go of wanting to change the object or situation, the next step is to go back and check on whether or not you actually *did* let go of wanting to change it. Consider your object or situation and see how you feel about it now.

Then write down how it looks and feels to you as you view it now:_____

_____

In the future there will be no need for you to write down the releases you perform. This is done only in the first chapter to help you learn. When you're on your own, releasing is an immediate mental process.

Does the object or situation feel in any way *different* to you than it did before (even slightly)? If it does, this means that your "monitor"—the evaluative part of your mind—has opened up somewhat because you let go of wanting to change this object or situation. When you find that the letting-go experience results in a change of perspective, you know that you have experienced a release. It's as simple as that.

POINTER: When you have released on something, the matter in question always looks, seems, or feels "different" when you go back to it.

If you don't see any change in the situation that you chose to "let go" of this first time, this may be because it was such a relatively unimportant matter that the change was not noticeable. Later on, when you release on more important issues, you will notice changes.

The second step is the same as the first one. You do another release. For this, select another object or situation in your immediate surroundings that you'd like to change (but which you don't feel too strong a need to change) and ask yourself whether you would like to change *that*. If the answer is "yes", then think to yourself, or say out loud:

"Could I let go of wanting to change that?"

Answer:_____

HINT: Suit yourself. You may find yourself releasing as soon as you ask the question. Later, you may find yourself releasing as soon as you think the mere word could. *Later still, you may find yourself releasing merely by* thinking *of releasing, or find yourself releasing automatically without thinking of it at all!*

You may be surprised to find that Releasing is fun. Since we never know in advance exactly what will happen when we let go of wanting to change something, releasing on anything, even the most trivial object, can bring surprises. Letting go of wanting to change anything changes our relationship to that thing—finding out *how* it will be changed is an adventure.

If you did "let go" (even a little bit) of wanting to change this second object or situation, take the important next step of going back to check on how that object or situation looks or feels to you now. This is like using a compass. Checking tells you exactly where you stand. You may want to jot down your observations.

How that situation (object) seems to me at the present moment:_____

On checking, you may sense a change in your overall mood as well as in your attitude toward the object or event in question. Releasing on wanting to change even a seemingly trivial thing can lighten a portion of the total emotional burdens that we carry. With each experience of "letting go," we free a certain amount of energy which has been tied up in that issue (or similar issues), and a quantum of our own energy is restored to us to use creatively. This released energy now goes into our energy reservoir, increasing by a small but important amount the total energy available to us for other tasks in life.

Now we come to another principle.

Releasing is instantly blocked if effort or force is introduced. To set ourselves free, all we need to do is "let go"—that is all *we need to do.*

SUGGESTION: Never force yourself to "let go." If, when you ask yourself whether you can let go of wanting to change something, you find that you don't want to let go—simply accept your feeling of not wanting to let go, and don't try to change that! "Not wanting" means that you're not ready to let go of this thing, at this moment. There's always another way to achieve a release. With this method, "All roads lead to Rome." You will learn more about this later.

In trying your two releases, if you answered "yes" to the "letting-go" question, then you have "let go" of two feelings or strivings. Perhaps you think this is trivial because the situations which you chose were trivial. Not so! The world and life itself are made up of little things—little moments and our relationship to them. As we let go of wanting to change any one thing (however insignificant it may seem to us at the moment), we simultaneously let go of whole networks of related events which are stored in our memory banks. The smallest release sets off a chain reaction that reverberates through our entire being and leaves us in quite a different place than we were before the release.

There is an ancient saying: In each raindrop, we see the whole sky.

The smallest contains the great. How we relate to little things reflects how we relate to big things. If we release ourselves from wanting to change the tiniest, most unimportant objects or situations, we have released ourselves to achieve a new kind of relationship to all things which make up our lives. This happens whether or not we are thinking about it. It just happens.

Maxim: Whether we realize it or not, a little release is always a big release.

SUGGESTION: When harassed by a "big" problem, release on some "little" unimportant detail in your surroundings that you would like to change—let go of wanting to change that—and the big problem will seem different.

IN EACH RAINDROP, WE SEE THE WHOLE SKY.

General Principles

1 *Wanting* can be dropped at will. It is like dropping a pencil and letting it fall to the ground. All we need to do to drop a pencil is open our fingers.
2 Our feeling of *wanting* does not hold us in its grip; we hold it in our grip. Because of this, we can choose not to hold on to it—to open our fingers, to let go. We can release.
3 When we let go of a *want*, its control over us is gone. If you

released on the two simple situations that you chose, you experienced this for yourself.

4   It is much more productive to let go of a want than to hold on to it—"holding on" saps energy from us; "letting go" returns energy to us.

5   It always feels satisfying or relieving to let go of wanting to change something; releasing is experiencing freedom.

6   Letting go of wanting to change something doesn't make us passive or take away motivation. On the contrary, it sets us free to realize our goals more effectively, or to change them in order to better serve our interests. We now have freedom of choice. That is the difference.

So far you have had two experiences of Releasing. This means that you have learned the basic method that you will be using from now on. If you have "let go" even a tiny bit, you know that it can take place, and how it feels. If you have not yet been able to release, you will soon be doing so.

At this point, if you have released at least *once*, you are ready to practice Releasing on your own. You may want to spend the next few days or even weeks just getting used to Releasing. This is a very good idea. If you are able to take it slowly, to put aside this book and experience the pleasure of releasing on small matters, your leisurely way of learning will free you. You can absorb the principles of Releasing simply by picking up this volume every few days and reading it until you finish a new exercise, then "letting go" of the book itself.

This way you will set the book's pace. You will move forward only when you wish to, and your learning will unfold at a tempo that matches your needs.

To practice Releasing on your own, each day select a few small, relatively unimportant situations and release on them as we did here. Do this any time of day you want and as often as you wish. Just be sure to remember that at this point the situations you choose should be relatively unimportant to you—just objects or events that you would like to have somewhat different from the way they are. If an appliance doesn't work, release on wanting to change it. If the weather doesn't suit you, release on wanting to change that. You can do the same with the temperature, food in a restaurant, traffic conditions, elevators, subways—there are endless possibilities.

During this phase of your experience, simply avoid releasing on situations that involve important or emotionally loaded relationships with *other people*. Complex interpersonal situations require special releasing techniques which you will learn later. Some of the situations that you will select now will contain people in an incidental fashion (such as drivers in cars or waiters in restaurants), but as long as these people aren't central in your life—as long as you don't know them well, or like them or dislike them too much—it will be easy to handle the release. Simply concentrate on wanting to change the situations themselves, not the people who appear incidentally in them.

SUGGESTION: Let Releasing be a game. Try your wings. Experiment.

When you are on your own, after identifying what it is that you want to change, then ask yourself:

"Could I let go of wanting to change that?"

And then let go . . . but only if this feels comfortable. Give yourself the right to answer honestly any questions that you ask yourself—to say "no" to yourself if you need to. You are learning how to set your energies free.

If you are on medication, Releasing could have an effect on the amount of medication you need, and you will want to check this out (see page 268, the section entitled "For Those Taking Prescribed Medication"). By the time you are ready for the next step in your learning process, you will have made many observations on your own and will therefore be in a somewhat different place when you start the next exercise. You will have had a chance to experiment by releasing on small matters and to discover how pleasant it feels to let go. When you are ready to learn more about this method, we will meet in the next chapter.

Chapter 3

SAMPLING THE EXPERIENCE

At this point, it will be helpful for you to learn what your own personal Releasing style is so that you can make use of this information when you want to release on a particularly difficult situation. Often you will be able to release automatically simply by remembering *how* it feels to release.

To find out what your Releasing style is, select some relatively simple situation to release on, then notice exactly how you experience the process.

Do you *feel* the release happening? Do you *picture* it happening? Do you *hear* it occurring? Or do you experience some combination of these things?

For me, a release is experienced as:_____

_____

For some people, releasing is a physical sensation. It may feel as though something in their head or chest had let go of tension, or as though they were being cleansed or had become lighter in weight, or as another bodily sensation. A woman in one of my Releasing workshops described her bodily feeling of releasing as a "sudden, very pleasurable sensation—a sort of honeylike feeling. It's a lovely sort of dropping-down feeling, definitely a *physical sensation*. Then the shift in perspective comes and I feel relaxed. I can look outside of me then, and I'm happy and peaceful."

Other people experience releasing as a *visual* change. They may imagine a slate being wiped clean, a blackboard being erased, an image coming into focus; or have another experience that involves making a picture in their mind.

Still others may "hear" the release occur. It may seem to them like a whooshing sound or as though something were clicking into place. Or they may notice a sudden stopping of their own internal chatter (thinking), as though a radio had suddenly been switched off.

It's important to remember that people experience the releasing process in their own ways.

The Aftereffects

Just as you experience releasing in your own individual way, you will also notice certain characteristic aftereffects that follow quickly upon your release. It's useful to identify these aftereffects because they will let you know when you have obtained a full release.

To find out what they are, select some situation to release on, let go of wanting to change it, and then notice how you feel *after* you have let go. How do you react physically to your surroundings now? How do you see the world around you after releasing? How do you experience sounds after you have released?

What you want to catch is the experience that comes directly after and *on the heels* of the release:

Directly after releasing, I experience:_____

_____

_____

_____

The aftereffects of releasing differ from person to person. Some people feel the air against their face or the temperature of the day more sharply. Others see more clearly—objects seem more brightly lit or more focused, or colors become sharper. Others experience a sense of inner silence. For still others, releasing brings muscular relaxation, laughter, a sense of relief, or a feeling of expansiveness.

But suppose at this point you have not yet released. You may have tried but are not sure that you've caught on. If this is the case, it may reassure you to know that about half the people who read this book will also not have released *as yet*. If you're one of them, simply let go of wanting to change the fact that you *haven't yet released*. This should take the pressure off you.

While it's important to recognize the special characteristics of your own Releasing experience, the reason you are learning Releasing is to improve your handling of difficult situations. Here are some of the most common general effects that people report from Releasing:

A Changed Viewpoint

The way you respond to the situation you choose to release on often undergoes a marked change after you have released on it. It looks, sounds, or feels different. A member of a Releasing workshop, after releasing on something that had been annoying him, experienced an interesting change.

He had been gazing out of the window at a pool in a Japanese garden, where a reddish stain just above the waterline had caught his eye. Although he enjoyed looking at the pool and the trees surrounding it, his eyes kept returning to that rusty-looking mark. This annoyed him because it detracted from the tranquillity of the scene. Then he let go of wanting to change the watermark. When he did so, he immediately noticed something in the scene that had not attracted his attention before. *Some of the leaves on a tree near the pool had a rusty-red color that he now saw was identical to the color of the pool stain*. The rusty line and the rust of the leaves seemed to match. When he noticed this relationship, he found that he could look directly at the reddish mark without having his eyes *drawn* to it anymore. He was now free to enjoy the garden in a different way. The rusty line had merged into a larger pattern of related colors.

This man's experience of having the object which he had wanted to change form part of a harmonious whole after releasing is not unusual. When we are involved in wanting to change something, we can concentrate on our wish to change it to such an extent that the thing itself becomes relatively unimportant to us—all we are concerned with is getting it to be different. When we let go of wanting to change something, we are free to sense its genuine qualities. This can be like having blinders removed.

A Change in Attitude

When we release, our attitude towards the situation or object in question shifts from negative to less negative, or changes to neutral or positive. After releasing on wanting to change an object that formerly seemed useless, we may be less disturbed by its "useless" quality, become comfortably indifferent to it, or spontaneously become aware of unexpected uses for it. After releasing on someone's behavior, her actions may simply be less annoying or not bother us at all anymore, or we may suddenly discover *advantages* in her behavior.

A woman who had learned the Releasing technique reported a negative reaction which turned into a positive one after releasing. She had grown up with the superstition that if a bird tries to force its way into your home, imminent disaster will strike a member of your family. Soon after she had acquired releasing skill, she awoke one morning to find a small bird pecking at her bedroom window. A chill went through her as she thought of her two young children in light of the superstition. Then she released, asking herself to let go of wanting to change the fact that the bird was trying to force its way into her home. As she did so, she suddenly felt a burden lift, and a new thought came into her mind.

"Oh!" she thought. "How nice! The bird likes me enough to want to get into my home—how incredible that it found its way to my window!" She felt close to this bird, as though it had come personally to awaken her in order to get the food that she was accustomed to feed to the neighborhood birds each morning. She then went out into the yard, scattered seeds for the fledgling, and watched as he gobbled them up. Her day was pleasant afterwards, and her family healthy and happy. She tells me that if she hadn't released on this incident, she would have carried her anxiety with her for the entire day.

A shift from negative to positive after releasing can take many forms. Suppose you were at the theater, seated in a chair which pressed uncomfortably against your back. To release on this situation, you might let go of wanting to change the way the chair was constructed. Suppose that as soon as you did so, positive thoughts about the chair entered your mind. You might think, "This pressure against my back is giving my back some support." Or you might decide that the pressure was helping you stay alert at what was a rather boring performance, or have some other positive thought.

Such a change in thinking wouldn't mean that you have reasoned your way out of your annoyance, but rather that a genuine change in perspective had occurred *after* (or possibly simultaneously with) letting go of wanting to change the situation. While logical thoughts can occur along with a release, Releasing is *not* a way of talking ourselves out of things. On the contrary, it is a process that alters the way we *experience* things.

While making sense of a release is useful for many people, never try to talk yourself into a release. Let it happen. Only when the "letting go" is experienced *can it bring about a powerful change.*

With respect to the uncomfortable chair, after releasing on the discomfort, you might decide to change your seat to a more comfortable one; but the act of moving to another chair would now be a different experience than it would have been before you released. Now you wouldn't feel compelled to look for a new seat because you couldn't stand the old one. Instead you would be free to shift seats or not, as you wished. Having a choice can take the distress out of a situation.

A Change in Physical State

Releasing can result in a beneficial change in your physical state. A man attending a lecture on Releasing had developed an allergic reaction to the smell of mold in the auditorium. Soon after he sat down, his nose began to run and his eyes to water. In the course of the lecture, I suggested that each person in the audience let go of wanting to change something in their immediate environment. He decided that he would let go of wanting to change the fact that there was mold in the air. When he did, he discovered to his surprise that now when he tried to detect the smell of mold, he was unable to do so! What was even more impressive to him was the fact that his allergic reaction had disappeared. Ironically, when we let go of wanting to change something, it may change—in its own way. The end result may be the very goal we wanted in the first place!

When you let go of wanting to change something, you allow it to change.

If you have emotional problems which require psychotherapy, you will want to consider how Releasing fits into your treatment plan. If so, turn to page 268 in the section in the back of the book entitled, "For Those Requiring Psychotherapy."

You are now ready to take the next step in learning to release, a step which will insure that you do not mistakenly think that you have to give up your reasonable intentions and goals when releasing. Knowing how to remind yourself of this fact will make your Releasing practice far easier.

Chapter 4

HOLDING ON TO YOUR INTENTIONS

What sensible person wouldn't want to change a distressing situation to a comfortable one? Who wouldn't want to put an end to pain? Who doesn't want to find a solution to a distressing problem? If you are going to release successfully, you should know that the Releasing technique recognizes normal human strivings such as these as desirable. Not only does it not suggest that such goals be abandoned, it offers you a more effective way to achieve them.

There are several ways to remind yourself of this fact at the point when such a reminder counts most—the moment of releasing.

The Clarifying Phrase

The first way is to introduce an additional phrase into your mental self-questioning which instructs you to hold on to your intention, even as you simultaneously give up the *wanting*. Many different phrases can be used. I will list some of my own, but you may think up one which works even better for you.

After you have identified a situation you would like to change, think to yourself or say out loud:

"It would certainly be reasonable to change that . . . but could I let go of wanting to change it?"

Or:

"It's OK to intend to change that . . . but could I let go of wanting to change it?"

Or:

"It would be nice if (such and such) were different . . . but could I get go of wanting to change it?"

Or:

"Granted that it would be nice (convenient, useful, fun, relieving, etc.) to have such and such different . . . could I let go of wanting to change it?"

As you see, a new twist has been added. A short statement now precedes the question. It reminds you that it's reasonable, OK, desirable to wish that the situation in question be different. In other words, it's all right to hold on to your reasonable intention. All you are asked to do is to let go of the *wanting*.

The clarifying phrase is extremely valuable when releasing on a difficult situation. Starting out by thinking this phrase, you are reminding yourself that you are not being asked to give up your sensible wishes or practical goals at all, only the troublesome overpush.

Dramatizing the Holding On

You may also find it effective to remind yourself that you can hold on to your intention by demonstrating this fact to yourself. To dramatize holding on to an intention, after you have identified the situation you'd like to change, write down on a sheet of paper or on an index card:

"I can keep my *intention* of (description of intention)."

When you have done this, read the card over to yourself; then, holding it in front of you, let go of your feeling of *wanting*.

If you don't have a card handy, imagine this sentence written on a large blackboard, or hear it in your mind as though it were being repeated several times over a loudspeaker.

As an example, suppose you were annoyed because someone was demanding your attention while you were busy working. To release on this, you would write down the phrase:

"I can *keep* my intention of not being interrupted."

Holding the card in front of you, you could then read this statement over several times while thinking to yourself:

"Could I let go of wanting (this person) to stop interrupting me?"

The card would serve as a reminder that you are allowing yourself to retain your very reasonable intention of not being interrupted. The concrete gesture of writing down your intention has made an all-important distinction between holding on to your intention and simultaneously letting go of the *wanting*. As soon as you make this distinction, virtually any release becomes easy.

Realizing that you can hold on to your intention while letting go of your wanting is itself *a release!*

The Releasing Chart

Another way to remind yourself of the fact that your desired goal can be retained while you let go of the unproductive *wanting* is through the use of a device known as a Releasing Chart. This device often appeals to people who like to write things down in a methodical manner. You will find instructions for its use in Appendix A.

Releasing on the Past

Much of the releasing in our daily lives has to be done after the event has occurred (it is frequently difficult to find time to release during an event), so you will want to know how to release after the smoke has cleared away. Here is the technique for doing that.

Select a past event where you experienced some difficulty with an inanimate object or with a person who was not vital in your life. The event should be sufficiently troublesome so that it feels somewhat—but not too—uncomfortable.

Now imagine this situation, allowing yourself to see it, feel it, and hear it almost as clearly as though you were right there. Then jot down what you would like to change in the situation exactly as you would if the past *were* the present.

"I would like to change _____."

For example, suppose a clerk at a checkout counter had jammed your groceries haphazardly into a bag, crushing some fragile purchases like eggs. To release on this later in the day, you would imagine this past situation as vividly as possibly, as though it were occurring in the present, and think to yourself:

"Could I let go of wanting to change the fact that he/she *is jamming* (present tense) my purchases into the bag?"

In other words, you would act as though you had been

transported backward in time so that the situation were happening right now. Then you would let go of wanting to change it just as you would let go of wanting to change a present situation.

Now take an event in the recent past that you would like to change, and think to yourself or say out loud:

> **"Could I let go of wanting to change the fact that (such and such)** *is happening***?"**

After you have let go of wanting to change it, go back to check on how you are experiencing this same situation. Has it shifted from being negative to being less negative, or to being neutral, or positive? If so, then it is a release. If not, remember this particular situation for later use. It will come in handy when you arrive at your next releasing exercise.

Releasing on Rewriting History

Since many of the goals that we set for ourselves in emotionally loaded situations are goals located in the *past*, this means that to realize them it would literally be necessary for us to rewrite history. Past goals can arouse the strongest kind of feelings and direct some of our best energies at an impossible target—to make something which has already happened *not* happen.

"If only I hadn't done such and such!"

"If I could just do such and such over again!"

"Why didn't I think of doing *that* instead of what I did?"

"Why didn't this person act the way I would have *liked* him to have acted?"

Listing all of our urgent desires to rewrite the past would take up volumes. Trying to change the past is such a commonplace occurrence, in fact, that we usually don't recognize that it is happening.

A good strategy to use when you realize that you are caught in this all-too-human attempt to rewrite the past is to release directly on the problem of "wanting to rewrite the past." To do this, think to yourself or say out loud:

"Could I let go of *wanting to rewrite the past?*"

This question often brings a full release without any further steps.

Releasing on the Future

Because many of our fears also relate to events which we anticipate in the future, releasing on the future is a valuable maneuver. To do this, select a forthcoming event about which you are concerned. Mentally rehearse this event exactly as if it were occurring in the present—and release on wanting to change it. From that point on, act exactly as you would if you were releasing on a present situation. You will see how useful this method is when you read in part 2 of this book about people who have used anticipatory Releasing to cope with upcoming difficulties.

Now we are ready to proceed to a crucial feature of the Releasing technique—finding those keys which can unlock a release under circumstances where it may at first seem impossible to release because the situation is so emotionally loaded.

Chapter 5

USING UNLOCKING TACTICS

Most of the time you will be able to release easily whenever you want. Occasionally you may find yourself unable to let go. Knowing how to release when you *can't* readily do so is an essential skill. It is at those precise moments when it's most difficult to release that you may need Releasing the most.

This chapter presents the "unlocking" tactics, simple but highly effective devices that can help you release successfully in *any* situation.

At this moment, you are in one of two conditions. Either you haven't yet been able to release—in which case you will want to apply the unlocking tactics immediately—or else you've already released on at least one simple situation, in which case you will need to select a more difficult type of situation to use for the exercises in this chapter.

If you need a more challenging event to release on, allow your mind to wander until you think of several emotionally loaded situations. Try to release on each of them in turn, and keep doing this until you find a situation that *resists* releasing, one that's "locked in." When you have found one, you are ready to apply the unlocking tactics.

I will list the unlocking tactics one by one so that you can try each in turn. When one of these tactics "unlocks" a release for you, you may want to rest for a while before moving on to another locked-in situation. Then you will be ready to test out the next unlocking tactic.

Most people find it interesting to try these strategies. You should give yourself an opportunity to experience every one of them. Each adds to your repertoire of unlocking tactics, forming a group of Releasing aids which you can keep conveniently on hand to deal with high-pressure situations.

The 1 Percent Solution

When you locate a locked-in situation, one that you can't readily release on, think to yourself or say out loud:

"Could I let go of *only 1 percent* of wanting to change (that situation)?"

You will discover that letting go of 1 percent of the *wanting* is often much easier than letting go of all of the *wanting*. Application of the 1 percent solution will usually result in at least a partial release. Sometimes it is all that is required for a full release.

If you can let go at all ... you can let go.

There is also a helpful addition to the 1 percent solution which you may want to use in heavily locked-in situations. Point out to yourself that you can *hold on to* 99 percent of the *wanting*. The question now goes as follows:

"Could I let go of *only 1 percent* of wanting to change (such-and-such situation) and hold on to the other 99 *percent* of wanting to change it?"

The addition of the "99 percent" phrase emphasizes the fact that you're not being asked to give up any more of the *wanting* than you are ready to at this moment. *Never use force when releasing*. It should be entirely comfortable, merely an effortless letting go. However, you should not try *not* to use force, either.

To try not to make an effort is to make an effort.

It doesn't work to force a release. The 1 percent solution, or letting go of only 1 percent and also reminding yourself that you can hold on to 99 percent of your wanting, *removes the forcing from the process.*

Another way to use the 1 percent solution is to switch the releasing phrase around so that you don't ask yourself to let go of 1 percent of wanting—but rather ask yourself if you can *accept* 1 percent of the situation. The phrase now goes like this:

"Could I *accept* 1 percent of (such-and-such situation)?"

Some individuals find this acceptance of 1 percent of what is happening particularly appealing (after all, this is an easy amount of unpleasantness to accept even under adverse circumstances), and they obtain an immediate release this way. I suggest you try both ways of phrasing the 1 percent solution— the letting-go and the accepting approach. You will probably find that one works better for you in a particular situation than the other, but the opposite approach might fit the bill under different circumstances. Experiment!

Now let's consider what to do when you have already released partially by using the 1 percent solution, so that some of the pressure has been lifted from the situation but some still remains.

At this point, you can continue using this "divide-and-conquer" strategy. You have let go of part of the *wanting* (or have accepted a tiny portion of the situation). Now ask yourself once more, in the same words, to do exactly the *same* thing again:

"Could I let go of the same 1 percent of wanting to change (this situation)? Or could I accept the same 1 percent of (this situation)?"

Remember, you are not asking yourself to let go of (or to accept) an *additional* 1 percent. You are not increasing your percentage of releasing to 2 percent. You are exactly duplicating your original question. If you still can't get a full release, then just keep on letting go of that same tiny percentage of the *wanting*—or accepting the same percentage—until you feel the situation neutralized.

A member of one of my Releasing workshops complained about glare from a window. It was interfering with his concentration on the workshop. I asked him to let go of wanting to change the glare. He couldn't readily do this, so I suggested that he let go of only *1 percent* of wanting to change the glare and "hold on to" the other 99 percent of wanting to change it.

After pausing for a few seconds he was able to let go of 1 percent, "but no more." Actually, that was plenty. When we checked to see where he stood in his feelings about it, the glare didn't seem important to him now. He was then able to let go once more of that same 1 percent of *wanting* and at this point was no longer disturbed by the glare at all.

You will have ample opportunity to observe the 1 percent solution when you read about those people who have applied Releasing to more serious life problems. It you don't fully understand how it works at this point, simply let go of wanting to change the fact that you don't understand! This is a way to "release on Releasing," one of the most successful procedures I know.

The Cumulative Percentage

One way to increase the effectiveness of the 1 percent solution is to start by letting go of 1 percent of your *wanting*. Then, after that, if you find that some of the original problem remains (that is, if you've obtained only a partial release at this point), let go of another 1 percent (or another 5 percent or 10 percent) of the *wanting*. Rest for a few minutes; think about something else; then go for a few more percentage points of the *wanting*. Repeat this process every minute or so until you can let go of 100 percent (or nearly 100 percent) of your *wanting*.

With this method, waiting between releases is important, and it can be helpful in the interim to distract yourself by doing something completely unrelated to Releasing. By waiting in this manner you avoid pushing yourself, which can create resistance. You need to give yourself time to assimilate the fact that you have to let go of, say, 40 percent of the *wanting* before you move on to let go of 45 percent or 50 percent of it, or whatever amount you are up to.

Given a little time, you will find that you can reach a very high percentage of release. Often you will be able to let go of 100 percent of the wanting. . . . But never force yourself to reach 100 percent. Only do what is comfortable.

The "Suspend" Tactic

When you find yourself locked in to a situation and unable to release, the challenge is to convince yourself that you *can* let go. Ninety-nine percent of the time you will have forgotten this fact, and that is why you are stuck.

Here is an unlocking tactic to handle this.

Locate a situation on which you can't readily release; then think to yourself or say out loud:

"Could I let go—for only two seconds—of wanting to change (this situation)? . . . then I can *take back* the *wanting*.

This creates a temporary suspension of the *wanting*, which allows you to experience how it feels to let go of it. You are trying it on for size. Since this involves no commitment on your part to let go completely, it is easier to do than going for a full release. If you prefer, you can use the following phrasing:

"Could I *postpone* wanting to change (this situation) *for only two seconds*?"

When you find yourself locked in, you can repeat this procedure several times, each time suspending the *wanting* for only one or two seconds. This should be all you need to do in order to experience a partial release. You may very well experience a full release.

If you can let go at all—you can let go.

When you realize that you can release on a situation, you may have *already* released on that situation!

A workshop member was unhappy with the location of his chair in the room. He had tried releasing on this but was unable to do so. I asked him to let go for only *two seconds* of wanting to change the location of his chair, then to *take back* the wanting. This he found he could do easily, and we repeated the process. After he had released in this manner, he was now much less aware of his chair. He could allow the chair to be where it was, even though its position wasn't ideal. He could also move it to a more comfortable place, which he eventually decided to do but now was able to do this in a relaxed, unpressured manner.

Once you have let go of the wanting *even for a split second, you have established the fact that you have control over letting go of the* wanting *. . . then you can let go.*

Divide and Conquer

Most locked-in situations have a high impact on us, and sometimes we feel so strongly about them that we can't conceive of *not* making an effort to change them, or not *wanting* a change. To try to release on them in totality under these circumstances can be like tackling a whole army at once, instead of individual foot soldiers one at a time—much too big a task.

An effective way to deal with the problem is to "divide and conquer." I have already mentioned some related methods— dividing the total *wanting* so that you let go of only 1 percent of your *wanting* at a time, and dividing the time factor so that you can let go for only one or two seconds at a time. Another powerful tactic is to divide the situation itself into such small portions that you can release on each of these separately without difficulty.

Suppose that you had noticed that someone's hair was badly

snarled and were bothered by this. You had tried to release on wanting to change the way his hair looked but had found that you were locked in because you felt so strongly about it. To use the divide-and-conquer tactic, you might select *one single strand* of his hair—a strand that you could easily see—and release only on that. You would isolate this strand from the rest of his hair in your mind and then let go of wanting to change it:

"Could I let go of wanting to change the way *that particular strand* **is disarranged?"**

The difference between releasing on a whole situation and releasing on only a tiny portion of it is considerable. There is usually no reason not to let go of wanting to change some minor aspect of a situation (such as a single strand of hair), but you may be able to think of many reasons for not letting go of wanting to change the whole situation. In fact, common sense suggests that we let go of wanting to change unimportant details!

This can be a surprising tactic to use, however, because once you have been successful in releasing on a portion (or several portions) of a situation, your feeling about the entire situation may have changed.

A little release is always a big release.

A member of one of my workshops complained that her back hurt. This was distracting her from the workshop, but she felt unable to release on it. I suggested that she divide her total feeling of discomfort into discrete areas, making these areas as small as possible. Could she locate one square inch of discomfort somewhere on her back?

She was startled by this request but was eventually able to locate a "square inch of pain" over to the right, a little below her waist. I then asked her to let go of wanting to change the fact that *that particular square inch* on her back was hurting. This she was able to do because the area was so small, but when she had released on the square inch, to her surprise her whole back felt easier.

When you divide and conquer, it is seldom necessary to release on all portions of the original experience. Often you need to release on only one or two small components to change the entire situation.

In each raindrop, we can see the whole sky.

Another example of dividing and conquering was demonstrated by a workshop member who found the noise of an air conditioner troublesome. Because it was difficult for him to release on this, I asked him to isolate one particular element of the air-conditioner noise—perhaps a high or low tone, or a clicking, or a rhythmic pulsation—a single element only.

He identified a "funny little whine" that seemed to pulsate under the heavy roaring noise. When I suggested that he let go of wanting to change that whine, he couldn't do this because now that he had singled it out, the whine seemed to him to be the most annoying part of the noise.

To help him break down the situation even further, I asked him to let go of wanting to change the fact that the whine *pulsated*—that it seemed to come and go. This he could do, and when he had released on it, he found that the entire situation had changed. Now, to his surprise, he *liked* the way the whine was pulsating! When he checked back to see how he felt about the total air-conditioner sound, he discovered that he now liked the noise of the air conditioner as well—the very noise which had formerly annoyed him. After releasing, it seemed to him as though all components of this sound went together like an orchestra, and were vibrant and energetic.

When we let go of wanting to change something, we experience its true quality. Most things are interesting once we are able to experience them.

The divide-and-conquer tactic can be used for major as well as minor events and is one of the most effective ways of handling situations that are extremely resistant to other approaches. When it is used on a very difficult situation, the dividing is done in an exceptionally detailed way. I sometimes call this tactic "divide the divide." You will have an opportunity to see how it works later as you read about people who have released in more serious situations, in part 2 of this book.

Remember the Feeling

When you are locked in to a situation so that you can't readily release, you have an excellent strategy that will always be available no matter what the circumstances—*you can remember how it felt to release in the past*. Your own distinctive experience of Releasing is a major unlocking tactic. That's why we took the time to have you identify this experience in chapter 3. In the future, the memory of it can be enough to trigger a complete release.

To evoke this memory, when you find yourself heavily locked in, first think the answer "yes" to the Releasing question ("Could I let go of? . . . Yes!") Do this automatically whether or not you really feel the answer is "yes"—then recall the exact sensation (impression, image) of how it feels for *you* to release—or if you have established a Releasing signal, use that to bring back the feeling.

Remembering the releasing sensation can be a powerful method of Releasing.

Use a Releasing Signal

If you have been releasing easily right from the start and so didn't need to establish a Releasing signal, you may now want to do so for future use in tight spots. To create a Releasing signal you can either use the thumb-pinkie technique described before, or select some other easily relocated spot on your skin (such as your right earlobe, the knuckle of your left thumb, etc.) to use as an anchor, or reminder, for your release. Just be sure that you have located a spot which you will be able to relocate *exactly* and then press again when you want to in the future.

When you have done this, release on some simple situation. At the precise moment when you feel yourself releasing, lightly press the special spot which you have selected. Hold your finger on that spot for about three to five seconds; then let go.

Later on, pressing this exact spot (with roughly the same amount of pressure) will bring back the experience of releasing in a compelling manner and with exceptional vividness. You have "associated" the feeling of releasing with your finger touch. The one now evokes the other. This anchoring tactic will often trigger a new release—immediately.

Letting Go "for Now"

By asking yourself if you can let go of wanting to change something "only for now," you often give yourself the freedom necessary to bring about a release. The question goes like this:

> **"Could I let go *just for now* of wanting to change (such and such)?"**

The phrase "for now" reduces your commitment.

The Exaggeration Effect

When we were children, my brother and I used to play a game where the rules were to stare into each other's eyes for as long as we could without laughing. We tried as hard as we could not to laugh, and we always ended up laughing so hard that the tears rolled down our cheeks and our stomachs ached. We loved to play this game because it never failed to make us laugh!

Try not to laugh. *Try* not to think of a white elephant. *Try* not to release. . . . What happens?

This "going-contrary" aspect of human nature is the basis for two very effective unlocking methods—the "exaggeration effect" and the "forbidding tactic."

Both these methods are useful when a situation calls forth reactions so strong that the regular unlocking tactics don't work. At such times, something in us may resist releasing with a stubborn insistence. When we feel such resistance, it is as though a little voice within us cried, "Never!"

If you run into this kind of resistance and find yourself trapped in your own determination to win at all costs (even your own), *holding on to* the resistance, or exaggerating it, can be the best strategy. In one of those "I can't . . . I won't release" situations, try thinking to yourself, or saying out loud to yourself in a *commanding* voice.

"Increase **wanting to change (the situation, feeling)! . . .** *Increase* **it more . . .** *increase* **it more . . .** *increase* **it even more! . . ." (and so on)**

Or tell yourself:

"Hold on to **wanting to change (the situation, feeling). . . . Hold on more tightly . . .** *hold on* **. . . keep on wanting to change it. . . . Increase wanting to change it. . . . Hold on even more tightly . . . etc."**

Your exact words are not important. The point is to push yourself to the limit, to keep on wanting whatever you want and to want it more and more, until finally, like a soap bubble blown up to the bursting point, the problem suddenly vanishes.

This is not unlike our childhood game of staring into each other's eyes with intense seriousness until we had to laugh. There is humor somewhere in the universe. When it hits us, the crisis is over.

The exaggeration effect sometimes results in laughter and sometimes it doesn't. Whichever way, it restores perspective rapidly. That is what Releasing is all about.

The Forbidding Tactic

There is another way to capitalize on our human tendency to "go opposite." This is to sternly *forbid* ourselves to release!

To do this, think to yourself, or say out loud:

"I *won't* let myself release (on this situation or feeling). . . . I will not let myself release on it! . . . I *won't* allow myself to release! . . ." (and so on)

Try telling somebody that they are not allowed to do something *under any circumstances* and are not even to *think* about it. What happens?

In the same way, when you use the forbidding tactic, you are motivating yourself to do exactly what you are telling yourself *not* to do—that is, to release. This may sound like playing games with yourself, but it works (games can be serious). Both the exaggeration effect and the forbidding tactic drive us to the limit. It is hard to keep on indefinitely with either of these maneuvers without running out of steam. When you run out of steam, you have automatically released.

One workshop member reported that her husband had cut down a lovely tree in their garden against her wishes. She was extremely upset about this because she had told him many times that the tree was important to her, and she felt that he had cut it down just to annoy her. She was so distressed that she was unable to release on the incident.

This woman's goal was to have the tree "back where it was" and to have her husband "observe her wishes"—two reasonable goals but both of them located in the past, which was impractical, to say the least, since to realize them she would have had to rewrite history.

To help her obtain a release, I asked her to *increase* her feeling of wanting to have this tree back in the garden. "Intensify your feeling of wanting to have the tree back in the garden," I advised her. "Now make a *stronger* effort to *want* that tree back in the garden! . . . Keep on holding on to wanting that tree back in the garden. . . . Keep on wanting to control that tree getting itself back in the garden. . . . Keep on wanting to put that tree back in the garden! Keep on imaging yourself getting that tree back in the garden! Make your wanting to get that tree back in the garden *stronger* and *stronger*. . . ."

She followed me by exaggerating her *wanting* and finally was able to continue the process silently on her own. She worked to make her feeling of wanting the tree back in the garden stronger and stronger. She put everything she had into wanting to change that situation. After about thirty seconds or so of this intense effort, she broke into a broad smile.

"I can't do it anymore!" she cried. "That tree is never going to be back in that garden!"

When we checked on how she felt now about her husband cutting down the tree, she reported that she still felt it was a strange thing for him to do, but it didn't bother her any longer. Now she felt that the important thing was to get another tree in there, a young one, to get it planted and start it growing. She thought that maybe her husband would help her with that. She added that for her the whole upset was now "over and done with."

Shifting Gears

When we find ourselves locked in, we can often start ourselves releasing again by shifting to an entirely different activity. It doesn't make any difference what activity we choose for this. We can do some physical exercise, attend to an errand, listen to music, chat with a friend, read a book, or occupy ourselves with anything else—*except* releasing. This serves to distract us and break up the "lock-in." When we come back to the original situation later on, we can often release on it without difficulty.

Another way of shifting to a different activity was mentioned in chapter 3. When you find yourself locked in, turn to a situation that you know will be easy to release on, and let go of wanting to change *that*. After that, you may be able to release on the difficult situation without any trouble. Releasing fully and easily on *anything* greases the wheels of the releasing process.

Physical Releasing

If you demonstrate to yourself that it is possible for you to let go on a physical level, this often serves to unlock the releasing process immediately. Two excellent exercises for this purpose are included in Appendix D. Use them liberally whenever you find yourself 'locked in' and unable to release.

When to Use Unlocking Tactics

An important point to remember about unlocking tactics, however, is that they are for locked-in situations only. Many times you won't need more than a simple release to obtain the full effect you want. When you first start releasing on any situation, try to release on it *in its totality* first ("Could I let go of wanting to change such and such?"). If that doesn't work, then use an unlocking tactic, or several, until you get a release.

You will be learning some other unlocking tactics as we go along, but you now know enough to handle many difficult situations. At this point, you can anticipate noticing some benefits from your Releasing practice. When this happens, you will probably find yourself wanting to share this new skill with family members, friends, and others. This is constructive, but it is important to realize that Releasing is not easy to teach. Many misunderstandings can arise in transmitting the basic principles and details of the practice. Unfortunately, if the person learning it misinterprets the spirit or intent of Releasing, or if he or she is confused about the tactics to be used, this can lead to serious errors in its practice.

If you want to help someone you know to learn to release, the appropriate way to do this is to have them read this book. After they have gone through the step-by-step exercises here, they will understand the nature of Releasing and be able to apply it properly. You and they can then practice Releasing together if you like. This can be enjoyable and a valuable pastime which we will consider later when we discuss Releasing Partners.

Now you may want to put aside this book and give yourself a chance to try your Releasing skills on problems which are somewhat more serious in nature. Life affords many opportunities to release, and you can benefit from these by discovering ways to release under pressure which are particularly useful to you.

As you do this, remember that you are setting your own pace in this learning process. When you feel that you are familiar with the unlocking tactics, you will be ready to experience one of the most useful steps of all—learning to release on unwanted emotions.

Chapter 6

RELEASING ON FEELINGS

When you find it difficult to release, whether you realize it or not, this is because you have such strong feelings about the event at hand that you can't see how you could possibly "let go." Basically, it is emotional reactions that block releasing. For this reason, a major unlocking tactic is to go directly to the source of difficulty and release on the feeling itself. You will be learning how to do so in this chapter.

At first, the process of Releasing on feelings may appear startling. You will be asked to allow an unpleasant feeling to "just be there," rather than to push it away. This can seem illogical unless you are aware of something about the nature of emotions which most people don't realize.

The general belief is that the way to handle unpleasant feelings is to suppress them. Unfortunately, however, as a friend of mine use to say, "when you bury a feeling, you bury it alive." The feeling always returns in some form to cause trouble. When you suppress a feeling, you are actually lending strength to that feeling. As a result, it becomes deeply entrenched, difficult to deal with, and lasts longer. The dilemma is like that of a political candidate who faces slander by her opposition. If the candidate engages with her critics by trying to prove them wrong or attempts to suppress their criticism, this only lends strength to the opposition. So it is with feelings.

The Releasing technique is effective in dealing with difficult feelings because it neither suppresses nor opposes them. Instead, it deals with these feelings in a realistic fashion that reduces or dissolves roadblocks.

How We Learned to Control Our Feelings

As infants we all experienced feelings freely without actively fighting them. When we felt distress, we cried with our whole hearts. When we felt angry, our bodies contorted with rage. When we were pleased, we wriggled with delight. But since that time, most of us have been fighting our feelings in a subtle fashion.

This struggle began for us early in life when we learned that it was not acceptable to express openly everything we feel.

For example, when we got mad at people, we were not supposed to hit them over the head. This is generally sound advice, except that, through no fault of our parents (who probably didn't have the skills either), we were not taught how to stop ourselves from acting on our feelings (from hitting other people over the head) while *at the same time* experiencing our feelings fully the way we did when we were infants.

It is, however, possible to do this. The Releasing method offers a healthy way to exert control over our feelings—a way born of acceptance rather than opposition.

If you observe what you presently do when you have a strong negative feeling—fear, anger, sadness, frustration, whatever—you will probably find that you automatically judge that feeling and then make a decision. You think to yourself, "I shouldn't have that feeling," or, "It's all right for me to have that feeling *because it's justified.*"

You may think that when you justify a feeling, you are accepting that feeling but this is not the case. Whenever you have to justify a feeling, you can be sure you are *not* accepting it.

Let's go back to the infant. When it screams in rage, or squeals with pleasure, or cries with hunger, it totally *accepts* its own behavior; it makes no judgment about what it is doing. It feels what it feels. That is all.

Now imagine a three-year-old girl who becomes angry when a playmate grabs her toy. She has been taught not to hit other children when they do this, and so, in her preschooler way, she now judges her own anger. Her thoughts may go something like this: "I'm mad. . . . No, Mommy wouldn't like that. . . . I'm still mad! . . . Oh, it's *OK* to be mad because he took my toy and that's *unfair!*"

First this (already somewhat grown-up) child fights against her own feelings ("Mommy wouldn't like me to feel this way"). Then she justifies them (It's "OK" to be mad because he was "unfair"). Now she is free to attack her playmate, perhaps with words if she's learned how to use them well enough. She may even recapture her toy. But her anger is not simple or innocent as it was when she was a baby. It is now contaminated by her justifications.

When we have to justify a feeling, it is no longer a pure feeling. It has become self-conscious. When we justify a feeling, its innocence and simplicity are gone.

Pure, unjustified feelings can be handled like the innocents they are—honestly, simply, and with respect for their true nature. Feelings put on the defensive behave like anything else under attack. They are stubborn, defensive, and can resort to cunning. If we fight them ruthlessly enough, they may become monstrous. At best, they are no longer our friends.

To handle our emotions with ease and courage, we need to accept them *without acting on them*. Then (and only then) can we let go of these feelings, allowing them either to slip away or to become transformed. When it is not obstructed (but at the same time not acted upon), a feeling will, like water, rapidly find its own level. It will soon start to change as reflections in water do—moving and shifting and dissolving. If we let our feelings be, without opposition *but* without putting them hastily into action either (this is important), they will transform themselves in a positive way and without any effort on our part.

Releasing on Feelings

An effective unlocking tactic to use when we are heavily locked in and can't release is to identify the *feeling* we have about the situation and release on this feeling first. When we allow our feelings to "just be," they work for us. Friendly feelings don't block Releasing but move the Releasing process forward.

Every locked-in situation involves at least one single "pure" feeling. A good rule-of-thumb then is: When you find yourself locked into a situation, identify the purest, strongest feeling that accompanies it. Is it anger? Discouragement? Shame? Guilt? Sadness? Frustration? Fear? Something else?

When you have identified that feeling, try to state it to yourself as strongly as possible, to give it a powerful name. Pure feelings are intense; they are not stated diplomatically. Anger is a pure feeling, but partly concealed, it becomes "irritation." Fear is a pure feeling, but partly concealed, it becomes "uneasiness"—and so on. Go for the pure feeling (if you can) and use the *stronger* word. This helps. But if it doesn't feel right to you, then go for the concealed, watered-down feeling and release on that. It will work, too. And if you can't locate any specific feeling (but just know that you feel strongly about something), then let go of wanting to change "that feeling" without naming it. This will work, too. Any form of Releasing is always useful.

When you have identified the feeling that is giving you trouble (even if it has no name), think to yourself, or say out loud:

> **"Could I let go of wanting to change (that feeling) and just let it be ...** *without acting on it* **in any way? ..."**

Or, if you don't want to change the feeling, think to yourself:

> **"Could I let go of wanting to** *justify* **(that feeling) and simply let it be there ...** *without acting on it* **in any way? ..."**

Then allow the feeling to exist within you, strongly and without having to be justified. Don't think about why you have the feeling; just let yourself feel it throughout your entire body, experiencing it physically. Let the feeling just "be there" for about thirty seconds (or whatever period of time feels comfortable). If the feeling doesn't change in quality, or fade away after you have done this, then you haven't released on it. In this case, release on wanting to release, and turn to another unlocking tactic for the time being.

Now let's review what you just did. You did *not* ask yourself to let go of your feeling or banish it. On the contrary, you asked yourself to let go of wanting to change that feeling, or of wanting to justify it. In a sense, then, you asked yourself to hold on to the feeling. This is, of course, exactly the reverse of what most of us ordinarily do!

This means that if you are angry and want to release on your anger, you don't try to get rid of the anger, but at the same time you don't act on it either. You don't bury or evade the anger—but neither do you hit someone, shout at someone, smash an object, or tear your hair out. All you need to do to release on anger is allow the anger to *be there, fully.*

When releasing on an emotion, do not act on your feelings. Do nothing to try to get rid of those feelings. Instead, behave like the captain of a sailing ship who decides to make a complete about-face and head straight into the wind. If you face directly *toward, go straight into, and sail right through a feeling—on the other side, there is a release.*

> **To release on a feeling, locate some recent event that has made you feel uncomfortable, identify the feeling involved, then try to *hold on to* this feeling for as long as you can. . . . Keep this feeling in the center of your awareness, but without feeding it any thoughts or images to justify it. . . . Just hold on to the pure *physical* feeling, by itself.**

If you can do this, the feeling will change. Feelings have to be fed to remain strong. we usually feed them with thoughts about why we have them (scenes that explain them). When we allow a feeling to "be," without feeding it, then, like a fire which is no longer fueled, the feeling will die down.

A member of a releasing workshop wanted to—but couldn't—release on the behavior of the superintendent of her building. He had failed to repair an annoying leak in her kitchen ceiling for more than a week, and she had had to keep changing pails under the spot. The leak was getting worse, but neither the super nor her landlord had responded to her urgent requests. Her reaction was one of helpless fury.

I suggested that she let go of wanting to change or justify her feeling of anger and just let it "be" for thirty seconds. At first she was bewildered by this request. She said she had been angry at the super all week and it hadn't helped. I explained that I was not asking her to allow herself to *get angry* at the super (that is, act on it), but merely to feel the anger itself, without thinking about any of the reasons for it. "Just feel the pure, strong anger. Feel it physically through your whole body."

Actually, she had been so busy frantically trying to change the leaking ceiling, her super, and the landlord that she had not had any time to fully experience her anger. Now she was able to forget about these people and their behavior and about the leaky ceiling, too, at least for half a minute, and allow herself to feel the anger all through her body—with no need to justify or explain it. She was able to allow the anger simply to exist.

As she did this, the muscles in her cheeks and around her mouth softened, and her breathing became slower and fuller. She reported that she felt the anger "balance out" and was no longer overwhelmed by it. She was not even sure that she was angry anymore. It was, she pointed out, a relief just to feel the anger without having to explain it. At this point, she decided she could take care of what had to be done about the leaking ceiling without putting this strain on herself.

When we stop making mental pictures of the situation that has upset us but accept our feelings in their raw, pure form—we experience a release.

I am reminded of an experience of my own. I was conducting an all-day workshop which was going extremely well. Group members who had never seen each other before were working together like old friends, and I found myself relaxed and at my best.

Then we took a ten-minute break during which I routinely checked my makeup in the mirror. The lighting in the hotel room where I had stayed the night before had been dim. As I looked in the mirror now, I discovered that in the inadequate light I had put on too much rouge and had been over made-up all morning!

Since my style is the natural look, I found myself extremely embarrassed at the thought of having conducted that morning session looking totally unlike myself. "Of all things, *me* over made-up?" For a moment the embarrassment was so painful that I couldn't imagine facing the group again. Then, while wiping the excess color off my cheeks, it occurred to me to release on the embarrassment.

"Could I let go of wanting to change the embarrassment and just let it exist?" As soon as I thought this, the embarrassment flared up even more and my cheeks began to burn. Then the feeling commenced to change. I allowed myself to be "in" the embarrassment fully. It was like being carried by an ocean wave which crested and then receded. As I waited out this experience for about thirty seconds, I felt an immense relief flowing through me. I thought "How incredible. I can be that embarrassed and still live through it! Embarrassment isn't as devastating as I thought!"

During the following hour, I experienced several returns of the feeling of embarrassment, but this time they were less intense. My mind was simply reliving the situation of having conducted the group all morning while not looking my best. It was similar to the way one might push against a painful tooth to see if it still hurts. Each time I remembered the scene, I released once more on wanting to change the embarrassment. As I repeatedly let the feeling be there, it became progressively weaker. Finally the embarrassment disappeared entirely. Now, even when I intentionally rehearsed the scene in her mind, I couldn't bring back that feeling.

It was then that I experienced the most important aspect of this release. I realized that I would never fear embarrassment in the same way again. I would try my best to avoid it in the future—who wouldn't?—but now I knew that anytime I found myself in an embarrassing position again, I would release on it and the embarrassment would be bearable. I had won a permanent freedom.

Since that time, whenever I have been threatened by a sense of embarrassment, I have automatically released on the situation. This occurs with the instantaneous thought, "It's only embarrassment! I can stand *that*. Remember the meeting when I had on too much rouge?"

Letting Go of Feelings

There is another way to release on emotions. This consists of letting go *directly* of the feeling that is bothering us. I personally don't find this method as profound in its effects as releasing by allowing the feeling to remain "unchanged and unjustified," but some people find that releasing directly on feelings this way works even better for them than the first approach. You will decide for yourself and therefore should try both. Here is how to let go of a feeling directly:

When bothered by an unpleasant feeling, think to yourself, or say out loud:

"Could I let go of (the feeling)?"

Then simply "let go" of the feeling. Don't *try* to let go; just let go. To illustrate what I mean by this, try the following experiment.

Pick up a pencil, hold it in front of you, and say out loud in a determined tone:

"I'm going to *try* to get rid of this pencil!"

Then try to get rid of it!

Are you confused? Do you really know how to "get rid" of a pencil? Do you hide the pencil? Give it away to someone else? Break it into pieces? Drop it into a scrap basket? Bury it in the ground? Or use some other means of getting rid of it? All you really know is that since you are to "try" to get rid of it, you have to use effort. Other than that, you may be confused.

Now do another experiment.

Pick up the same pencil again, hold it in front of you, and say out loud in an easy, offhand manner:

"I'm going to let go of this pencil."

Then simply let go. The pencil will fall, thanks to gravity.

To release directly on a feeling, you just "let go" of the feeling, as lightly and easily as you would open your fingers to let a pencil drop. It's only when you try to let go of a feeling that you get locked into it. As water becomes transformed into ice, feelings which we try to manipulate are frozen into permanent form. Befriending our feelings (or simply letting go of them without fuss) allows them to flow once more.

You will have an opportunity to see how this method operates for some of the people whose experiences are recounted later on. For now, the point to remember is that there are two ways of releasing on feelings. One is to stop trying to change or justify them and just allow them to "be." The other is to let go of them directly.

Surprising as it may seem, we can let go of any feeling, just as easily as we can let go of "wanting to change" something.

The Layering Effect

An interesting aspect of releasing on feelings is the discovery that underneath one feeling another may be hidden, and beneath that still another. Sometimes we have to release on a whole string of emotions before we obtain a full release. Imagine the following.

A stray dog stands with his back against the fence, facing a group of children and snarling. The children are trying to capture the dog in order to befriend him, but the dog doesn't know this. He has experienced only cruelty in the streets, and to him the children are enemies. The dog bares his teeth, the hair on his neck bristles ominously, and he lowers his head for attack.

Then one of the children asks the others to step back. He breaks off part of a sandwich which he is carrying and throws it to the dog and speaks to the dog in a quiet voice, "Good boy ... good dog." The dog makes a frantic leap for the food, swallowing it in one gulp. Then the boy throws another piece of food, still talking quietly to the dog. He continues to do this until the dog has devoured the whole sandwich.

Now the animal cowers against the fence. He is no longer snarling. His anger is gone. Now he is trembling, every inch of his skinny body shuddering as though with a chill. The dog was terrified to begin with. His fear was the main cause of his anger, but before the boy fed the dog, anger held the center of the stage. Now that anger had died down, the dog's underlying fear has surfaced.

The boy stays with the dog, talking to him quietly for a long time, until finally the dog looks up and meets the boy's eyes. This is a signal to the boy that he can step forward and quietly slip a rope around the animal's neck. He does this and leads the dog to his home. When the two of them arrive there, the boy finds the dog a place to sleep. The dog is weary and lies down with a deep sadness in his eyes. The dog's fear had hidden the sadness and loneliness of his ordeal in the streets. Now that fear has been stilled, the sadness surfaces.

As the dog becomes accustomed to his new home and learns to trust the boy, the sadness, too, will fade away. Now the dog's expression will become one of love. The situation will have been transformed.

Feelings occur in layers. When we release on one feeling, the feeling that was underneath it surfaces. This gives us an opportunity to release on this other feeling, bringing us even greater relief. Many of us have warm and loving feelings that are buried beneath negative feelings. When the negative feelings are released, we are free to be more loving of others and of ourselves.

Recognizing Your Feelings

Recognizing your own feelings in a troublesome situation is a keystone to successful releasing. Most people don't pay much attention to their feelings except when this is unavoidable. The reason is simple. They think that there is nothing to be gained from focusing on their feelings, so that looking at those feelings seems like an exercise in futility. When we learn to release, the situation is different. Now we have a tool for getting rid of the harmful effects of those feelings. This provides a good reason for paying attention to them. It is now to our *advantage* to do so.

It is useful to identify the feelings you have about any problem that you confront. If a feeling is getting in the way and making it difficult for you to release—then go straight to the feeling and release on that *first*. Later you can release on other aspects of the situation—if you still need to.

The question of releasing on feelings sometimes leads to a misunderstanding of what Releasing actually is, however. I have often had people ask me whether releasing on their anger would simply make them into a wimp—"sweet and understanding" all the time. The answer to this is, or course, "no." Releasing on your anger won't get rid of your capacity to become angry (fortunately, because anger can be essential for your survival in certain situations). What releasing will do is give you a choice in any given situation as to whether or not you *want* to be angry.

Greg's fifteen-month-old daughter was showing signs of pulmonary stress, accompanied by a fever of 105 degrees which was mounting by the minute, when he and his wife rushed her to the emergency room of the hospital. There they were met by a clerk who presented them with elaborate forms and admonitions to "be patient" and wait for a doctor. This could, they learned, mean a wait of an hour or more; all physicians were "very busy." Since the baby was now struggling to catch her breath and had become deathly pale, Greg chose not to suppress his mounting anger. In a voice ringing with the rage of a parent whose child's life is in danger, he shouted to the clerk to move out of his way. With his little girl in his arms, he then pushed his way through the closed doors into the medical examining room and demanded that the first doctor he saw examine his daughter. When the physician did so, he found it was necessary to administer emergency treatment. The little girl might not have lived had Greg not given vent to his anger.

The point of this story is that expressing anger can be the best possible behavior in some situations. Greg had not yet learned to release when this incident occurred (he did learn later), but he might not have wanted to release on his anger under these circumstances. On the other hand, he might have decided to release on the *feeling* of anger, but to have *acted* very angry indeed. Often this is an extremely effective maneuver.

He also might have decided to release on his anxiety. Had he released in any manner, his distress would probably not have persisted as a bodily tension long after his little girl was out of danger. After releasing his expression of anger would not have taken as great a physical toll.

The main point to remember about releasing on anger is that it allows you to make the choice to be outraged rather than having the "knee-jerk" response—anger. This puts *you* in the driver's seat. If you release on the anger, you may still choose to assume a posture of anger. This can be a powerful way of attracting attention. It is, in fact, the strategy of experienced trial lawyers who use their anger in the courtroom with devastating effectiveness but are not consumed by the emotion so that it pounds away at their gut. Anger of choice may even be the most effective kind of anger because it allows you to know what to do next. After you storm the bastions, you will now be clearheaded enough to be able to organize your actions to take the next step and achieve what you want.

Releasing, therefore, gives you a choice with respect to your emotions. If you decide not to release under certain circumstances, that is fine, too, but you will still sense the control that comes with having had a say in the matter.

Just as with anger, releasing on anxiety doesn't lead to inaction. If action is required, it can be undertaken more effectively after releasing on the anxiety involved in the situation. One member of a Releasing workshop released on his worry that his wife might never be able to find a new house that she wanted to move into, although their present house had already been sold and the family would be forced to move in a matter of weeks. He was then able to be more resourceful in assisting her to find a new home that would meet their standards. And now he was able to do this without causing his stomach to contract and his throat to dry up. He was efficient without paying the physical price that anxiety would have brought.

Because identifying feelings is crucial to the releasing process, the following is a useful rule-of-thumb:

When in doubt about how to release on a situation, first locate your *feeling* about the situation. Release on that, and the rest will follow easily.

One of the benefits of releasing on feelings is that our minds seem to open up so that we can now see the pertinent facts more clearly and make appropriate decisions. I call this process *opening the monitor*. We will look at it in the next chapter.

Chapter 7

OPENING THE
MONITOR

The "monitor" is a word used in the Releasing technique to describe that part of our minds which scans and evaluates incoming information and selects an appropriate response from the many which are stored in our memories. Our monitor might be compared to the beacon of a lighthouse continually sweeping across sea and land. The more information its searchlight picks up, the more valuable it is to its owner.

Unfortunately, however, when we experience strong negative feelings such as anger, fear, grief, and the like, our monitor closes down. At such times, it is as though the lighthouse keeper had readjusted the searchlight so that instead of swinging in a wide arc of 180 degrees or more, surveying sea and land to all sides, it now swings in a narrow 15-degree or 10-degree arc. The searchlight beam now illuminates only that small portion of the landscape where an "emergency" seems to lie.

This shutting-down of the monitor under strong emotion results in tunnel vision, and the effect is as though we were wearing blinders. We see no more than a tiny portion of what is "out there," or "in here" in our minds. Not only do we not see the forest for the trees, we are lucky if we see even an individual tree, or part of one! Meanwhile, the forest might be burning down, and we wouldn't know it. Restricting awareness to such a narrow focus can be dangerous, and it drastically reduces our effectiveness.

The way the monitor shuts down under strong emotion is illustrated by the following tale. The details are not to be taken seriously (they are not true), but the point the story makes is important.

Let's suppose that a woman named Beth is driving some distance to attend a convention where she is due to address a group of business associates at 2:00 P.M. It is now 1:00 P.M. As she drives through unfamiliar countryside, her car develops a flat tire. She stops to change the tire but on opening the trunk discovers that her automobile jack is not there. Because of this, she has to get help and must do so within the next few minutes if she is to make it to her speaking engagement on time.

Beth walks anxiously up the road and spots a house with an ordinary doorway (picture 1). Relieved, she hastens up the path and rings the doorbell. No one answers. She rings again. Still no answer. She pounds on the door, panic welling up within her. This door has now become the center of her universe. She feels she must get through the door and into that house at all costs to get help or to telephone her colleagues at the convention.

Picture 1: The darkened portions in the circle above represent the closed monitor. Subsequent pictures on page 66 show the opening up of the monitor with Releasing.

Now, let's assume that Beth has learned Releasing and that at this point she decides to release on wanting to change the situation. As she does so, her monitor opens up. Now she can see a wider scene (picture 2 on page 66). (The beacon light is swinging in a wider arc.)

At first, in her intense need to get to the door, she didn't notice a path leading somewhere else—to another part of the house, perhaps? At this point, let's assume she releases once more. When she does so, her monitor finally opens fully, and she now finds herself surveying a wide panorama (picture 3 on page 66).

Now she sees many options. There is another door in another part of the house. She could go over and try that. She sees people in the yard doing some landscaping and a man jogging along the sidewalk. She could ask any of these people for help, and possibly they would let her into the house.

If she can't get into this particular house, not all is lost either. A road leads up a slope to another house nearby. There are people on that road, too, any of whom might be able to offer help or advice, and the house on the slope is also likely to have a telephone.

Beth's mental capacities have opened up as her monitor has been reactivated. The situation now seems soluble. Her awareness has returned to the present, and she feels as though the outcome of the incident is in her own hands. She promptly works out the problem, arrives at the convention on time, and walks calmly up to the podium.

When we release, we notice that we have choices.

Negative Triggers

There are many reasons why the monitor closes down. Certain situations will trigger strong emotions that cause the monitor to shut down in almost everyone. Each individual also reacts to special situations that shut down the monitor for them but not necessarily for others. It is useful to know about both types of triggers, the universal ones and the personal ones. This helps to

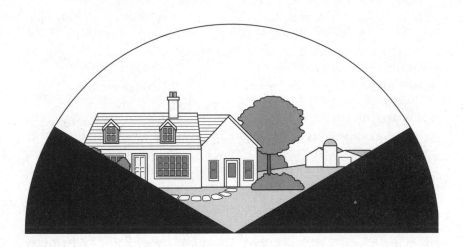

Picture 2.

Picture 3.

identify opportunities to release that we might otherwise overlook.

Any life-threatening situation can trigger a shutdown of the monitor. Panic is capable of closing the monitor to a point where perception and judgment are severely distorted. A friend of mine recalls an experience he had in a theater some years ago. He was sitting in the second row of the orchestra with his friend when a fire broke out backstage and the audience was abruptly requested to leave. Looking around, he quickly spotted an exit door nearby and started to guide his friend toward it. To his surprise, however, she broke away from him and began to push her way into the center aisle. The front door of the theater was at least a hundred feet away, and the center aisle was already jammed with people. He caught her by the arm, pointing out that they could leave by the side exit, but she acted as though totally deaf to his words. Her monitor was so shut down that all she could see was that the center aisle eventually led to the front door. She fought her way free and pushed herself into the mass of struggling bodies. He left by the side exit and waited for her in front of the theater for twenty minutes before she finally emerged, trembling, as the desperate crowd struggled out through that one set of doors.

Stories about panic closing down the monitor are common. Another friend of mine remembers being in a new auditorium when the foundations of the building began to sag under the weight of the crowd. The room was listing to one side like a sinking ship, but the audience was assured by the management that everything would be fine if they left in a quiet, orderly fashion.

Then someone cried out, "It's an earthquake!" Panic broke out and there was danger of a stampede which might have rocked the building, further weakening the foundations. The admonitions of the building staff were drowned in the rising cries of alarm.

At that point, a man from the audience leaped up on to the stage and in a resonant tenor voice began to sing, loudly and clearly the national anthem. As they heard him singing, one person after another in the audience stopped to look around and see what was happening. This broke the spell. The panic subsided. My friend remembers that she could feel the mood of panic leave the building, like a wave turning into ripples and flowing out through the doors. The man's wise and unexpected action had opened the collective monitor of the crowd. The audience quickly became orderly again and was able to evacuate the building safely.

There are many common situations that can close down the monitor. Here are some of the most frequent:

Physical Illness

Accident

Pain

Dangerous Attack

Threat to Security

Starvation

Intense Thirst

Action of Mind-Altering Substances (Alcohol, Drugs, etc.)

Fatigue; Loss of Sleep

These situations shut down the monitor because of the strong emotions involved. Any overwhelming emotion can have this effect. Terror, grief, anger, intense shame, or other powerful feelings decrease our effectiveness radically.

Under the above conditions, releasing can be particularly valuable.

Aside from these universal situations, individual situations that trigger a shutdown are frequent. Some people are distressed by certain social situations to such a degree that their monitor closes down rapidly and they stop noticing anything except the way they think people are responding to them—and they often can't gauge even this correctly.

Other people discover their monitor snapping shut whenever they feel guilty, even if their guilt is about a trivial matter. For example, a college student who had forgotten to phone his mother about a minor issue the previous night felt so guilty about this (because of his particular relationship with this mother) that he couldn't concentrate on answering the questions in an examination he had to take in the morning. As a result, he almost failed the exam, although he had studied well and had a good grasp of the subject. His guilt had shut down his monitor. Similarly, being unfairly accused can close down some people's monitors to a point where they can become either depressed or angrily riveted on the idea of revenge.

Still others find their monitors regularly closing down whenever they have to meet a deadline, speak in public, face a job interview, deal with in-laws, handle children's disobedience, be alone, or under any number of other situations. Each of us can have personal triggers that close down our own monitor to a point where we can scarcely function, although under ordinary circumstances we may function extremely well.

What Are Your Triggers?

It can be helpful at this point to make a list of your own personal triggers, those situations that leave you not acting at your best or which cause you such discomfort that your effectiveness is severely hampered. Once you know them, any one of these negative situations can become a positive signal for you to start releasing.

It's a good idea to rate each of your personal triggers according to the degree to which it shuts down your monitor. Suppose, for example, that one of your personal triggers is having someone criticize a piece of work that you have done; when this happens, your attention is removed from more constructive things for a while, but the situation doesn't immobilize you and you are apt to recover from it before the day is over. In this case, you might estimate that the situation shuts down your monitor by about 30 percent. If another trigger upsets you to the point of affecting your entire day thereafter and making concentration on problems at hand difficult, then you might want to give this trigger a "shutdown rating" of 50 percent. A truly immobilizing trigger, such as an emergency situation, can rate as high as 90 percent or 100 percent.

When assigning your shutdown rating, don't think about it. Simply jot down the first percentage figure that pops into your mind. Your intuition will help you make this an accurate figure.

Your monitor-shutdown ratings can then be used to give you an idea of how much releasing may be necessary in order to open up your monitor in any particular situation. The situations which have lower shutdown ratings may respond readily to releasing directly on the situation. ("Could I let go of wanting to change the fact that_____?") The situations with the highest ratings (80–100 percent shutdown) will usually require you to release on the *feelings* involved first. ("Could I let go of wanting to change (or justify) this feeling—and just let it *be* for about thirty seconds?")

In general, the more closed your monitor, the more intense your emotion, and therefore the more important it becomes to release on the emotion itself first, before turning to the situation and working directly on that. Take your time in making up your list of personal triggers. It can be extremely valuable for you when the monitor closes down. Closing of the monitor may block out the thought of releasing, along with all other options. You will want to remember to release when you need to. Having made up the list in advance can help you to remember.

Releasing is always indicated whenever the monitor has shut down!

Taking Time Out

Another key factor whenever the monitor closes down is—*time*. When you take time out—you can release.

A successful business executive I know has been using this kind of "time-out" strategy for years. Whenever he is confronted by a challenging business situation he retreats to the men's room. When he returns, his emotional reactions are completely under control and his business judgment is masterful.

This story points up an important aspect of releasing under pressure. Some people find it easy to release while in the midst of a highly emotional situation, but others cannot. For those who can't readily release under pressure, it is essential for them to take time out as quickly as possible. When confronted by an upsetting challenge, they should take a break *on any excuse*, use it to release, and then return to the situation with their monitor opened.

Now we come to a major shortcut to releasing—the way in which you can release on wanting approval and wanting to control. These issues will be taken up next.

Chapter 8

DO YOU WANT
APPROVAL OR
CONTROL?

So far, you have learned how to use unlocking tactics in difficult situations. Now you are going to learn a shortcut. Certain feelings occur so frequently that releasing on the *general categories* they represent can save valuable time.

Releasing on Wanting to Control

The opening phrase you have been using to release has been,

"Could I let go of wanting to change? . . ."

When you want to change someone (or something), you are, of course, trying to control that person or thing. Unfortunately, we often feel the need to control anything and everything around us. When we don't succeed in this, and we often don't, we can make ourselves very unhappy.

Being in control is certainly useful, however. Human inventiveness is born from the need to control, and a healthy wish to control forms the basis of all learning. When I talk about letting go of wanting to control, therefore, I will mean letting go of the need to *over*control—the desire to manipulate facets of life which either cannot be manipulated or which can only be manipulated at too heavy a cost to ourselves.

A great many things are partially or completely outside of our control. These can range from abstract matters such as air pollution, our own mortality, and the political-economic situation to such minor inconveniences as a mechanical device that doesn't work, a person who speaks to us in an "edgy" tone of voice, or being unable to locate something. If we noted down how many things failed to go the way we wanted them to go during a typical day, we would all find ourselves with a long list.

Since we can't make everything go the way we want it to, we need to learn how to let go of our overinvolvement in unchangeable situations and concentrate instead on those matters which *can* be affected by our actions.

The philosophy behind this is similar to that of mutual-help organizations such as Alcoholics Anonymous, which teach their members to let go of making impossible demands on life and turn their energies toward realizing the possible. AA members sum up this philosophy in their Serenity Prayer which goes as follows:

God grant me the
Serenity to accept the things I cannot change;
The courage to change the things I can;
And the wisdom to know the difference.

This verse reflects the experience of countless people who have struggled to find constructive ways to deal with the uncontrollable aspects of life. Releasing is a device for putting such philosophies of acceptance into action by helping the person to relinquish his or her drive towards *overcontrol*.

To release on wanting to "control," first consider the situation and find out if you want to change it in any way.

If you do, you are wanting to control it, and you can simply substitute the phrase, "wanting to control," for the phrase, "wanting to change." Then think of yourself, or say out loud:

"Could I let go of wanting to control (this situation)?"

Or simply:

"Could I let go of wanting to control (in general)?"

The way you phrase the question will be determined by your objectives. Mentioning a specific situation ("Could I let go of wanting to control this situation?") is useful in driving home a special point. Releasing on wanting to control in *general* ("Could I let go of wanting to control?") affects your basic need to control.

You may also revert part of the time to your original phrase, "Could I let go of wanting to *change* that?" Some people (myself included) use this "change" phrase more than any other for Releasing. Others prefer the "control" phrase for almost all situations. Many people switch back and forth between the two. These phrases say the same thing in different ways. Both are effective. In a particular instance, one may work better than another, so it is useful to have both alternatives at your fingertips.

Wanting Approval

There is no human need which causes more mental anguish than the need for approval. Receiving approval can bring us much pleasure, closeness and warmth, but when we seek approval from people whose approval is not forthcoming or from whom it is inappropriate, or when we seek it in situations where it is impossible to know whether we are really getting approval, this need can cause great distress.

Our drive to win approval is not limited to seeking it from others, either. Although we may not realize it, we are constantly seeking approval from ourselves. There are special ways to deal with this need for our own approval by releasing on it. We will work with these shortly. In the meantime, let's first deal with wanting approval from others.

As we grow from total dependence on other people in infancy and early childhood to relative independence and self-reliance, we usually work out a balance between seeking approval from others and being able to give approval to ourselves. There are times, however, when no matter how independent we may be, we can get caught up in a frantic need for outside approval. At such times we may become locked in to the need for outside approval, and can experience anxiety, anger, or even despair if the other person's (or people's) approval is not forthcoming. At these times, releasing on approval can be the most valuable unlocking strategy we can use.

To do this, think to yourself, or say out loud:

"Can I let go of wanting (that person's) approval?"

Or:

"Can I accept the loss of 1 percent of his/her approval?"

Then let go of the *wanting* (the *overpush*), or accept this very small loss of approval, just as you have let go in other releasing situations.

Because the need for approval is an exceptionally strong need, you may sometimes find yourself feeling that you "can't survive" without a certain person's approval or that it would be "unthinkable" not to have it. In such a case, it may be useful to phrase the Releasing question to yourself somewhat differently. For some people the following wording can be very effective:

Think to yourself, or say out loud:

"Could I let go of wanting to *control* (that person's) approval?"

This way you are not asking yourself to let go of wanting the approval itself. You are simply asking yourself to let go of wanting to control when and how the approval occurs or is expressed. Basically, wanting to control the approval is the root of the problem anyway. We are apt to want to run the show and decide how the approval is to come to us; we want to move the chessmen around on the board in a way that will satisfy us. Unfortunately, it is impossible to control how, when, or why others will approve of us. When we let go of wanting to control their approval, we experience relief.

Still another helpful strategy is to think to yourself, or say out loud:

"Could I let go of the feeling of wanting (that person's) approval? . . . Just the *feeling*?"

After all, a feeling is just a feeling; you can always let go of it.

It may also help to write down on a card your intention of experiencing approval. Then hold the card in front of you as you release. This way you are reminding yourself that you are not required to give up your *intention* of having approval—just the *feeling* of wanting approval.

Wanting Your Own Approval

Approving of ourselves is essential to a happy, meaningful life, but when we are approving of ourselves, we are seldom aware that this is happening. At such times, our sense of self-approval is simply present in the background, as a solid support. It is when we *don't* have our own approval that we become aware of the approval issue. At this point, we may try desperately to win our own approval.

The Releasing technique can help by lessening this strong desire. When we release on wanting our own approval, we allow our approval to return to us naturally. We feel at ease with who we really are.

If you feel uncomfortable about anything, it is useful to ask yourself whether the issue at hand involves seeking your own approval. It often does. To release on your own approval, think to yourself, or say out loud:

"Could I let go of wanting my own approval?"

Or:

"Could I let go of wanting to *control* my own approval?"

Or:

"Could I accept the loss of 1 percent of my own approval?"

The second question ("Could I let go of wanting to control my own approval?") asks only that you let go of wanting to control whether you will approve of yourself *now* or in the ten next minutes, or in the next hour, or over the next day, or of just how you will approve of yourself, or of exactly what things you're going to approve. With this question, you are simply asking yourself to let go of trying to manipulate the whole process of approval; for example, having it now instead of later. It may, therefore, be easier than the other questions. You can also let go of wanting to change the *feeling* of wanting approval ("just the feeling"). This can sometimes be the most helpful move of all.

A member of one of my releasing workshops wanted to speak up in the group but was hesitant to do so because she was afraid that her observations might not be the most "brilliant and fascinating" in the room. She clearly wanted approval.

When I pointed that out to this woman, she was able to easily let go of wanting the approval of other people for being "brilliant," but found it extremely difficult to let go of wanting her *own* approval because this seemed far more important to her. I pointed out that when a person wants her own approval *too strenuously*, it can make that approval recede into the distance and become unattainable. The process is like trying to swim after a beach ball. The harder you try to reach the ball, the more you create waves. The waves keep pushing the beach ball ahead, and so it stays maddeningly just one foot in front of you and you may never catch up to it. Or it is similar to the way you feel when you try to get a speck out of a glass of water with your fingertip. Each time your finger approaches the speck, it creates a bubble that pushes the speck further out of reach. This continues for as long as you keep creating the bubble with your fingers.

Striving too hard to get what you want can prevent you from getting it.

This group member had difficulty releasing on her own approval because she thought I was asking her to *relinquish* her self-approval. To help her understand why this was not the case, I suggested that she imagine sitting down to eat a delightful dinner with close friends somewhere in the country on a lovely summer's day. She should imagine the air as being fresh and sweet-smelling and herself as feeling that all is right with the world. At that moment as she experienced herself fully and happily, she was to observe whether she was thinking to herself, "Now I approve of myself. . . . Now I really accept myself." She would probably not be thinking this, because in most happy moments people don't think about approving or disapproving of themselves; they simply experience themselves in an accepting way. The reason they won't be thinking about approving of themselves is because at that moment they *have* their own approval.

When we *want* something, that always means that we do not, at the moment, *have* that something. When we have something, there is no need to want it.

Conscious approval and disapproval are both judgments. When we accept ourselves fully, we don't judge.

The woman who had been concerned about her own approval was now able to release fully on her need for it. When she did so, she was no longer concerned about being brilliant before the group and began to contribute openly to the discussion.

If you stop trying to control whether you have your own approval, you experience a "rightness" about yourself, whether you want to call it "approval" or by some other name. Actually, this feeling is the most important approval of all.

Approval and Support

Often we feel we cannot let go of wanting someone's approval because we are afraid of losing her support. This reaction harks back to the days when as very young children we actually required outside support in order to survive. We had a great deal to lose *at that time* if we incurred the disapproval of our parents, older brothers or sisters, or others on whom we depended.

When we feel it is too difficult to release on wanting someone's approval, the issue is usually support (or security).

Can we let go of wanting support (or security)?

Think about this before you object, "Of course I can't let go of wanting those things! Doesn't everyone want security?" You should remind yourself that you are not to let go of your *intention* to have support or security when you need it. You are to *keep* the intention of having security and merely let go of the *wanting* of it.

To drive home this point to yourself, you might write down on a card in large clear letters:

Having security (support) is an excellent goal—I can keep it!

Then hold this card firmly in your hand, and, looking straight at it, think to yourself or say out loud:

"Could I let go of the feeling of wanting the support (or security)? Remember, it's only a *feeling*."

You are asking yourself to let go only of the *wanting*. If you still have difficulty after that, you can ask yourself:

"Could I accept the loss of *1 percent* of his/her support?"

Then you might proceed to build up by increments (over a period of time) the percentage points you can let go of, until you are able to let go of 100 percent of your wanting support (you learned in chapter 5 how to add percentage points to the 1 percent solution until you reach 100 percent).

You may be astonished to discover what this strategy does for you. It will probably make it far easier for you to let go of wanting approval from others. Also, if you were particularly dependent on the approval of one of your parents (grandparents, etc.) as a child, it can be a very effective strategy (after having let go of wanting support or security) to ask yourself if you could let go of wanting *that parent's* approval. Do this as though he or she were standing before you right now:

"Could I let go of 1 percent of the feeling of wanting (mother's, father's, etc.) approval?"

Or:

"Could I accept the loss of 1 percent of his/her approval?"

When you have let go of 1 percent of the wanting, then work your way up gradually by increments to the point where you are able to let go of 100 percent (or near that) of wanting this important person's approval. This is such an effective device that it might be considered a form of therapy, serving to put to rest the feelings from your past which may interfere with your effective functioning in the present.

The Approval of Your Conscience

Perhaps you are wondering how people can influence themselves to behave properly if they don't seek their own approval. This raises an important issue. The human conscience is necessary for the functioning of society and is maintained by a deep need to feel right about what we do, to have our behavior match our ethical standards. We need to retain these moral standards because they give depth and meaning to human life.

Letting go of wanting our own approval, however, as done in the releasing method, does not mean letting go of our basic intention to seek the kind of self-approval involved in moral decisions. Releasing merely helps us get rid of unproductive harassment of ourselves. It stops us from forcing ourselves to be "good" in little things at the expense of more important things.

When we release on wanting our own approval, we get off our own backs and stop plaguing ourselves. This allows us to retain our moral values and the joy of feeling good about ourselves, while letting go of trifling approval (or disapproval) issues. When we release, we dispense with tendencies to come down hard on ourselves, or to pat ourselves condescendingly on the head as though we were truculent children who had to be incessantly managed.

Releasing on wanting our own approval allows us to stand up to the "preachy parent" in ourselves and place our self-criticism in perspective. When we do this, our moral sense is freed to guard our genuine values. Because we have stopped pestering ourselves about matters that are best looked upon merely as practical issues, we are often more willing to cooperate with our own consciences when *big* issues are at stake. Our conscience has become reasonable and balanced in its approach to us and we in turn are more willing to listen to it. We can now take major self-approval issues more seriously because we have gotten the paltry ones out of the way.

Because an oversevere and unreasonable conscience (as opposed to an enlightened and reasonable one) is a frequent cause of depression, releasing on your own approval can be an excellent strategy when experiencing feelings of depression. If you feel depressed about something, simply ask yourself:

"Could I let go of wanting my own approval?"

Or:

"Could I accept the loss of 1 percent of my own approval?"

There is not even a need for you to figure out what the issue is you might want your own approval for. Just ask the question. It can lead to a release.

Do You Want Approval or Control?

Wanting approval or wanting to control are such fundamental drives that a good rule-of-thumb is to check routinely on whether approval or control is involved in any situation that is causing you difficulty. Most situations involve one of these motivations, and many involve both. To check on what is involved, think to yourself or say out loud:

"Does this situation have to do with approval or control?"

Or just use the shortcut phrase:

"Approval or control?"

Once you identify whether the issue is approval or control, release on that category. If both issues are involved, release on each in turn. To do this, you can use any unlocking tactics you need.

The Giving-Approval Tactic

Another excellent way of releasing on approval is to use what I call the Giving-Approval Tactic. It is a means of supplying approval to yourself when you need it most, so that you can then let go of the need for it. The tactic involves three steps:

Step One: Think to yourself, or say out loud:

"Could I give myself a lot of approval—right now?"

You may be able to give yourself a feeling of approval immediately and effortlessly. If not, then think of some experience you have had recently where you did thoroughly approve of yourself. Recreate this experience for yourself as vividly as possible, and enjoy it.

Step Two: Think to yourself, or say out loud:

"Could I feel approval from some other person?"

Allow yourself to identify a person who approves of you in some way (even in a small way), and then feel their approval—really let it in.

Step Three: Think to yourself, or say out loud:

"Could I let go *for only five seconds* **of wanting approval?"**

When you realize you already have approval—your own and that of others—it is easy to let go of wanting approval. We only want what we don't have.

When you have been releasing for a period of time on wanting approval or wanting to control, you will begin to sense when you want approval or when you want to control, and you may find yourself releasing on these needs without even having to ask yourself about them. When this happens, you will experience considerably less pressure in your life.

With the basic approval-control issue now in hand, you are ready for the final step in your formal training in Releasing—learning how to release on arguments.

Chapter 9

USING RELEASING WITH ARGUMENTS

There is almost no occasion when we need Releasing more urgently than when we feel attacked. Feelings of anger or fear can become so intense at such moments that our monitor can close down drastically, making us far less effective.

Because of our distress we usually attempt to *control* our adversary in some manner, if only to try to change his or her behavior to a more reasonable one. If we are enraged, we may attempt to make the other person apologize, repent, feel badly, or in some other way submit to our will. How much we try to control depends on how strongly we want to win, or how much we insist on revenge.

In a similar manner, the individual who attacks us is basically trying to force *us* to behave in some particular fashion—to capitulate or feel regret, to go away, to make amends, or to act in some other way. Our response to adversaries is therefore likely to be to try to stop them in their tracks from saying or doing something. A vicious circle is thereby created. The more they try to control us, the more we try to control them, and so on back and forth in a never-ending spiral. Fortunately, however, as someone once wisely observed, "A vicious circle can be broken at any point."

One of the most effective of all ways to deal with an adversary was that used in traditional combat by the Samurai warriors of Japan. The Samurai were renowned for their extraordinary swordsmanship and expertise at maintaining balance and composure, even when faced with mortal danger. It is said that a samurai could remain deadly calm under all circumstances because instead of focusing on what his opponent was doing, he was trained to rivet his attention upon his own intent and allow his own actions to fill his awareness. This way a Samurai remained totally in *control* (rather than *controlling*) during any confrontation. Because he was not caught up in trying to change his enemy, he was free to become keenly observant of him. The Samurai warriors are said to have been invincible fighters.

When we focus on wanting to change an adversary's behavior (wanting to make him do or say or think something different), we lose our balance. When we let go of wanting to change his behavior and focus instead on our own goals, we achieve balance. It is hard to topple a balanced person.

To release on someone who is attacking you (or in any other fashion attempting to control you), think to yourself, or say out loud:

"Could I let go of wanting to *change* (that person)?"

Or:

"Could I let go of wanting to *control* (that person)?"

When you do this, your monitor will open, and you will be able to handle the situation more effectively. You will have a number of opportunities to observe this strategy in action later on when you read about people who have used Releasing to deal with a variety of personal confrontations.

Releasing on Details

A strategy which can be particularly useful when you find yourself under attack, or when someone is attempting to control you, is to identify some unimportant detail of your opponent's appearance, speech, or behavior which you would like to change and let go of wanting to change that detail.

You can let go of wanting to change this same detail over and over again, or you can shift to other details and repeat this process. When you have released several times on some seemingly unimportant detail about a person, you will find it easier to deal constructively with his or her aggressive behavior. It, too, now becomes just part of that person.

In addition, as soon as you cease opposing your opponent's behavior or trying to change his or her feelings, the person's behavior may change! The principle in back of this is the same as when you release on your own feelings. When you stop opposing the feelings of another person, that person may be relieved of the intensity of his or her feelings toward *you*.

> **When we fight emotions or behaviors (our own or others'), we strengthen them. When we cease fighting those emotions or behaviors and instead allow them to be, we make room for change.**

The reason why your adversary's behavior may change when you release on it can be understood if you imagine yourself in the shoes of the aggressor. If you are on the offensive, having an active adversary makes it easier because the other person's opposition serves to direct you. If you are engaged in physical combat, you will know that if you make a swift move to the right, an actively involved adversary will make another swift move in the same direction. When you have an active adversary, there are rules to the game—your adversary's strength pitted against your own is something you can easily gauge. Active opposition tells you where you are at each moment.

Now, consider what happens if your adversary stops engaging in direct battle and becomes instead unavailable to your blows, seeming to yield and slip away from you instead of directly fighting back. How can you effectively fight a person who reacts to your blows by moving *with* them? If you aren't careful, you may inadvertently lunge at your opponent and, meeting no opposition to block your charge, catapult forward onto the floor! When you realize that the old rules don't apply, *your* behavior will have to change.

WARNING: Although releasing on wanting to control your opponent's behavior will often result in a change in his behavior, this does not mean that you can set out to change his behavior by releasing on it. Releasing won't work if it is deliberately used to control, even for a good cause.

Occasionally someone is tempted to use the Releasing method as a means of controlling others. "If I release on wanting to control people, then I can bring them around to my side," goes the reasoning. Actually, this is sneaking control in through the back door and doesn't work. Even if others should change their ways (and they may well not do so because they will probably sense that you are trying to control them), if you have released in order to control them, then you have not released. Not having released, you remain vulnerable. If anything goes wrong in the next step, then you are right back to square one, facing all the frustration which made trouble for you in the first place.

When you release on wanting to control others, you have to release *fully* on wanting to control them, right down to wanting to control their final reactions and the outcome of the Releasing experience itself. You have to employ the method honestly. When you do, then you set yourself free.

Releasing on Wanting to Protect Yourself

One of the most effective tactics to disarm someone who is trying to control you is to think to yourself, or say out loud:

"Could I let go of wanting to *protect* myself?"

Difficult as this may sound, when you do it, you free yourself to act in a way that can ensure your safety. The cartoon opposite illustrates this.

In the cartoon, you see a rabbit facing away from us. Directly in front of the rabbit is a boa constrictor, a type of snake that swallows small animals whole. The rabbit, understandably, thinks—if it manages to think at all, under the circumstances—"I must control what that boa's going to do, or it will eat me up!"

Thinking about this, the rabbit has become frozen to the spot. All it can see are the two beady eyes of the boa constrictor staring at it. The rabbit's monitor has closed down 100 percent.

Actually, there are several options available to the rabbit although you can't see these in the picture, any more than the rabbit with the closed monitor can: to the right stands a zoo attendant with a net, waiting to catch the boa constrictor as soon as it moves forward; and to the left is a snakeproof cage with an open door, which shuts automatically when a small animal enters the cage. The rabbit could jump into this cage, and the door would snap shut, affording it safety.

If the rabbit's attention were not hopelessly fixed upon its enemy, it might realize that if it were to step back, the boa constrictor would probably slither forward after it, and the zoo keeper could then move in with his net and trap the snake. Or the rabbit could make a quick leap to the left into the snake-proof cage. Unfortunately, the rabbit's attention is riveted on trying to change the boa constrictor's *attack*, and so it remains paralyzed.

Since this is a fanciful story, now let's imagine that the rabbit "releases" on wanting to protect itself. The minute it does so, its monitor opens up and it is no longer frozen to the spot, desperately hoping to change the behavior of the snake. Now it is free to change its *own* behavior and ultimately to achieve safety by doing this.

The phrase "can I let go of wanting to protect myself" does not mean letting go of the goal of protecting oneself. It means opening up the monitor so that we can move from seeking "protection" to initiating effective action against whatever danger faces us.

Releasing on Feelings in Arguments

When we are attacked (or when someone is attempting to control us), a useful strategy is to identify the specific feeling (anger, fear, whatever) which has been aroused in us by the attack—and then release on that *feeling*. This opens our monitor so that we can be more effective.

A member of one of my Releasing workshops reported that a man with whom she worked daily was deliberately mispronouncing her name to annoy her. Although she had corrected him many times, he persisted in this behavior.

When I asked her how she felt about this, she replied that she wanted to "kill him." She said this with great feeling and with tears in her eyes. Because this feeling was so strong, I suggested that she let go of wanting to change or in any way justify her feeling of wanting to "kill" this man and just let her anger "be there" for about thirty seconds.

As she turned inward and contacted her angry feelings, she became extremely still. Finally she nodded, indicating that she had allowed the anger to settle. Now she was able to picture herself more easily in her work place with this man pronouncing her name incorrectly. She was now ready to release on the situation itself.

I asked her to imagine him mispronouncing her name again and then to let go of wanting to change this annoying behavior. Her first reaction was that this was impossible to let go of because the situation was so humiliating, but when she had released on her feeling of humiliation (by letting it "be"), she was then able to identify her core problem. She could not let go of wanting to change his behavior because she wanted so strongly to *protect* herself. If she didn't protect herself by changing him, she felt that she would be seriously hurt. I pointed out to her that she could hold on to her goal of not wanting to be hurt and also the goal of remaining safe—all I was asking was that she let go of the *feeling* of wanting to protect herself, "just the feeling."

Making a distinction between her intention and her feeling allowed her to let go of the feeling while still holding on to the need for protection. When she did this, the situation seemed different to her. She realized that if she didn't have to protect herself, she wouldn't have to pay that much attention to this man. It was now easy for her to imagine him coming into the room where she was, looking straight into her eyes and mispronouncing her name. As she imagined this, a new thought came to her. "This is a funny little man," she said to herself and was grateful that he was not her regular supervisor.

Releasing had opened her monitor. Now she could imagine the man saying those "silly" things and herself simply shrugging her shoulders.

When she went to work the day after the workshop, whenever the man started mispronouncing her name, she released on wanting to protect herself. This tactic not only brought her relief, but to her surprise, after the first few times she tried it, it had an effect on the man as well. Eventually, he stopped mispronouncing her name. It may no longer have been so interesting to do when it didn't upset her.

Releasing on Wanting Your Opponent's Approval

When you are attacked (or when someone is attempting to control you), you can often regain your equilibrium by releasing on wanting your attacker's approval.

A member of one of my workshops who was a dentist had, some years ago, done a good deal of dental work for a particular family at low fees, allowing them to charge the work because they were unable to pay. When the family eventually left town, they owed him over seven hundred dollars, which he subsequently wrote off as a bad debt.

Within a year or two, however, the father of this family obtained an excellent position in another city. Despite this turnabout in the family's financial status, he made no effort to pay Len, the dentist, the debt he owed him and had failed to respond to repeated billings. Recently, to Len's surprise, he received a phone call from this man, now president of a flourishing company. He was phoning to ask for assistance in obtaining dental insurance.

Taken aback by his call, Len used the opportunity to tell him how disturbed he had been over the years because the family had never paid the bill they owed. To this the man responded curtly, "Do I owe you money? I have absolutely no memory of it!" The conversation ended there. Len knew that the man had received many bills over the years.

Afterwards, Len found himself hurt by this phone encounter. Since he had stood by to help out the family in hard times, he felt that he did not deserve this cursory dismissal. As a result, he began to feel depressed and could not get the incident out of his mind.

Since he had learned Releasing, he decided to release on wanting to change his depression and to allow the depression just to "be there" for him. When he did so, he realized that underneath he was actually wanting this man's approval. He knew that this was absurd, of course. There was no reason he should want the man's approval—the man should want his— but, nevertheless, he found himself thinking that he wanted this man to think that he was a "good guy." Having asked him for the money that was owed to him, Len felt that he himself no longer came over as the good guy in this situation.

This was a sticky issue for him. Len was habitually trying to help people but tended to feel uncomfortable when he needed to ask them for money. Now he realized that he had to deal with his need for his own approval. Len asked himself if he could let go of wanting to *control* when and how his own approval came to him. This rather novel way of putting the question to himself seemed to do the trick. When he had let go of trying to control, manage, and regulate how he received his own approval, a sense of relief swept over him and a number of thoughts which were quite new occurred to him.

He realized that during the course of any single day he actually did approve of himself at many different times, and that the rest of this day he would undoubtedly be approving of himself in ways that he could not even anticipate at the present. This thought allowed him to decide that there was no need to insist that he approve of himself on this particular issue. All that was left now was for Len to do a little bit of cleanup releasing. This he did by releasing on wanting to change the man's curt behavior on the phone. As he did so, he found himself allowing that man for the first time to "own his own actions, whatever they were." This brought the final release that Len needed, and he found himself thinking that the man had every right to be "as low as he wants, and by the same token, I have the right to ask for the money that is owed me."

Now he could accept the fact that the man would probably never pay him the money. If by any chance the man should get back to him, he would say to him something like, "If you want to believe what you say, that's your privilege, but, for my part, I certainly don't feel inclined to do a favor for you."

Later that day, just for good measure, Len released several more times on wanting to be the good guy (that was an old, entrenched habit), but his distress about this man's phone call had been resolved once and for all. He subsequently wrote an appropriate letter, requesting payment and enclosing copies of the delinquent bills, and allowed himself to put the matter to rest in his mind.

Releasing on "Fairness"

For most people justice is a major value. We respect people who are just, dislike those who are not, and feel better about ourselves when we know that we have behaved fairly toward someone else.

To *demand* that someone else be fair to us is unproductive, however. Much of the residual pain that comes from being attacked or wronged—the pain that lasts far longer than the attack itself—comes from a smoldering resentment at having been unfairly treated.

Releasing on fairness is, therefore, a particularly liberating thing to do, making life easier and greatly increasing our coping ability. To release on wanting another person to be fair, think to yourself, or say out loud:

"Could I let go of wanting (that person, institution, etc.) to be fair?"

This can defuse the conflict, leaving you stronger to deal with the other person (or people) involved in a realistic and effective manner.

Reversing Roles

One final way to release on someone who is trying to control you (or even whom you may *suspect* may be trying to control you) is to switch roles (mentally) with that person and then release on wanting to control *yourself*. This may sound like a strange maneuver, but it's the approach that I use when I feel that anyone is trying to control me, and I find it extremely effective. Here is how it works:

Let us suppose that someone (let's call him John) has criticized your way of doing a certain piece of work and that you feel he is attempting to make you work the way he wants you to. The beauty of the reversing-roles tactic is that it makes no difference whether you are actually correct in thinking John wants to control you. It's enough that you *feel* as though this were the case.

Now put yourself mentally in John's place, and imagine as clearly as possible what it is about your behavior (or your attitude) that *he* (John) wants to control. Then release on wanting to control *that feature of yourself*.

If, for example, you felt that John wanted to control the speed with which you were getting a project completed, then your Releasing tactic would go something like this:

"As *John*—could I let go of wanting to control whether (insert your own name) gets the project completed on time?"

From that point on, proceed as with any other release. It is surprising how much relief comes from this tactic of reversing roles. You will discover how well it works as we explore actual accounts of people who have used releasing for home and work problems.

Releasing and Ethical Values

Releasing on arguments can be extremely helpful in furthering relationships and assisting one to behave in a manner in which he or she would actually like to behave—usually as a decent, reasonable person. Many individuals with strong religious or ethical convictions have found Releasing invaluable in helping them put their principles into practice.

Howard was a devout churchman with serious religious interests. His standards of behavior were high, and he demanded a great deal from himself. This made it particularly difficult for him when he found himself experiencing uncontrollable temper outbursts at what he considered the unreasonable behavior of his teenage daughter. It seemed that the more he tried to control his own outbursts, the less he succeeded. Increasingly, he found himself carried away by a rage that led him to do and say things that he later regretted.

When he talked this matter over with his minister, the latter suggested that he learn to release, believing this might help Howard put into practice his convictions about how to be a better father.

When Howard attended a Releasing workshop, intent upon learning the technique as rapidly as possible, one of the first things he needed to do, therefore, was to let go of *wanting* so strongly to *control* himself. His very intensity about improving his behavior was creating an overpush that was preventing him from achieving effective self-control. When he had released enough to reduce this initial urgency, he then learned to let go of wanting to change his daughter's unruly behavior. As soon as he was able to do this successfully, he experienced great relief. Now he no longer felt helplessly engaged in a battle to change her ways.

As he put his Releasing skills into practice, he found himself able to roll with the punch when she did something of which he might formerly have disapproved. He noticed that his tone of voice seemed to have changed to a softer, more reasonable one as he spoke to her, and he found himself able to listen to her side of the story in a way that had been impossible before. The result was the restoration of a truly workable relationship between father and daughter.

Howard's comments about his Releasing experience were particularly interesting. He felt it was doing more for him than simply improving his father-daughter situation. He had always attempted to accept what he considered to be "divine will," rather than fight it—but now he felt that he had a tool which enabled him to put this belief into practice in a way that was deeply gratifying to him.

While Releasing is not linked to any religious orientation, and certainly does not lead to acceptance of anything one does not believe in, it is worth observing that a number of people with deep religious convictions or strong ethical convictions have noted similar results. Releasing can be used to implement spiritual and ethical values, as well as for such purposes as stress reduction and personality development.

Part 2

RELEASING IN LIFE SITUATIONS

Part 2 of this book deals with people—individuals who have learned Releasing through attending Releasing workshops or in the course of counseling or psychotherapy. In one instance, the person I report on learned releasing by typing the manuscript of this book. This was my secretary, Marianne Dobi, whose anecdote about her subsequent Releasing when engaging in a sports activity has made an interesting addition to these pages.

The accounts in this section of the book afford valuable practice in Releasing with all kinds of situations, some of them situations that you personally may never encounter. They will be very useful to you, nonetheless. As you read about the experiences of others, you will find that your own feelings surface and that you can benefit from releasing on them. I suggest you use these accounts of others' experiences as opportunities to identify your own feelings and sharpen your Releasing skills. Most of us are accustomed to paying little attention to feelings as they arise because we are not supposed to be able to do anything about them. Now that you know how to change your feelings (without suppressing them), you are in a position to benefit from the wide variety of situations presented here.

Finally, I suggest that you not skip over any chapter because at first glance it doesn't seem to apply to you. You may not be facing any formal evaluations at this point in your life, for example, and therefore think you don't need to read the chapter on releasing evaluation situations. If you read it, however, you might gain valuable information on how to release during ordinary social evaluations—which all of us do face. Or you might decide the chapters on Releasing at the work place (or on careers) don't apply to you because you aren't currently employed or don't have a career. This would be a mistake. These chapters contain many examples of Releasing that apply to everybody. They will enlarge your repertoire of Releasing tactics as you see these tactics in operation.

Your next step is to relax, enjoy the anecdotes you will encounter, identify with them fully, and allow yourself to recognize the feelings they elicit in you. Then release on those feelings. If you do this, you will have advanced your understanding of Releasing considerably by the time you finish part 2.

Chapter 10

RELEASING FOR COUPLES' PROBLEMS

The use of Releasing for difficult life situations can be one of its most important benefits. This section of the book deals with people who have coped with many different types of problems by releasing on them. The first of these is the use of Releasing in the couple's relationship.

A couple need not be a pair of lovers within or without the bonds of marriage but can consist of any two people who live in the same household or who in some other manner are emotionally bound to each other in a two-person "system." The main difficulty in the couple relationship stems from the fact that it involves a personal commitment and often a physical proximity as well, which limits the freedom of one or both parties concerned.

Members of a couple are forced to get along with each other in order to live a pleasant life. Each individual's needs still persist, however, and this can lead to unfortunate deadlocks, with each partner trying to control the other's behavior. Attempts to control can range from subtle, unconscious maneuvers to outright battles and can involve such issues as the way the two spend their leisure time, allocate their money, handle their social relationships, their children, their relatives or their sex life.

While the issues of control is often paramount, issues of

approval are also sources of much difficulty. One partner may suspect the other of disapproval (failure to "appreciate"), or may try to control or monopolize the approval (love) of the other.

Releasing can play an important role in defusing these difficulties which couples face. The following accounts of couples who have used Releasing for this purpose will show you how this works.

Couple 1

Karen was an attractive woman who came for counseling because she was suffering from intense bouts of jealousy over Hal, her lover, with whom she had had a continuing relationship for three years.

Since Hal lived in a nearby city, their relationship had consisted of spending weekends together. Neither had seemed ready for marriage, and Hal was inclined to drink a bit too heavily and to flirt casually and openly with other women, although he remained basically faithful to Karen.

While Karen knew that she was the woman in Hal's life and that his flirtations were not serious, she was torn by jealousy over them, and much of her relationship with Hal was punctuated by bitter fights in which she would accuse him of infidelity. These fights would eventually end up on a childish level with Karen feeling foolish and defeated afterwards.

It became clear during her counseling sessions that Karen was involved in a relationship which caused her continual frustration. This was a problem which would need to be understood in time, but meanwhile, along with psychotherapy, I taught Karen the Releasing technique. I wanted her to have a tool which she could use on the spot to defuse her intense jealousy reactions.

She took quickly to the method and began applying it at once to her problems with Hal. For several weeks after she learned to release, each time she thought about Hal's dating other women, she paid close attention to these fantasies, allowing them to become vivid. Then she released on wanting to change the fact that Hal was with another woman.

The first time she tried this she found herself stubbornly resisting releasing on the scene—her feelings were too strong. Then she found that an effective way for her to release was to think, "Of course I can't let go of wanting him not to be with that woman—but could I let go of just the *feeling* of wanting him not to be with her? A feeling is just a feeling," she would think to herself.

Once she had let go of the feeling, the battle was won. Her fantasy no longer had the same power over her. As a result of Releasing, the couple's fights became much less frequent.

As so often happens, however, battling between members of a couple may constitute one of their main ways of relating to each other, so that when one partner begins to withdraw from the struggle, the other may (unconsciously) bring up issues which *will* result in a fight. Hal may not have been comfortable with the easier, non-battling Karen, because after several days of peaceful and pleasant relating to each other, he suddenly announced to her that he had to leave early one Sunday afternoon because he was due back to do some extra work on the job.

Karen suspected that he was planning to meet another woman, and, despite her ability to release, before she knew it she was in the middle of another one of her battles—she accusing, he defending himself. It never occurred to her to release during the fight itself (she was so emotional that her monitor closed down to a point where all she saw was that she was being "hurt and wronged"), but afterwards, when Hal had left for the city, she sat down to release after the fact.

She wanted to control Hal and make sure that he didn't go out with any other woman. The first step was to release on her need to control. When she tried to do this, however ("Could I let go of wanting to *control* Hal?"), her answer was a resounding "NO!" So she tried another tactic. She asked herself whether she could let go of "only 1 percent" of wanting to control him.

This worked. As she felt herself let go of a little corner of wanting to control Hal, she now thought to herself, "Same old Hal, same old story." The storm had blown over, her perspective had cleared.

In a relationship as complex as Karen and Hal's, however, the drama does not end with one release. A week later, Hal came back to visit, and the two of them, now in a pleasant mood, went out for the evening. As they sat in a bar, Hal began talking to an attractive brunette, who indicated that she lived in a nearby apartment complex. As he did so, Karen became acutely uncomfortable. She felt that she was unable to compete with this other woman in attractiveness. This feeling was so strong that at the time she did not even think of releasing on it.

Since Releasing had by now become a natural part of her life, however, after getting home that evening, she did release on the incident. When she compared herself with the tall, willowy brunette with the lovely tan and flashing eyes, she saw herself by contrast as a dumpy, faded blonde. She wanted Hal's approval, but more than anything else, she wanted her *own* approval and despaired of getting it.

When Karen was able to let go of the feeling of wanting her own approval, this left her more clearheaded. Now she was able to let go of a little bit of wanting Hal's approval, too. After releasing on that, the thought occurred to her that Hal's talking to the other woman might have nothing to do with how attractive she herself was. True, he seemed to have a compulsive need to flirt with other women, but why should this affect her feeling about herself? It felt different when she viewed it this way. The few minutes of Releasing had served to defuse the situation to such an extent that when Hal came back to the apartment, they had a delightful evening.

Hal's own needs as well as Karen's soon came into play again, however. The strongest challenge came the following weekend when Hal once again left at midafternoon on Sunday with an excuse about having to work. As he did so, Karen remembered the willowy brunette in the nearby apartment complex and suspected that Hal was going to meet her.

This time she said nothing, because for the first time she found herself determined to check out whether or not her suspicions were correct. She quietly bade Hal good-bye, accompanied him down to the parking lot, and watched him drive away in his car. As soon as his car had passed the row of trees at the edge of her driveway, she got into her own car and began to follow him at a safe distance. She knew where the apartment complex was, and it was not difficult for her to find her way there without being detected by Hal.

Outside the apartments she saw Hal's car drive up and pull into the parking lot. Backing up furtively, she waited on the road, and as she did so she experienced mounting suspense, as though she were a detective apprehending a criminal. She also felt relief at finally confronting the thing which she had thought about obsessively for years.

Her suspicions were confirmed when she saw Hal emerge from the apartment with the willowy brunette, step into his car, and drive off. She followed at a safe distance. They stopped at a roadside carnival, and she parked some distance from them and walked to the gates of the fairgrounds. She saw Hal buy tickets and the two of them enter and take a seat on the Ferris wheel. It was at this point that Karen realized that since she was alone, she could begin to release right there *on the spot*.

As she watched the blinking lights of the Ferris wheel and saw the couple silhouetted against the darkening sky, laughing together as the wheel turned, she was aware of powerful feelings of anger, defeat, and humiliation. Her cheeks were actually burning with humiliation. Since this was her strongest feeling, she remembered how to release on emotions and asked herself to let go of wanting to change the feeling of humiliation.

As she let go of wanting to change it, she felt herself sinking into the humiliation, almost trembling with the intensity of it. Then the feeling seemed to settle down. As she let the humiliation flow through her, it occurred to her that this feeling was not the worst experience in the world. She now saw the humiliation as something she could handle. This left her freer, and she could breathe more fully.

At this point, with some of her intense feelings cleared away, she was able to release on wanting her own approval in this situation (wanting to feel as "attractive and lovable" as her rival). She felt such a strong need for her own approval, however, that she could only release on 1 percent of the wanting at one time, then on 10 percent, and 20 percent, until finally she obtained a release. When she did so, she decided that whatever this woman was like was irrelevant—that the real issue was Hal and whether she wanted to live her life with him.

Now she was able to look once again at the Ferris wheel. Seeing Hal's arm around the slim brunette, she felt a stab of regret, almost a physical pain at the idea of losing him. This feeling overwhelmed her to such a degree that at this point she had to break up the situation into small components. "I have to get a handle on this," she thought, closing her eyes so that she wouldn't see them for the moment.

"I've got to keep going with the releasing," she thought, and started releasing on the most neutral thing she could think of—the Ferris wheel itself. Could she let go of wanting to change the way the Ferris wheel was turning around? Even this seemed too difficult for her to do, and she had to break it down into still smaller segments. Could she let go of wanting to change the *speed* at which the Ferris wheel was revolving? This she could, and this seemingly small release unlocked the roadblock.

Karen then proceeded to release in turn on wanting to change the way the seats swung from the Ferris wheel, the way the particular seat where Hal and his companion were sitting was attached to the Ferris wheel by its hinges, the fact that their seat was rocking back and forth as the wheel turned, and before she knew it, she found herself able to release on the fact that Hal was seated next to this woman on the Ferris wheel and that he had his arm around her! This was a triumph for Karen. By building up a series of little releases that she *could* do, she had eased herself into a position where she was able to accept the reality of the situation.

She at last realized that Hal's sitting with his arm around this woman was a fact of life, and for the first time since she had known him, she experienced a quiet acceptance of who Hal really was. As she released fully, she suddenly felt disinterested in what was going to happen next with the two of them. It was not within her control, and there seemed no point in her spying on them further. "What they'll do, they'll do," she thought, and walked away.

With this realization, Karen went to her car, drove home, released some more on the situation, and when she came in for her counseling session two days later, was ready to talk for the first time about why she had remained with Hal all these years, rather than moving on to a more promising relationship.

From that point on, her therapy became an effective agent for change. Eventually, she was able to break off with Hal and begin a new life for herself. Today Karen is married to a man with whom she finds herself living in a pleasant, peaceful relationship.

Couple 2

Sheila and Bruce had been married for twenty-eight years and during that time raised five children. Sheila described those years by saying, "There was absolutely nothing else in my life then except Bruce, his career, and the children."

Now, however, the children were grown, and Sheila found herself free to choose new directions in life. As a result, a battle had begun over her newfound independence. This battle was shaking the foundations of their marriage.

Sheila had applied for work in a community organization and soon discovered that her small but regular paycheck and the new friends she made on her own at work were exciting. Bruce, on the other hand, found himself inexplicably threatened by her venture into the working world. As a result, he had become increasingly withdrawn and frequently complained that she was no longer a good wife.

The result was a worsening of the situation as Sheila now began to refuse to do even simple things around the house, which formerly she had done automatically. She became so obsessed with the idea of winning her battle for independence that she was now refusing to handle very real contingencies, such as the need to call a repairman for urgent roof repairs or to take professional phone calls for Bruce. This annoyed him because she seemed to be letting him down in an area where he could have used her assistance and backup. She, on her part, was convinced that she couldn't "give an inch or he would take a mile," and her struggle to be a person in her own right lent constant fuel to the perpetual smoldering fire which underlay their present relationship.

When the two came for separate counseling (because they found it difficult to be in the room with each other), I worked to help them understand the crisis they were going through at this period of their lives and the manner in which their own personal problems might be contaminating it. In order to help them consolidate the marriage, which neither wished to abandon, in addition to using psychotherapy, I taught both partners to release.

Sheila seemed to take to Releasing with more enthusiasm, and so I suggested to her that she learn to view what she considered Bruce's efforts to "control her" as opportunities to release on wanting to control *him*.

Predictably, she was outraged by this suggestion. Wouldn't this be abandoning her fight for liberty? I pointed out that far from weakening her position, it might give her newfound strength that could win for her an even more genuine kind of liberty—without having to pay the price of destroying her marriage.

She finally agreed to "test out" releasing on wanting to control Bruce for a period of one week. If she didn't feel even freer to do those things that she wanted to do in her life *after* she had released on wanting to control Bruce's behavior, then she was to abandon the Releasing strategy. On this basis, she felt that there would be nothing to lose, and so she set about applying the method.

On the following morning, when she thought that Bruce looked like a thundercloud at the breakfast table after she had informed him that she was going to spend Saturday at the ballet with a woman friend, she tried releasing instead of withdrawing defensively. Watching him as he angrily twisted apart his breakfast roll and noticing his flushed face, she decided to release on his behavior by using the divide-and-conquer tactic.

"Could I let go of wanting to control the necktie he's wearing this morning?" she asked herself casually. She could. Then she tried releasing on wanting to control the way he clattered his fork and knife as he ate his eggs. This she found more difficult to do because it made her feel that he was angry, which in turn stirred up anger in her, so she asked herself instead if she could let go of the *feeling* of wanting to change the clatter—she let her wish (the intention) stay there; after all, it was only reasonable.

When she released on the clatter, Sheila found it easy to let go her feelings of anger as well. They seemed to consist of tensions that ran along her arms to her fingertips, with an accompanying vivid fantasy of tearing the knife and fork out of his hands! "A feeling is just a feeling," she said to herself, and this thought brought a surprising sense of ease and of being *in control* of herself.

As she watched Bruce now, she was able to let go of the feeling of wanting to control the flush of anger in his face. As she did this, something now struck her as slightly humorous about the whole situation. He was eating with jerky movements, probably because he was angry, and this looked almost clownish to her. It seemed ridiculous that he should be so annoyed by such a small incident. After all, he himself was planning to play golf on Saturday, whether or not she went to the ballet!

As she released again, the whole matter now seemed irrelevant. She felt that she had a right to go with a friend, and so it didn't seem an issue worth fighting about. It seemed obvious that they should both do something that they enjoyed on Saturday. She now felt her own position so clearly that she could smile about it.

This was a new experience for Sheila, and she cleared the dishes off the table in a pleasant mood. Watching her, Bruce noticed her calm and saw that when he called to her in the kitchen she even smiled to him and said quite naturally, "You're going to be late for work, but I don't really think it makes a darn bit of difference because they know the office can't get started without you, anyway."

He grunted and was silent, but he was no longer rattling dishes, forks, and knives about. In fact, he even turned to her as he left to say, "I'll pick up the cheese on the way home so we'll have something for the guests."

Both of them recognized that the tension had been broken and a fight averted.

This was the beginning of a systematic campaign on Sheila's part to release on wanting to control Bruce every time he pulled what she felt to be a "controlling act" on *her*. The result was a marked lessening of tension between them, but even more interesting was a surprising new acceptance on Bruce's part of Sheila's new plans for herself. He apparently responded to her change in attitude by being less threatened by her new independence. At their counseling sessions, Bruce now complained less about Sheila and tended more to work on some of his own problems, such as his sense of being outmoded in his work, a problem which had little if anything to do with his marital relationship. As he dealt with his problems and Sheila with hers, she continued to use Releasing to defuse the control issue between them, and their relationship steadily improved. Finally, both were able to discontinue counseling and resume their lives in a balanced fashion. They had gained renewed respect for each other.

Couple 3

Ronald's wife had been pleading with him for some time not to bring so much work home from the office and to take her out more often. He was distressed by what he perceived to be her need to control him. Since he was ambitious to climb the corporate ladder, he felt that he had to do a lot of work at home in this stage of his career.

At this point, neither Ronald nor Joan could see the other's viewpoint. Beth felt unreasonably pushed. In addition to the marriage counseling from which they had sought help, I taught the couple how to release and suggested that they use the tactic "reversing roles" to help them deal with their problem.

I suggested to Ronald that he imagine a specific scene in which Joan asked him to drop the work he had brought home with him and instead go out with her for an evening. He had no trouble envisioning such a scene. I then asked him to place himself, in his imagination, in Joan's shoes, as though he were she, and to feel how *she* wanted to control *his* behavior—feel her "controllingness" as though he were Joan. As he tried this, Ronald was able to feel "Joan" wanting to control him from her standpoint. I explained that he didn't have to sympathize with Joan's point of view, just feel it. Then, as "Joan," I asked him to release on wanting to control his own (Ronald's) behavior. That is, he was to pretend he was Joan and release on wanting to control Ronald.

When he got the hang of this, a smile crossed Ronald's face as he imagined this odd situation. In order to check out what this role-reversal tactic had accomplished, I requested Ronald once again to imagine a familiar scene in which Joan was asking him to go out when he had work to do at home. How did he feel about that?

To his surprise, when he reviewed the scene, Ronald felt that he had a choice he didn't have before. He thought that now he would be a lot calmer if Joan started insisting that they go out. If he felt the work was important and that he really couldn't go, he believed he could now explain it to Joan without creating any hassles. On thinking further, Ronald guessed that what was different was that now he didn't feel guilty about having brought home the work and therefore could be more low-key about it. He also added that he hadn't known that he *had* felt guilty about it!

We may be trying to control our own behavior much more than we think. This can cause trouble. As a result, when we imagine another person letting go of wanting to control *us*, this can help us release on wanting to control those aspects of ourselves that otherwise we might not think of releasing on. The result may be considerable relief, arrived at indirectly but just as powerful in its effects as though we had released directly on our own behavior.

Another reason that the role-reversal strategy works is that we often agree with much of the criticism directed against us without realizing that we are doing so. If this is the case, then by using the role-reversal tactic, we can get off our own backs.

There is also the possibility that putting ourselves in the other person's shoes may give us a surprising insight into how they really felt—it may not be what we thought at all—which, of course, automatically solves the original problem.

It is not necessary to understand *why* a Releasing tactic works *for it to work*, however. All you have to do for role-reversal is to reverse roles in your imagination—then let go of wanting to change your own self. Even if you don't fully understand why, you will feel better.

Joan tried this tactic next. She had felt that Ronald was trying to control her by forcing *her* to accept this curtailment of their social life. When she imagined herself in Ronald's shoes, she "felt" his attempt to control their social life and her behavior, and then released on it. Immediately she felt less threatened by his "controllingness."

Since now she had stopped thinking about whether he was trying to control her, she began to look at the situation in a practical light and decided that if she wanted to have more social life, she could have it anyway. She also realized that Ronald's bringing home an overload of work was not necessarily something that would continue for ever. Because of Releasing, the "charge" had been taken off the situation, and Ronald and Joan could explore practical solutions.

The role-reversal tactic is highly effective. It is, however, a strategy we are apt to forget in the heat of an argument. It is, therefore, particularly useful to find ways to remind yourself to use this tactic when needed. We will talk about "Releasing reminders" later in part 3 of this book.

Couple 4

Gina, a college student who lived in an apartment off campus, complained that her roommate was unwilling to keep the apartment clean. It seemed to her that she was constantly scattering junk around, and Gina was sick of tripping over it and having dirty dishes pile up in the sink. When she reported this at a Releasing workshop, she realized she wanted to control her roommate's behavior.

Since a great deal of anger was closing down her monitor, I suggested that she start by letting go of wanting to justify her anger and simply allow it to "be." When she did this, she began to feel steadier.

We then used the "divide-and-conquer" tactic. Could Gina imagine the dishes piled up in the sink and then let go of wanting to control *how* they were piled there? She could let go of 1 percent of wanting to control them, and that was all that was needed. She felt better already.

The next step for her was to let go for only *two seconds* of wanting to control the way the dishes were piled. This she did easily, and when thinking back about the dishes, she found herself looking at the situation differently and thinking,

"Oh, it's those dishes again." They now seemed merely an inconvenience.

Next, she pictured her roommate's clothes, notebooks, and letters scattered over the floor—disgusting! When asked to imagine one little corner of the mess, one "tiny, unimportant detail," she thought about a letter which had been kicked out of place and was lying where she might have stepped on it.

I asked her if she could see a postage stamp on that letter. Could she let go of wanting to control the way that stamp was positioned on the envelope? She laughed and let go of wanting to control it.

Next, she was able to picture the handwriting on the front of the envelope and let go of wanting to control the way the address was positioned there. After that, she let go of wanting to control the way the letter itself was lying on the floor—whether it was turned sideways, catty-corner, or straight. Then she was able to let go of wanting to control the whole letter. Finally, after having gone through these steps, she could let go of wanting to control the way *all* of the letters were scattered about.

The wheels had been greased; the Releasing process was rolling. It was easy now. Imaginging the whole "mess" of the apartment in front of her, she was able to let go of wanting to control that, too. By building up to the big challenge with little steps, Gina had arrived at a point where she could release on the thing that was troubling her most—the total disarray in her home.

To solve a problem of this sort you don't have to endure a perpetual state of disarray. Through Releasing, Gina was able to mobilize her energies for a realistic solution of what to many neat and orderly people is a burden. She saw that anger was not the answer but that she had available to her a more practical solution. If her roommate's life-style was not to her liking, she could move out and live under circumstances that would be more acceptable. She realized that eventually she would have to move to another apartment since her roommate held the lease, but that this didn't mean she had to move immediately. She decided she would start looking around for an apartment the following month. The problem had receded in importance. It was now manageable.

When we let go of wanting to control a situation, we may see ways of acting that can change that situation.

Couple 5

Barbara's divorced sister Nancy had been supporting herself and her child in a small town some distance away, but recently, unable to manage well on her own, she had fled to Barbara's house as though to a haven.

Barbara had always been a source of strength for her younger sister, but when she found Nancy anxious, depressed, and unable to plan constructively for her future, she regretted having suggested that she come to her house. She realized that her sister would need some counseling or other professional help in order to make a realistic decision about her future.

To add to Barbara's problems, her own husband and children were beginning to suffer from having the mother and baby in the house. While it was all right for a short while, the prolonged tension-filled visit was beginning to tell on all of them. It seemed like taking in flood victims to help them out during an emergency and having them settle down to stay indefinitely.

Barbara decided to do some anticipatory releasing on a coming scene, which she dreaded. When Barbara had recently suggested counseling, Nancy had seemed alarmed by the idea. In many ways, Barbara seemed to be Nancy's only "lifeline," and she feared asking her to leave because this might cause Nancy emotional distress. As she thought about this, Barbara realized this was because she wanted her sister to love her. Obviously, love is a form of "approval." If, by magic, she could arrange things so that Nancy could move out of the house without being disillusioned in her, Barbara felt that this would solve everything.

The first step was to let go of wanting her sister's approval. She was able to let go of 1 percent of wanting this approval, allowing herself to "keep the other 99 percent." This lifted a weight from her shoulders, and Barbara now imagined telling her sister that the family was having some difficulty with the sleeping arrangements at home and that she would like a better plan worked out for her and her child.

In her imagination she saw a hurt, angry look on Nancy's face as she said this but immediately released on wanting to control whether or not Nancy would "like her." At this point, she finally felt ready to face her sister.

When Barbara put her anticipated behavior into action, she was able to tell her sister in a quiet manner that it would be useful if she left. Since she no longer felt it was a disaster to confront Nancy, she was able to do this in such a way that the words came easily, without tension or any seeming attempt to force her opinions upon her sister. Barbara knew that she was willing to help her sister our with the arrangements and that what she was asking was reasonable. When one person is calm, this tends to calm others. Nancy was not nearly as upset as anticipated and was able to go along with these new plans in a constructive fashion.

Releasing on approval from others allows us to see them as they really are—this can help us deal with them more effectively.

Releasing can also be used in other ways to handle the problems that couples face. One partner can release on wanting to change the fact that the other does not seem sufficiently cooperative, understanding, loving, patient, neat, etc. He or she can also release on wanting to control the other partner's "indifference" or "impatience" or any other behavior which seems objectionable, with the result that certain key aspects of the relationship are almost certain to change in response to Releasing.

Partners can also release on wanting each other's approval (or love) and on wanting their own approval for their own attractiveness, their own ways of behaving, or any other attribute about which they have doubts. This can remove pressure from the relationship and automatically improve the manner in which the partners deal with each other.

If both partners have learned Releasing, leading each other through releases can be extremely beneficial. How to do this will be dealt with later when we come to discuss Releasing partners.

One problem that couples frequently face, where Releasing is particularly effective, requires a separate chapter. We will now look at the ways Releasing can be used to handle sexual difficulties.

Chapter 11

RELEASING FOR SEXUAL PROBLEMS

Despite the much talked-about sexual revolution, sexual problems are still common. Even people from liberated backgrounds grow up with an unspoken puritanism ingrained in them by families, schools, and community. Because of this they may experience a vague, illogical shame about their bodies which is in direct opposition to their conscious acceptance of their sexual self. Such feelings defy logic because they are carry-overs from early childhood.

Other frequent causes of sexual difficulties include physical disabilities, sexual assaults or seductions that may have occurred in the person's childhood, the experience of parents who had their own sexual problems, feelings of inadequacy about oneself as a person, or other disturbances associated with sex. In addition, in a world where achievement is a prime value, sex has become a proving ground for many. It is no longer enough for some people to enjoy themselves when engaging in sexual activity. Instead, they may feel compelled to be "fully liberated," or always to experience ecstatic sex, or to make the sex act radically different and superior each time.

Since sex is a form of play, it is, of course, immediately hampered by any forcing or effort to succeed. This is why, in the new sex therapies, the therapist teaches those who are experiencing difficulties in their sex lives to forget about *trying* for any particular result. They are not to attempt to achieve orgasm or, in fact, to try to achieve at all. Instead, they are instructed to view sex as a leisurely, nonstriving experience, free from demands and judgments about performing "correctly" or "incorrectly." Sex is no place to strive for outstanding success of any sort.

While this advice is useful, letting go of performance anxiety is more easily said than done. Many people keep track, on some level, of what the "score is" in whatever they do. It is scarcely surprising, therefore, that such concerns invade the sexual realm, diminishing spontaneity and pleasure.

Those who use the Releasing method before engaging in sex have reported a striking improvement in the quality of their sexual experience. The following are accounts of couples who used Releasing in this way.

Sexual Problem 1

To the guests at their wedding, Terry and Mark seemed the ideal couple. Terry, who had just graduated from an Ivy League college, was an exquisite bride. As she walked down the aisle, her fine blonde hair drawn back into a simple bun, her family, who were leading citizens of the community, looked on with pride. Mark, who towered above her, had recently graduated from law school and was starting a promising career. He, too, was an impressive figure as he walked arm in arm with her out of the church.

There was a shadow over this relationship, however. Although Terry and Mark had been living together for more than two years, they had not yet resolved a troublesome sexual problem which made their wedding stressful for both of them.

Terry was "nonorgasmic" (she disliked the word frigid) and unless she smoked marijuana could not engage in sex with any ease. At the thought of sexual relations, her body would become tense and she would talk compulsively—about anything and everything. Her talking jags happened regularly, even though she clearly found Mark to be the most desirable man she had ever known. To her bewilderment, it seemed to her that it was precisely because he *was* so attractive and so "right" for her that the thought of getting into bed with him would make her stiffen up and become what she termed later in their marriage-counseling sessions "the proper boarding-school pupil."

Terry had attended fine schools and observed all the correct churchgoing traditions. Her father was a professor and her grandfather a leading clergyman in the community, and she had prided herself from early childhood on being extraordinarily dignified and self-controlled. Not surprisingly, she had become an expert horse-woman and had exceeded all the family's expectations at horse shows throughout childhood and adolescence. She was an elegantly poised rider, perfectly in control of her horse and herself at all times. Her show manners were impeccable.

Terry's exquisite poise was not an asset when in bed with her husband, however. It was as though some of the very qualities which had attracted Mark to her—the fact that she was a popular campus figure, self-assured, attractive, and sought after—were the qualities which now got in the way of her freedom in lovemaking. Being less than perfect in bed with Mark was frightening to Terry.

Like many another college student, she had smoked marijuana occasionally and was then sometimes able to respond sexually in a temporary mist of drug-induced relaxation. Taking the drug created new problems for her, however. Her need to remain in control was so strong that she tended to steer away from more than superficial contact with any drug substance, including alcohol, which might lessen control. The result was that when she and Mark went to bed, she would often find herself remote from the sexual experience.

For Mark, Terry was still the girl of his dreams, and so her lack of response made him doubt his own sexual competency. This in turn led to arguments, which at times had endangered their relationship but which both of them had attributed to the instabilities and insecurities of not yet being officially married.

It came as a shock to them, therefore, to discover that their wedding ceremony did not improve their sexual life. The problem continued. It even seemed to worsen. Terry then sought to solve the impasse by escaping into social life, horseback riding, and community activities to the point where Mark accused her of being a "dinner-party wife."

It became increasingly evident that the couple needed professional help, but it was difficult for Terry to agree to discuss her sex life with a stranger, even in marriage-counseling sessions. Eventually, however, the couple did seek counseling, and, to facilitate progress of their treatment, I taught both Terry and Mark the Releasing technique.

When they had mastered the basic method, I suggested to Mark that he let go of his need for his own approval when engaging in sexual relations (preferably just before starting), and also release on wanting Terry's approval. This was intended to help Mark handle his problems with respect to Terry's difficulties in responding. It was also aimed at helping him with some residual sexual insecurities of his own.

I suggested to Terry that she use the Releasing technique somewhat differently. In her counseling sessions she had indicated that when she began to feel warm and responsive to Mark and became aware that she was responding to him with mounting excitement, it was as if, in her words, "a whole array of family faces came into my mind." She saw her mother straightening her little white Sunday dress and white socks, or her mother's face disapproving of her when her room wasn't clean enough or her hands weren't scrubbed. At such times she would also imagine her grandfather's face as he had looked when in the pulpit, eminently dignified and approving of Terry's *own* great *self-control*. Or she had fleeting visions of herself riding in horse shows, holding herself erect and balanced over the most difficult jumps. There were, it seemed, many different forms of approval that Terry had to learn to "let go of."

When she started releasing on wanting approval, it was difficult for her to tackle the issue head on, but she could let go of the *feeling* of wanting approval. She was familiar with that feeling and found she could let go of a little bit, perhaps 1 percent of it at a time. Even this little bit seemed to lift a weight off her shoulders, and, following her Releasing sessions, the disapproving family faces seemed to recede into the background and leave her free to be herself, alone with Mark.

Coupled with Terry's need for approval was an extraordinary need to exert tight control over herself. From the time when as an infant she had managed to please her mother by allowing herself to be toilet trained at seven months of age, controlling bowel functions which were extremely difficult for her immature nervous system to handle, to the times when she had stoically taken falls from horses, picked herself up out of the dirt, gritted her teeth and refused to cry, Terry had always placed a premium on having tight control over her surroundings, her feelings, and her physical reactions.

In some respect, this control had enabled her to become very effective in her own way. Unfortunately, however, she was unable to choose *when* to exert tight control over herself. There were times when strong control was desirable, as at a horse show or when serving guests at a party. The problem was that she couldn't dispense with the reins when this sort of control was not appropriate.

Learning to release on wanting to control her own self was crucial in Terry's sexual re-education. To help her, I suggested that she first release while *imagining* that she was having sexual relations with Mark. As she thought about making love, she was to let go of wanting to control her reactions to him. She was also to let go of wanting approval—*everyone's* approval—her own, Mark's, her family's, her friends'. This was a crucial step for Terry because for her, sexual freedom seemed a frightening loss of control. It felt similar, she said, to the loss of control that a very little girl might feel if she were to wet her pants at a birthday party, soil her beautiful party dress, and then feel deeply ashamed. Terry was able to recall such an incident in her own childhood. It had remained with her for years.

Today, Terry often felt a sense of shame envelop her when she approached orgasm. It was important for her to release on this shame. This she could do by letting go of wanting to *change* the shame—just letting it "be." The first time she did this, it was an extraordinary experience. She had never imagined that she could live through shame of this sort without something dreadful happening to her. However, as she allowed herself in her imagination to fully experience the shame, to feel it burning throughout her, she found herself riding out the experience and emerging on the other side. This was a revelation to her. She felt never again would she have quite the same fear of shame and realized, wordlessly, that she was no longer that little girl who wet her pants at the party.

Terry soon acquired the habit of releasing whenever she began to feel herself tense up as Mark approached her sexually. When she let go of wanting to control his behavior (and her own), she would think, "I don't have to *think* about this now; I'll just relax and enjoy myself for a little while."

As a result, the overcontrol began to leave her sexual experiences and she was able to allow herself to live more in the moment. Although the tightness would come back again periodically—the memory of disapproving words or looks from her family and the need to be impeccably neat—she soon learned to release every time this occurred. It became her spontaneous pattern to think:

"Can I let go of wanting to control my body?

"Can I let go of wanting to control my feelings?

"Can I let go of wanting to control my excitement?

"Can I let go of wanting to control the fun?"

Terry then became bolder in her releasing. "Can I let go of wanting to control fucking?" she asked herself one day. The question felt like a declaration of independence. Finally, she felt human, rather than like the little girl in the all-too-white dress.

Terry now found herself beginning to enjoy sex more. She had become more spontaneous during the sex act, experiencing a sense of fun and freedom that she had never known. She also found to her relief that, despite this freedom, when it was necessary to exert control under other circumstances in her life, she could still do this easily when she wished to. In short, she still could wear the "white dress" when that was appropriate, but now she did this only when *she* chose to do so.

As for Mark, releasing on his need for his own approval and his increasing relaxation in light of Terry's greater freedom began to give him the feeling that the two of them were on the same wavelength. Both were now freer to express themselves the way they actually wanted to—in bed and out. From that point on, they made rapid progress in their marriage counseling and soon were able to taper off their treatment as they assumed responsibility for their own new life.

Sexual Problem 2

Natalie and Jim had enjoyed each other sexually and in many other ways when they were first married, but the memory of those days now seemed distant. Eleven years later, after the birth of their three children, a dullness had set in. It now seemed to them that they were always talking about the same old things with each other—their children, relatives, friends—and there was a routine quality to their sex life which made it seem always the same.

When the couple attended a Releasing workshop, they were both enthusiastic about the value of the technique, and it wasn't long before Natalie thought up the idea of releasing before they want to bed together. She suggested it to Jim, who had been using Releasing in other aspects of his life, including his business, and finding it useful. He was immediately interested, and as they sat in their living room one evening, they began releasing on wanting to control what the other person would do when they finally got to bed—whether that person would make the first advance, how they would both caress, how they would behave in other aspects of the sex act, and so on.

When they finally went up to bed, they found to their surprise that they were anticipating making love, a feeling which they had almost forgotten. There was an aura of excitement, of the unknown, about the anticipated experience.

As they began to caress each other, they released out loud on wanting to control the other's reactions and began to find it quite amusing. Natalie giggled (something she hadn't done for a long time when making love), and it struck them both as amusing that it was necessary to let go of so many elaborate ways of controlling each other, themselves, and their own bodies.

They then got into the swing of the thing and began letting go of wanting to control how different strokes, various movements, and different positions felt to them. They then let go of wanting to control each other's genitals, each other's physical responsiveness, and their own sexual reactions. Finally, they lapsed into silence. The Releasing process, having been started, was like a snowball rolling downhill. It continued to increase in strength as they now released silently on wanting to control all aspects of their sexual experience.

To their amazement, their lovemaking that day was spontaneous, playful, and *new*. It was as though each one of them were discovering a new sex partner. As Natalie commented when she reported the experience to me later, "I felt as though I were having an illicit affair! It was wonderful!"

Jim had the same reaction, and from that time on the two of them never went to bed without releasing first. In his words, Releasing was "an incredible discovery."

Interestingly, their bedtime Releasing had impressive effects on the rest of their lives. They soon found themselves doing things together which they hadn't done for years—tramping through the woods together, taking long drives to visit distant friends, taking up tennis together, and finding other activities in common, whereas before they had each pursued individual interests alone.

Releasing on wanting to control each other sexually had built a habit of releasing on wanting to control each other in general. Now they found themselves automatically letting go of wanting to control the way the other partner swam at the beach, the way he grilled hamburgers over the fire, or the way she talked at dinner parties. For this couple, Releasing brought spontaneity back into their lives. It refreshed their imaginations and gave them new youth and freedom.

Sexual Problem 3

Lawrence, an executive of a large corporation, was divorced, and there seemed no end of women who were interested in him. His feelings were not those of elation, however. He had not yet recovered from the blow to his self-esteem that the failure of his marriage had brought. Whenever he thought of the trouble between himself and his once-admiring wife, Lawrence became depressed. Secretly he harbored guilt about the failure of that marriage. While he told himself many times over that he had outgrown Roxanne, he was haunted by the thought that he had never really satisfied her, either as a husband or as a lover. The shadow of what he considered to be his sexual failure remained with him.

It was not that Lawrence hadn't been active sexually. He had, in fact, been adamant in his sexual demands on Roxanne, insisting that they make love every night without fail and that they seek out the most exciting and different sexual experiences. At first Roxanne had responded to this frenzied sex, but soon she began to withdraw. There was something in her husband's behavior that bothered her. His insistence on ever new, unusual variations of the sex act seemed to have little if anything to do with *her*. She felt as though his behavior had more to do with some image of himself that he was trying to uphold for his own reasons.

Perhaps it was the look on Lawrence's face, a distant, self-absorbed look that she noticed more and more often, that made Roxanne eventually begin to find excuses for not engaging in sex as often as before. The result was an increased insistence on frequent sex on his part, an apparent determination to storm the bastions and win back her admiration.

This was a self-defeating maneuver, however. The more Lawrence tried to be an exceptional lover, the more Roxanne felt left out of the act and became defensive and withdrawn. This led him to try even more strenuously, until finally, enraged at Roxanne for his own seeming failure, Lawrence turned to another woman.

In his relationship with this new woman, he found that with the help of a few drinks he could achieve what he described as "absolutely wild sex." However, he conveniently ignored the fact that this woman, who was herself married, could only meet with him occasionally for short periods of time and was therefore not subjected, as Roxanne had been, to his daily efforts to prove his virility. The few hours that the two managed to grab at a motel seemed to him to be ecstatic, and he didn't have to worry about how this new woman was going to respond to his advances on a regular basis.

Eventually, Lawrence's prolonged affair resulted in a confrontation with Roxanne, which led to bitterness, reproaches, and finally to separation and divorce. After this, he quickly broke with this new woman and embarked on a different course of amorous activity.

He now avoided any ongoing love relationship that might bring about the kind of rejection, humiliation, and failure he had experienced with Roxanne. Instead, he started a series of cursory affairs. Usually, these affairs were with women who were married and therefore unattainable. His reputation, at first glowing, gradually became tarnished as numbers of disenchanted women discovered that he was playing the field broadly and had no intention of committing himself to any of them. They detected a frantic quality in his effort to seduce the female sex.

It was at this point that Lawrence developed severe tension headaches which would occur when he should have been having a good time. He found himself particularly prone to such a headache when he was about to meet an attractive woman for an experience which promised to be especially exciting. This was the symptom that led him into treatment with a psychologist colleague, who, in turn, recommended that Lawrence attend one of my Releasing workshops. His therapist felt it would be useful for him to acquire skill in Releasing in order to deal with the over-intensity with which he seemed to invest sexual encounters.

At this point, Lawrence suffered from what is known as "performance anxiety," an intense fear (frequently not conscious) that he would not be able to perform sexually in an adequate manner. He seemed to fear that he would be unable to elicit the rave reviews from women that would prove, once and for all, that he was a "true man."

This pattern of behavior had roots in Lawrence's life history, and his therapist worked with him to uncover those elements in his life that might account for his frantic need to prove his maleness. Among these was his memory of his own weak and ineffectual father, who had been a poor role model for a growing boy.

Added to the insights which Lawrence was attaining through psychotherapy, Releasing proved of great help in lessening his performance anxiety. His therapist suggested to him that he use Releasing as a form of sex therapy. As soon as he had learned it, the therapist advised him to take out a few moments before engaging in any sexual activity and to let go of wanting to be "fantastic in bed." The therapist also suggested that Lawrence let go of wanting to control the specific reactions of the woman to him and that he let go of wanting to control his own erections.

Lawrence enthusiastically applied the technique of Releasing to his sexual experiences, rapidly inventing ways of releasing on wanting to control all aspects of his own body and his partner's reactions. As he did so, he began to find himself becoming more at ease with his sex partners and less apt to develop headaches before having sex. He also discovered to his surprise that at times he could even be quiet and passive during the sex act and feel no particular need to change *that*. This was something he had never experienced before, and his acceptance of occasional passivity was a major triumph for Lawrence. It helped to remove the self-destructive habit of using sex only as a way of bolstering his self-esteem as a "true man" and allowed him to experience it as a means of achieving genuine pleasure.

Each person finds his own particular phrases which work best for him or her when releasing on sex. These often involve four-letter words that really "talk" to the person. Not surprisingly, Lawrence found an ingenious number of ways to ask himself to let go of wanting to control his own penis. Each time he did this, he felt his anxiety lighten, and eventually the issue of sexual performance became less important. Sex was becoming more fun, and he was no longer so apt to terrify his love partner by an over-intensity that seemed unnatural to the woman involved.

The use of Releasing along with intensive psychotherapy eventually helped Lawrence deal successfully with his sexual problems and resulted in a changed relationship both to women and to himself. His need to drink before engaging in sex dropped away, and eventually he was able to establish a permanent relationship with one woman, this time on a less hectic basis than his whirlwind marriage with Roxanne. Interestingly, he did not drop the use of the Releasing technique when things got better but chose to weave it into his sex life as an integral part of that experience, viewing sex much more as fun and a game rather than life's goal.

Releasing thus helps people cope with many differing types of sexual problems. It deals directly with the approval-disapproval

To Release on Sexual Experiences

Think to yourself, or say out loud:

"COULD I LET GO OF WANTING
TO CONTROL_____?"

List of Possible Categories
(Substitute words or phrases
that have a meaning for you.)

HIM/HER_____

THE FUN_____

HOW I DO_____

WHAT HAPPENS_____

MY RESPONSES_____

MY BODY_____

(Others)_____
_____
_____
_____
_____

Also release on wanting your partner's, or your own,
APPROVAL!

issues that can inhibit sexual freedom—those unpleasant leftovers from early childhood. It can also relieve performance anxiety, returning sex to its proper function of providing pleasure rather than amassing score points. It can renew sexual responsiveness, introducing freedom when dullness may have set in.

The latter is particularly important. If sex becomes mechanical, many couples seek out new sexual partners because these others seem to offer the promised land. This may start a restless search for the lost dreams of youth or the return of a once-viable relationship. Releasing before engaging in sex permits a couple to shed repetitive, outworn routines. It introduces a refreshing, invigorating tone of expectancy and the freedom to experiment. This can do away with the need to seek out a new sex partner by giving the person a new sex *experience*.

You need not have problems involving sex in order to benefit from Releasing, however. Releasing can enhance an already delightful experience. Many people enjoy using it this way.

Chapter 12

RELEASING FOR PARENT-CHILD PROBLEMS

Even the best parents run into difficulties in child rearing. Problems involved in the relationships of family members to each other and in the child's experience with the outer world make the raising of children both rewarding and frustrating. Children frequently experience difficulties with their parents, too.

Releasing can dissipate potential conflicts within a family and simplify day-to-day existence in the home. The following accounts of people who have used Releasing for parent-child problems represent only a few of the possibilities for stabilizing family life by use of the technique.

Parent-Child Difficulty 1

When Beatrice came to counseling, she was at the end of her rope. Despite the fact that her seven-year-old son, John, was receiving psychotherapy in a guidance clinic, her difficulty with him remained a central focus in her life.

Beatrice's oldest child, a girl of eleven, was well liked by her classmates and friends, and her youngest boy was fun-loving. But her middle son, John, seemed intent upon making her life miserable. John's ready temper, habitual sulking, and inability to get along with other children without outbursts of anger was a constant source of distress to both his parents. He seemed more like someone else's child than their own. Unlike anyone else in the family, he could spend hours alone with his Erector set but could not relate well to others.

In addition, Beatrice herself had gone through a difficult and unhappy period in her own childhood when she, too, had not gotten along well with other children. Later, she had developed ways of getting along with others which had worked out well, but in her heart she was never totally certain of being accepted by a group, one of the reasons why it bothered her so much when John alienated the children of neighbors whose friendships she had worked hard to attain.

As Beatrice faced these facets of her relationship to John in her psychotherapy sessions, it was clear that something was needed to help her handle her everyday confrontations with him. Despite a promising reaction to therapy, the fact remained that *at the moment* she was thin-skinned with regard to anything John did. The least threat from him would make her jump in an effort to control him and avert the behavior she feared. She understood that she was aggravating his behavior by opposing it—she often thought John was actually forcing her to pay attention to him by his annoying behavior—but she could not seem to change her reactions. In short, John was still able to press the buttons that made his mother go into an intensely emotional state from which both of them suffered.

At this point in her therapy, I taught Beatrice the Releasing technique. She learned it readily and was able to apply it immediately to her reactions to John. First she asked herself if she could let go of wanting to *control* John, "even a little bit." She soon found that the tactic of suspending wanting to control her son for *just one or two seconds* was the most effective way for her to do this. If she could suspend the feeling, then she had a sense of being relieved of her impulse to control him. After that, she found it fairly easy to let go of larger portions of this urgency to control John.

As Beatrice mentally rehearsed releasing on John (before going home to try it out), she suddenly felt less responsibility for John's behavior. The thought now crossed her mind that if he was going to act that way with the neighborhood children, then that was *his* business. She in turn could act as she wished with their parents. This brought a sense of perspective on the whole problem, and for the first time she seemed to see John as a separate person. True, he was only seven years old, but he was separate. She now saw him as "doing his own thing" and in a sense being responsible for it, just as she was responsible for how she behaved with her friends.

She left my office feeling that a burden had been lightened and indicated she was going to use the technique at home as much as possible. I pointed out that in the beginning she might forget to use it in the heat of an argument with John—after all, it was a habit of hers to respond to his triggers—but that in such cases she could always go off by herself as soon as she realized that she had been pulled into a battle, and when alone could relive the scene and release on it.

She agreed to try this. When I saw her a week later, her attitude toward her son had changed remarkably. She told me that she had re-entered her home after her first Releasing session to find John sitting on her younger son and punching him in a way that she considered dangerous. What struck her immediately, however, was the difference in the way she handled the situation this time.

As she walked into the room she thought to herself, "Could I let go of wanting to *control* John's punching?" While at the moment she could not let go completely, something eased up in her as soon as she thought the Releasing question. This allowed her to walk forward quietly. Instead of shouting to the children to stop fighting, she found instead that she walked right up to them, stood by their side, and placed one of her hands gently but firmly on John's shoulder and said to him, "I want you to stop immediately."

While at first he seemed not to hear her, she heard herself repeating in a strong but still well-modulated tone; "Immediately." She was not expressing anger now but a confident firmness, something which had been noticeably absent before when she had gotten into her battles to control John. Because of her releasing, her frantic behavior disappeared, and within a short time, John, apparently sensing a difference in the way she was reacting to him, let go of his brother and sulked out of the room *without battling*.

This was the beginning of a week of intensive releasing for Beatrice. Sometimes she had to use a variety of unlocking tactics to achieve a release. One evening when John came to dinner sulkily, she was annoyed because she placed a high value on families being friendly and "relating." Beatrice used the divide-and-conquer tactic to cope with her feelings. She began by letting go of her wish to change the way John's hair was falling over his forehead; then on wanting to control the fact that his shirt was not tucked in; then on wanting to change the flush on his cheeks; and so on through a long list of details about her son, each of which she successively *let go of wanting to control*.

The result of this Releasing was that she began to observe some interesting things. For the first time she noticed that John was watching his father much of the time out of the corner of his eye. Several times he tried to speak to him, only to have his father ignore him and talk to one of the other children instead. This made Beatrice realize that something was going on between father and son which she had never stopped to notice. She had been so absorbed in her wish to force John to change that she had not been able to look closely at what he was doing. Now this observation on her part led to her feeling that she wanted to change her *husband*, and she let go of wanting to control *him*, too.

She then had a quiet talk with her husband. Since she had already let go of wanting to control the way he behaved with John, her comments were casual and factual, and he didn't react to them as criticism. In fact, he was listening to her with more interest than usual. This started a friendly conversation in the course of which he said he would give thought to his reactions to John. Apparently he did, because later in the evening she noticed him taking John out for a ride in the car. The two of them went to the auto store together. He didn't take the other children along. As Beatrice continued releasing on wanting to change her husband's attitude towards John, she found herself beginning to regret that she herself had not been more sensitive to her son's needs. She was now seeing important aspects of the situation she had formerly overlooked. Fortunately, she recognized at this point that it might be useful if she could now release on her need to control (change) her *own* actions.

Beatrice then let go of wanting to change the fact that *in the past* she had made mistakes with John and had overlooked certain crucial facts. She even ended up saying to herself, "Could I let go of wanting to change the fact that in some ways I haven't been a good mother to him?" As she let go of her inner push to change how she had behaved in the past, a pressure seemed to be lifted from her, and to her surprise she now felt more interested in doing something for John. It even occurred to her that it would be pleasant to deal with him so that she could "gain back a son" by finding values in him that she hadn't seen before.

This thought led her to proceed with her program of releasing on John with renewed enthusiasm. Now there seemed to be a positive reward in this. She was going to find out about her middle child, the one she had not really known about and, up until now, had been unable to enjoy.

Beatrice's new optimism about John had an immediate effect on her son. He was quick to sense that he was now a source of interest to her and probably recognized from the expression on her face and her tone of voice that she was beginning to look upon him as a source of pleasure. Uncharacteristically, he looked up and met her eyes with long, interested stares whenever she began to talk to him. When he did this, Beatrice realized that previously he had been averting his eyes from her, an action that had made her feel rejected and then angry and vengeful.

What was happening was the beginning of a "fortunate circle" (the opposite of a vicious circle). As John looked his mother in the eyes, she felt a sense of contact with him that she hadn't experienced before, and he in turn sensed a goodwill from her that he had never experienced before. His behavior with his younger brother now began to improve, so markedly, in fact, that Beatrice described this as "almost miraculous." He was also fighting much less with the neighborhood children.

John would still retreat to his own room to build his elaborate Erector-set constructions, but Beatrice now began to think this a rather interesting phenomenon. One day when she found him in his room absorbed in building a toy merry-go-round, she let go of wanting to control him, using all the unlocking tactics she could think of. As she let go of wanting to change his behavior, the object he was building seemed quite unusual to her. It looked intricate and almost ingenious. She found herself unexpectedly saying, "That's an unusual merry-go-round. What's it supposed to do?" Contrary to his ordinary way of shutting her out when absorbed in his model building, John looked up and answered, "It's supposed to stop and start a lot of times as it turns, so that the little seats will jiggle back and forth and the people on the merry-go-round will have more fun." Involuntarily, she laughed with delight. It seemed to her a good idea. John in turn smiled back to her.

Releasing on John's behavior gradually led to changes in Beatrice which enabled her to rebuild her relationship with him and actually to find many unexpected sources of pleasure in her son. Her husband was also able to see interesting features to John's "different" behavior. A new and fulfilling era had begun in the family.

Releasing on Being a "Good Parent"

The question, "Could I let go of wanting to change the fact that I wasn't a good parent?" has been used by other parents too (with appropriate variations) to excellent effect. One young mother who was trying conscientiously to cope with two preschoolers, each of them a handful, found her ability to deal effectively with them greatly increased when she would ask herself, "Could I let go of wanting to be a good mother?"

She knew exactly what she meant by this. She didn't mean that she actually wanted to let go of being a *good* mother. She was asking herself if she could let go of wanting to be an extraordinary mother, beyond reproach, one who could do everything perfectly. When she let go of this overpush, she found herself more surefooted, quieter, and more patient with her children than before, and even better able to discipline them effectively when this was necessary.

She also found that Releasing helped her when her children encountered difficulties in nursery school. If she walked into the classroom and noticed her son in a scrap with another child, or if her daughter was not as "unselfish" as the teacher wanted her to be, she let go of wanting the approval of the other mothers or of the teacher. Such releasing relieved her of any feeling of awkwardness about her child's behavior. As a result, she no longer stepped in to intervene where it wasn't necessary, which left her more able to step in effectively where it *was* required.

This mother found that having two preschoolers meant that she needed to release repeatedly each day. According to her, this, more than any other single factor, has enabled her to take care of her children at an easy, relaxed pace.

Problems of Adolescence

Although the early years of childhood can create many frustrations for parents, probably no era gives rise to more stress between parents and children than adolescence. Strife between adolescent youngsters and bewildered, anxious, or resentful parents forms the basis for a large proportion of referrals to any guidance clinic.

The reasons for this are many. Our society does not provide for a smooth transition from childhood to the competitive challenges of adult life. Unlike their predecessors of several generations ago who often shared in the tasks of the household (particularly in rural households), the typical child of today is a relatively protected, carefree individual until his midteens. Then, with a suddenness taken for granted by most of us because it is our own way of life, the child is propelled into a position where he must compete strenuously with many other young people for admission to an institution of higher learning or a well-paying job.

Increasingly, this kind of competitive demand is made on women as well as men, and the protectiveness of older societies (whatever their own drawbacks may have been), where youngsters at least knew that they were going to fit into a well-defined niche and were prepared for it by adolescence, is gone. Children can no longer slide imperceptibly into adult roles. They must adjust to a switch in their basic way of life.

These factors contribute to the dilemma of young people when they reach the official age of growing up, making it a time of maximum stress. This stress is in turn reflected back on the family unit. If a youngster's transition is relatively smooth and uneventful, the family congratulates itself on not having had the usual troubles that other families face with their teenagers. However, if former tensions and family problems are revived in the teenage years, or if the family faces a crisis at this time such as economic instability, ill health, divorce, or separation, then the adolescent, with his already unstable adjustment, can be thrown badly out of gear and troublesome behavior problems can result.

Releasing can play an extremely valuable role for parents who are trying to cope with the bewildering behavior of a son or daughter who has entered the teens or early adulthood in a manner that is causing distress to other family members or perhaps an outright family crisis.

Parent-Child Difficulty 2

Arthur prided himself on the fact that while other fathers might have children who failed to cooperate with their parents, his own family was run with the precision of a superbly commanded ship. He himself had been a captain in the Navy and often used the expression "shipshape" to describe the manner in which his household was organized. Each person in the family knew his place, his duties. Since there was a generally friendly attitude among family members, Arthur's rather strict demands upon his children to conform were seldom resisted. It actually never occurred to his sons to rebel, in fact—until they reached adolescence.

When Dan, the oldest boy, turned seventeen, it was a year of change for him. While Dan's crisis was actually an inner one, it manifested itself in behavior which seemed to depart sharply from the military model within which the family had operated. In other families, Dan's behavior might not have been looked upon as particularly unusual, but within the context of this particular home, it stood out like a sore thumb.

Dan had noticed that independence of judgment was a requirement in the teenage world in which he functioned, and he found himself increasingly called upon by his friends and classmates, and by role models he saw on TV, in the movies, and elsewhere, to "stand up" and be "himself." This concept came as somewhat of a shock to him at first, since he had always deferred to the judgment of his father. Because of his authoritarian upbringing, he had a lot to learn in a brief time to catch up with his friends, who seemed to him to be masters of the art of expressing their own opinions and exerting their independent wills. In order not to appear to be "weakwilled," Dan felt that he had to declare some sort of independence from his father's absolute control.

In this family it did not take an act of violence to declare independence. It was merely necessary to step out of line. Dan found the family car an appropriate symbol of personal freedom. The car was especially meaningful to him because throughout his childhood he had helped his father care for it and keep it "shipshape." When Dan got his driving license, the issue of driving seemed an obvious place for him to prove that he had more independence of judgment than anyone had realized until now.

A series of incidents then followed, all centered on whether or not Dan would observe his father's strict curfew of 11:00 P.M. For several weeks, Dan had failed to do so but had carefully called in and made explanations over the telephone as to why he could not get home on time. Even this appeared to Dan to be a daring move when confronting absolute authority as he had known it in his family. Since his explanations were, however, grudgingly accepted by his father, it seemed that a more drastic declaration of independence was needed before Dan could feel himself to be an "individual" in his own right.

It was at about this time that Arthur and his wife Alice attended a Releasing workshop, at her request. Arthur had simply come along to find out what a stress-management technique was all about, as well as to assuage a gnawing awareness that he should do something about reducing stress in his life, because his physician had told him he might be suffering from an incipient ulcer and his regular regime of jogging had not helped this condition.

Two days before his parents attended the Releasing workshop, Dan had declared his independence more forcefully, and a family crisis had been precipitated. With his father's permission he had borrowed the family car, but this time, when the eleven o'clock curfew rolled around, he had not phoned to say he would be late. He simply didn't turn up, the silent phone serving as the opening barrage in what promised to be a crucial skirmish.

Alerted to some form of danger which he could scarcely believe was occurring, Arthur had waited up for his son to return home. He had waited for an hour and three-quarters, sitting in front of the television set, a drink in his hand to steady him. What was unusual about the experience was that Arthur was not only angry, but he had a vague sense of fear. Things which had gone smoothly ever since his household had been established now seemed in danger of slipping out of his hands. The episode was particularly distressing to him because he had always had a good relationship with Dan, never having had a conflict with him about family values. There was also another source of worry. Arthur sensed a growing rebellion in Dan and was afraid that his son might turn out to be uncontrollable, the kind of boy who would reflect poorly on him as a parent.

When Dan finally entered the house at 12:45 A.M., his father was pale, his mouth set in a firm line. He made few comments but promptly pronounced the penalty. Dan was to be "grounded" for a week. He was to come home directly after school and not leave the premises at any time until he left again for school the next morning. This was the initial penalty. If he ever did it again, he would be grounded for two weeks. If a third time, he would be grounded for a month. A fourth time, and he would lose all driving privileges.

As he spoke to his son, Arthur noticed an expression on Dan's face he had never seen there before. It was a firm, distant expression. In that moment of proclaiming the penalty and enforcing it, Arthur knew that he might be making a rift in their relationship which it would be difficult to repair. He was not triumphant as he went to bed that night. Instead, his sleep was a troubled one, his mind turning to thoughts of dire consequences which he could scarcely formulate to himself.

Dan accepted the grounding wordlessly, barely speaking to his father at the breakfast table, or anytime after that. An approaching storm could be felt in the house, and it was in this state of uneasiness that both Arthur and Alice arrived at the Releasing workshop for which they had previously registered.

Alice learned Releasing easily and well, but Arthur seemed to have more difficulty with it, claiming that "a practical thought, such as 'letting go' of what you can't do anyway, is only what every sensible person does." As he sat through the first day of the workshop, he absorbed more than he seemed to be absorbing, however; and at the end of the second day, when I went around the group asking each participant in turn to choose a problem which had occurred *outside* of the workshop to release on, Arthur found himself admitting in front of strangers (something which was surprising to him) that he did have a problem about which he was greatly concerned. He seemed in some manner relieved that the structure of the workshop allowed him to talk about this, and he told us, with as much control and precision as possible, of the dilemma in which he found himself.

In order to help him get the feel of what Releasing could be like, I then led Arthur through a release. I asked him if he could "go back in time" to that evening when Dan did not bring the car home until 12:45 A.M. Could he remember the first moment that he realized Dan was not going to bring the car back on time? Where was he seated at that moment? What was he doing? How did he feel inside?

Arthur was able to recall the situation easily, and since he described a feeling of anxiety rather than one of anger, I asked him if he could let go of wanting to change that "vague fear" and just let it be there a moment . . . see how it felt to let the fear "be."

Arthur sat tensely on the edge of his chair, allowing the fear to "find its own level." He pressed his fist against his mouth and became very still. Then his breathing seemed to become easier and he looked up with an expression of surprise in his eyes. When he had been able to allow the anxiety to be there, it was no longer overwhelming him in the same way.

We then went through several more exercises of allowing the anxiety just to "be there." I asked Arthur how he now viewed the scene of Dan coming home late. At this point, Arthur's jaw was set in a determined manner, his cheeks were flushed, and he was experiencing much more clearly the anger which had welled up in him then and which once again had come to the surface. "Goddamn it!" he cried, "He's declaring war!"

I suggested that Arthur allow his anger "just to be" without having to justify it, and without trying to stop it, for about thirty seconds. When he had done this, he sat back in his chair, his shoulders more relaxed.

I was not about to try to change Arthur's standards or his goals for his son. These had a long history, and the Releasing technique doesn't try to change personal goals. What it does is change people's feelings about how they may want to reach their goals. Sometimes, after releasing, people may switch to new goals, but if so it is entirely their own choice. I asked Arthur if he could let go of just the *feeling* of wanting to control Dan's walking into the house well after midnight.

He struggled with this and as he did so was able to reason to himself, "Why not let go of the *feeling*? I can't lose by that." He was then able to let go of it.

We repeated this several times. Each time Arthur let go of more of his feeling of urgency. I never questioned whether or not he should control Dan, or whether it was reasonable to try, but after Arthur had let go of the feeling of wanting to control his son, he experienced great relief and commented that it was "already over and done with by the time Dan got home. His walking in was just the end of the story. Now it's past history."

I then asked Arthur if he could let go of the *feeling* (the *feeling*, not the intention) of wanting Dan to obey him. The word *obey* seemed a key one. Interestingly, since he had already let go of one feeling (of wanting to control), Arthur surprised himself by being able to let go quite easily of *wanting* his son to obey him. He didn't let go of the goal of having his son obey, but he relinquished the feeling that went with that goal, and this allowed his monitor to open up.

As a result, Arthur was now able to see that his son's being late was a practical problem that needed to be handled, rather than necessarily a "declaration of war." He also saw his son's behavior more clearly. He was now able to see the good things in Dan which he had always enjoyed, as well as Dan's present rebellion. He even remembered a rather similar incident in his own teenage years when he had disobeyed his own father on some relatively minor issue. He realized he had actually done the same kind of thing, and *he* hadn't turned out so badly. With this thought there came another release, and the issue seemed to swing into perspective.

Arthur felt that if he were talking to his son at this moment, he wouldn't feel that there was so much riding on it. He would simply discuss with Dan the situation about the family car and work out some better plan with him. This was the first time that it had occurred to Arthur that there was any solution other than to "make or break" Dan.

He began to think about how he could discuss the entire situation with Dan in a rational way and as he did so, it seemed reasonable to suppose that the two of them could work out something which could satisfy each of them to some extent. He then realized that he didn't have to keep to the grounding rule; it seemed more important to him that he and Dan agree on a plan. This way, instead of the boy sulking for having been grounded, the incident could be over and done with, and the family could settle down.

Arthur's monitor was now open. He could see other options. He knew that if he needed to release on the situation again later on, he could do so, but he was already on his way to a solution. At the next meeting of the workshop, he reported that the family situation was working out well after he had had a talk with Dan. A crisis in the making appeared to have melted away as he let go of his need to overcontrol and reestablished a *reasonable* control within his family instead.

Arthur was able to respond positively to releasing on his problem with his son because he had a basically good relationship with Dan to begin with. Had this not been the case, family therapy or some other form of counseling or psychotherapy might have been needed, along with Releasing, to help the family regain its equilibrium.

Parent-Child Difficulty 3

There are times when a parent's problem with a child may stem from the fact that the parent is seeking the child's approval. This appeared to be the case with Sarah, whose fourteen-year-old daughter had begun to criticize her mother's appearance and behavior.

This critical behavior had come at a time when her daughter, Marsha, had begun to take an intense interest in her own appearance. A bit of a tomboy in her earlier years, Marsha had only recently become conscious of her own femininity. It was at this point that she began to criticize the way her mother styled her hair, the shoes her mother wore, the fact that her mother's dresses were too low-necked, and a number of other details about her mother's behavior.

Sarah found herself hurt by this sudden barrage of criticism. She had always been close to Marsha. The two had been great pals. Now, in spite of her better judgment, Sarah felt somehow betrayed by this behavior on the part of her daughter. Having learned Releasing several months before, she decided to apply it to this problem.

Sarah asked herself if she could let go of her need for Marsha's approval but found this surprisingly difficult to do, so she turned the Releasing question around and stated it positively to herself. Could she *accept* only 1 percent of Marsha's *disapproval*? This she found herself able to do. The 1 percent of disapproval that Sarah could accept was her daughter's "silly comments" that morning as she watched her mother putting the finishing touches on her makeup—her words seemed trivial now and she could accept *them* at least. As she did this, Sarah experienced an immediate sense of relief; Marsha's disapproval suddenly seemed much less threatening.

Accepting 1 percent of her daughter's critical behavior had brought Sarah the release she needed. Now she began to see Marsha in perspective, as a young girl sufficiently unsure of herself so that she had to battle with her own mother, who was an attractive and poised woman. As her monitor opened up, Sarah no longer felt distressed by Marsha's dilemma. She now was able to think about helping her daughter learn to do things, such as style her own hair, which she felt would help her gain more confidence as a young woman. The result was a restoration of closeness between mother and daughter. Through releasing on wanting Marsha's approval, Sarah averted a potentially serious problem.

Parent-Child Difficulty 4

Not all difficulties which parents encounter with children are related to differing points of views or rebellious attitudes. Worry about a child can be a source of much distress.

The worries parents have about their adolescent youngsters may be particularly strong. Adolescents often try out new ways of behaving and in so doing may engage in activities which are unsafe. This can include anything from playing too rough a game of football, skiing down a particularly dangerous trail, traveling in a distant land with inadequate protection against disease, hitchhiking, or any number of other escapades which may trigger deep concerns in parents.

Olivia expressed such a concern at a Releasing workshop. Her son had recently graduated from college and was traveling alone in an underdeveloped country. The family had not heard from him for three weeks and had no address where they could reach him. The country where they believed him to be at this time had received considerable play in the newspapers because of a political crisis and was clearly not safe for Americans. Being a sensible person, Olivia felt that she should not be "fussing" about this, but it made her uneasy when she read about this country's upheaval and had no idea where her son was.

It would have been helpful, she thought, if he had phoned to say that he was all right, but she knew that youngsters "don't do that easily today." Then she hastily commented that her son was a "wonderfully independent person" and that she wouldn't want him to be otherwise. It was clear that Olivia was holding back her feelings and keeping a stiff upper lip. While this is an admirable trait under certain circumstances, it is not the best strategy when you want to release.

When she commented that she was worried about her son, I suggested that she change the word worried to "scared." It might be more dignified to use a watered-down expression like "worried," but a word like "scared" is easier to release on because it is stronger. Would she say that she was scared about Steven?

Olivia had to admit that she was scared that something had happened to him. When she found it difficult to let go of her feeling of being scared, I asked if she had been able to release satisfactorily at any time during the workshop. She had. I then asked her if she remembered how it felt to release. She remembered this easily.

I then suggested she do exactly the same thing—let go of the feeling of being scared and let the familiar sensation of releasing be there. Then I repeated a version of my original question, "Olivia, could you let go of being scared about your son?"

She sat quietly, intently staring into space, a slight frown on her brow. Then the tautness in her cheek muscles disappeared. She nodded her head slowly. When I asked her if she had let go of being scared, she nodded again. She had felt herself let go. It was a relief.

How did she feel now about the fact that she hadn't yet heard from her son? She said she was naturally concerned about it; he would certainly be on their minds until they heard that he was safe, but now she had an easier feeling. She knew she couldn't do anything about the situation at the present time and didn't feel any longer that she had to. If more time went by and then the family didn't hear, it occurred to her that they could try to trace him by contacting the embassy, but the situation was not getting to her the same way as before. She described herself as feeling more practical about it than emotional at this moment.

Olivia had released on her fears about her son by letting go of them (the direct method of Releasing on emotions). This enabled her to begin to cope more effectively with a situation where merely feeling frightened had not contributed to a solution.

Parent-Child Difficulty 5

Ruth faced anxiety with regard to her seventeen-year-old daughter, Susan. Susan had left the house early in the evening with a friend, a new girl from her class, whom she had introduced to her mother as Carolyn. She had mentioned they were both going over to Carolyn's house to study algebra. Susan was not permitted to stay out late on weekdays, but in order to encourage her daughter's independence (she was an only child and in many respects still very dependent on her parents), Ruth had stoically agreed to let her go out to study, mentally making note of the fact that there was usually no problem because Susan was always home by ten o'clock on week nights. Ruth didn't know where Carolyn lived or her last name, but again, to encourage Susan's independence, she purposely refrained from questioning her about this.

Later, when it was 12:30 and Susan had not returned home, Ruth began to panic. She found herself imagining any number of dire happenings—the car breaking down, Susan alone on a lonely road, Susan raped, Susan having been in an accident . . . her fears mounted at an alarming rate.

At this point, Ruth blamed herself bitterly for not having found out where her daughter was going. It was impossible for her to make a phone call to check on Susan's whereabouts. The evening became a nightmare for her. Her husband was calm about the matter, but she felt certain that something was wrong because her daughter was usually so reliable.

Susan finally walked into the house at 12:45, looking peaceful and her normal self, and explained that she and her friend had pored over their math for a long time to make sense of it. Ruth then found herself, for the first time that evening, remembering to use the Releasing technique which she had learned only a week before at a workshop. In the midst of her fear she had forgotten about Releasing. Now, as she experienced her relief at seeing Susan, she allowed herself to let go of wanting to change the situation. This steadied her so that she was better able to listen to what Susan had to say. After releasing on the situation once more, she turned to her daughter with a deeply serious look, stared into her eyes, and said quietly, "I simply don't want you to do this again. For my sake. I was very worried. In the future I want you to call when you're out late on a week night."

There was a note of quiet authority in her mother's voice to which Susan responded. She understood that she had inadvertently hurt her mother (something to which she had given little thought up until this point) and was able to agree earnestly not to do this again.

When Ruth came back for her second Releasing workshop a week later, she reported this incident to the group. She had mixed feelings about it. She was pleased that she had been able to release after seeing Susan and as a result handled the incident well. She was not happy, however, that she had gone into what she had considered an excessive panic at the time which had prevented her from thinking clearly about the situation *when* it was occurring. I suggested that Ruth do some "cleanup" releasing to take the remaining charge off the incident.

She described her feelings at the time when she was waiting for Susan to come home as "mounting panic." I asked her if she could first reexperience that panic and then *let go of wanting to change the panic* and let it "be there" for about thirty seconds. Ruth stiffened and waited a long time before replying. Then she relaxed perceptibly, sighed, and nodded.

I asked her to remember how she had felt sitting home, not knowing where Susan was, and I asked her to release on wanting to change the fact that she *hadn't known* where Susan was.

She was able to do this, and when we checked on how she was feeling now about the fact that Susan "wasn't home," she said the fear had lessened somewhat, but that she was still imagining terrible things that could have happened.

I now asked Ruth something that I knew might be difficult for her to handle. I explained that I wanted her to go along with me on this only if she felt she could. I suggested that she imagine herself back on that evening and ask herself the following question, "Could I let go of wanting to change the fact that Susan might have been seriously hurt?"

As I expected, Ruth found this extremely hard to do. How could she *not* wish her child to have avoided serious danger?

She couldn't, of course. What I was asking Ruth was to *accept* the fact that her daughter might have been in an accident. I was not suggesting that she cease wanting her daughter's safety.

"Let's change the wording," I suggested as I saw Ruth's look. "Could you *accept* the fact that she might have been seriously hurt?—Accept this as a possibility and move on from there?"

This Ruth could do. The word *accept* was the key. A possibility is, after all, something to be looked at seriously. If you look at it, perhaps you can do something about it.

At this point, Ruth was able to feel herself accept the fact that Susan might have been seriously hurt, and as she did so, possibilities opened up for her that had been closed up to this point. Her monitor was now open, so that she could scan these possibilities and come up with ideas. It occurred to Ruth that she would have had to verify an accident to be sure, and to do this she would have wanted to contact the police.

She could also have phoned one of her daughter's classmates and asked if they knew of Carolyn. Someone would certainly have heard of her.

I explained to Ruth that she hadn't been able to move on getting Carolyn's phone number at the time because she had been so emotionally involved that her monitor had closed down. Although she might have thought about some things that she could do at the time, they didn't become possibilities until she had released on the situation later on. When her monitor opened up, she was able to think of other ways to act.

Ruth's ideas were flowing now. Had she been able to release while waiting for Susan, she realized that she would have told the police that Susan could change a tire and that therefore it couldn't be a flat tire. She would also have asked the police if they had had any accident reports or if they had found any abandoned cars, and would have given them the license number of Susan's car and a description of it. She would also have checked the hospitals. If she had gotten word from one of Susan's friends as to where Carolyn lived, then she would have called the police and told them some probable places to look.

Ruth's monitor was now fully open. From here on, she could think of a number of constructive things she could have done. She also remembered again, with a sense of pleasure, how Susan did arrive home safely shortly after 12:45, with her homework finished, and how she was genuinely sorry to have caused her mother distress and was ready to cooperate in avoiding such a disturbing situation in the future.

Fully accepting a situation can be the first step towards *really* changing it.

Parent-Child Difficulty 6

While it requires special techniques to instruct a young child to release on a parent, adolescents readily learn this technique and can apply it usefully to difficulties which they may face from "problem parents."

Judy went to visit her father just after she had learned Releasing. Her parents had been divorced for a number of years, and her father was in many ways a stranger to her. She visited him only infrequently because she found these visits distinctly unpleasant.

Her father, a staid and critical math professor, seemed to find fault with her from the moment she entered his home. It was almost as if he had a prepared list of the faults which he had to find with the way she lived her life. After a few preliminary greetings, he would begin to criticize her friends, her grades at college, her lack of goals in life, her values, the books she enjoyed, her daily habits, and "just about everything else about me."

Since the visit inevitably turned into what seemed to be one long battle each time they met, she had been avoiding meeting with him for longer and longer periods of time, and now had not seen him for six months. After completing a Releasing workshop, however, she had the feeling that she could now cope better with her father and arranged to visit him. In a sense, she viewed this as a test of whether or not she could release on an unpleasant situation.

As soon as Judy arrived at her father's home, true to form, he began criticizing her for any number of things, including the fact that she had attended a Releasing workshop, which he characterized as "another one of your fads."

This time, as her father talked, Judy found that she was not following her usual pattern of trying to counter his attacks by marshaling arguments in her own defense. Instead, she spent the time listening and releasing on what he was saying:

"Could I let go of wanting to change what he is saying? . . .

"Could I let go of wanting to change how he is gesturing? . . .

"Could I let go of wanting to change his tone of voice? . . ."

Soon she felt unusually calm and, to her own surprise

unargumentative. In her words, she could let her father "rant and rave." When he became particularly abusive, she then used the divide-and-conquer tactic. This she did by placing her attention on his bushy eyebrows, or on some other minor characteristic which she didn't particularly like, and thinking to herself, "Could I let go of wanting to change the way his eyebrows are shaped? . . . Could I let go of wanting to change the way his hair is cut? . . . Could I let go of wanting to change the way he's holding his cigarette? . . ."

Releasing on these details about her father served to calm Judy so that what he was saying didn't register as deeply, and she felt more in control. It also helped her to feel that his attacks were far less important. Every so often he would say something which did arouse anger in her, and at these times she would ask herself, "Could I let go of wanting to protect myself?" This question seemed to clear up the problem. When she released on wanting to protect herself, it became, in her words "totally unnecessary to do anything more about the situation."

What was even more gratifying to Judy was the fact that as she continued to release on her father's behavior, she began to find his behavior interesting. She began to observe her father as one might watch someone in a movie, a character playing an unusual role. She even found herself feeling that he had a right to his "strange behavior": "It was as if he had to go through this act of his, and I didn't want to stop him. I could let him just carry on that way, if that's what he wanted. I didn't have to fight back desperately or get frightened."

One of the surprising results of this experiment was its effect on Judy's father. The more she released on wanting to change him, the more he seemed to be searching her face for evidence of her reactions to him. When she did occasionally speak, her own voice sounded to her unusually "reasonable." She wasn't pushing to make any particular point or to bring him around to her way of thinking.

Interestingly, every time Judy spoke to her father in this manner, he seemed to calm down more. Finally he became quiet, turned to her, and asked quite simply, "Shouldn't we make reservations to go out for dinner?"

Having released, Judy had no reason to stand on her pride

and refuse the invitation, so she accepted. They went to dinner, and she described this meal as the first time she can remember having "a really human conversation with my father." At dinner he began bringing up matters of interest to him, which he discussed with her as an equal. He asked for her opinions, and a genuine dialogue developed. The contest of wills was over.

Releasing can, then, be a tool which is equally useful for parents or for their children. The more members of a household who have learned the technique, the better, as far as the results are concerned, but even one person releasing in a context of family tension, as in the case of Judy, often alters the others' responses so that what I term a "fortunate circle" commences. From that point on, the tide can turn and the problem move toward resolution.

Releasing helps parents escape from the trap of trying to control a child's undesirable behavior through applying counterforce which can only result in resistance, which then creates further trouble. The technique reverses a vicious circle, instigating a fortunate one. It helps parents and teenagers alike to cope with seeming or actual rejections from other family members and to defuse family battles. It serves to handle some of the intense anxieties that parents feel about their children and helps them live comfortably with the mistakes they make in child rearing. It helps children to live with the limitations of their parents.

Releasing is also highly effective for problems encountered when at work. We will now turn to its use in this major area of life.

Chapter 13

RELEASING AT THE WORK PLACE

By removing inner obstacles to achievement, the work performance of "Releasers" can be enhanced and their satisfaction with their jobs increased.

Releasing may also have a beneficial effect on health problems related to work. A group of physicians, headed by Drs. Meyer Friedman and Ray Rosenman, have identified a behavior pattern which has been shown to be linked with coronary heart disease—"Type A Behavior." The complex of personality traits which are characteristic of "Type A" people are those of the well-known "workaholics"—persons driven by their own perfectionist standards and compulsive need to control their environment to a point where their health may suffer seriously.

The typical Type A person is described as having an excessive competitive drive, aggressiveness, impatience, and a harrying sense of time urgency. Type A individuals seem to be involved in a chronic, ceaseless struggle with themselves, with time, and with life in general.

There is also a "Type B" personality, which is the exact opposite of the Type A. These people are rarely harried by events or pressured by their own excessive need to control their environment. Interestingly, Type As are seven times more likely to incur clinical coronary heart disease than are Type Bs, although Type Bs may have as much or more ambition than their Type A counterparts. Type Bs may also have a considerable amount of "drive," but its character is such that it seems to steady them and give them confidence and security, rather than to goad, irritate, and infuriate them as does the drive of the Type A person. Interestingly, surveys have shown that there are as many Type B leaders in business, industry, and government as Type As. In fact, there appears to be tendency for top-level executives, such as corporate presidents or political leaders, to be Type B rather than Type A. This may be because it is important to be less driven by time urgency and less harried when handling high-level responsibilities with their inevitable frustrations.

Most people, of course, are a mixture of Type A and Type B traits. Since Type A traits are closely linked to an excessive need to control—the overpush—it is probably not surprising that those of us who have worked with the Releasing technique have noticed a tendency for predominantly Type A individuals to shift towards a Type B behavior pattern after having commenced the practice of Releasing. Along with this can come an increase in efficiency and decision-making capacities. The person using Releasing typically wastes less energy in trying to control the uncontrollable and focuses his efforts on more attainable goals. The following are accounts of people who have used releasing for work-related problems.

Work Problem 1

Richard relied for his livelihood on commissions from sales of life-insurance policies. Although he was in most respects an excellent insurance agent, well informed and attentive, the task of soliciting new customers had always been unpleasant for him. The result was that, notwithstanding his talents, he was achieving only small increases in income.

What bothered Richard were the cumulative turndowns from "cold" calls, where he was soliciting appointments with potential customers with whom he had had no previous contact. Like most other telephone salespeople, on many days he would encounter a string of "no" answers from those he phoned. After he had been refused repeatedly, he would begin to expect failure on the next call and would brace himself for this. His voice would then take on a tone of defensiveness, and he would talk faster than was customary for him. The result was that when he was turned down on several consecutive calls, he was likely to be turned down on the next few calls as well because his voice would betray his growing anxiety.

After he had learned Releasing, he decided to put the technique to work to solve this problem. Now, each time he picked up the phone to make a call, he first released on wanting to control how his customers would respond and then let go of wanting their approval. If he received a "no" answer, he would immediately let go of wanting to change the "no" after he had hung up the phone. This served to clear the decks, so that the next phone call he made was in the nature of a fresh start.

Richard's use of Releasing for his telephone soliciting made an immediate difference in his work. Unsuccessful phone calls now had a *positive* aspect as well as a negative one. This was because each unsuccessful call meant that he had to release. The more he released on the unsuccessful calls, the easier it was for him to release and, as a result, the better he could handle whatever problems arose. Often after he had received an unusual number of negative responses, he found himself finishing an hour of phone calls in an extremely relaxed mood. He laughingly reported to his wife that the days when he received the most rejections were now among his most productive days, since releasing on the phone calls put him in excellent shape for his meetings with both existing and potential customers later in the day.

The Releasing strategy led to a turnabout in Richard's career. He was now obtaining many more personal appointments with potential customers. The people whom he called apparently responded to the lack of urgency in his voice and felt confidence in a man who did not appear to need to struggle for their business. He was, therefore, able to increase his sales substantially and, accordingly, his income.

Improvement in performance at work through Releasing is not confined to people in sales, however. The president of a public company in the communications field, for example, reports that for the past three years he has released immediately before each of the annual stockholders' meetings. He has found it has resulted in his handling this most difficult day of the year much more easily.

The ability to make creative decisions, to work harmoniously with others, to withstand frustration, to learn from mistakes, to take criticism more easily, and to handle disagreements—these and many other attributes essential to success in business are greatly improved by the regular practice of Releasing. Work situations respond positively to an ability to let go of the overpush.

The following are accounts of people who have used Releasing to increase their ability to cope with problems at work.

Work Problem 2

Gertrude feared losing her job so much that even as she talked about this possibility, her hands became icy. She described her boss as a successful, hard-driving executive, who would berate her for each mistake she made but gave her little recognition for tasks well done. When this woman called her into her office, Gertrude's mind would "go numb" and she would feel as though she couldn't possibly meet her boss's demands.

Because she was so intimidated by her boss, Gertrude's first step was to release on her anxiety by simply accepting the anxiety and letting it "be." When she had done this for about thirty seconds, the fear seemed to settle and find its own level. She could breathe more easily now and didn't feel so confused. After she had released twice more in the same way, the fear had greatly lessened its hold on her.

Now Gertrude felt angry instead, and she released on her anger in the same manner. When she had done this, she still felt angry, but with a difference. This time she felt as though she were "getting something" out of her anger. She was beginning to feel that she would enjoy speaking up to her boss. It felt good to think about this, and Gertrude's face was now flushed, her eyes bright, her posture erect.

After she had accepted her fear fully by releasing on it,

Gertrude's sense of helpless anger, which had probably been beneath the surface all the time, emerged. When she had released on this helpless anger, she then felt constructive anger. At this point, she was able to think about protecting herself and to enjoy that thought.

The next day when she returned to the office, she was able to face her boss with more courage. Although she decided not to tell her off, she now felt in control. She knew she could speak up in her own defense if she wanted to.

Work Problem 3

Gary was relieved to have a job. He and his wife were expecting their second child, and she was planning to quit her own job to take care of the new baby. The mortgage on the home they had just bought was steep, and good jobs were becoming increasingly scarce. As a result, he was eager to make his mark in the department for which he worked.

Although Gary was well equipped for the position to which he had been assigned, his uncertainties about his future at the company sometimes led him to try too hard. Recently he attempted to land a major account for his firm and had been trying to get through on the telephone to George Chambers, the vice-president of the company he wanted to bring in.

When he finally spoke to Chambers, the conversation did not go as Gary had anticipated. Before he had gotten very far into his prepared sales pitch, Chambers interrupted with a barrage of questions, some of which required information that Gary didn't have at his fingertips and that needed considerable research before they could be answered.

Thrown by this unexpected turn of affairs, Gary made what he later considered to be a serious blunder. He tried to bluff rather than admitting that he didn't know the answers to some of the questions, and Chambers quickly picked up on Gary's areas of ignorance. Although the outcome was inconclusive, Gary was pessimistic about his chances of making the sale. Afterwards, he "kicked himself around the block" for not having told Chambers that he would get back to him with the requested information. When he came to a Releasing workshop several days later, the unfortunate incident was still rankling, and he welcomed the opportunity to work on it.

I asked Gary to commence by reenacting the phone call in detail and to let go of wanting to change what had happened. When he found this difficult, I suggested he release on small segments of it at a time (the divide-and-conquer tactic). First he let go of wanting to change that he had dialed a particular set of numbers on the phone; then on wanting to change the fact that Chambers' voice had sounded abrupt when he had come on the phone; then on wanting to change the content of his own opening remarks to Chambers; and finally on the fact that Chambers had interrupted him, not allowing him to make his prepared presentation. He then was ready to release on Chambers' rapidly fired questions.

He could almost hear in his mind the other man's voice saying, "I really haven't time for a long story, Mr. Stevens. I have some questions." This had thrown Gary. His reaction to the statement was so strong, in fact, that he had to divide Chambers' sentence into phrases and release on each phrase in turn. This is the "divide-the-divide" tactic, where one turns to minor details in order to handle a difficult situation.

Chambers' opening words in the sentence had been, "I really haven't time . . ." Gary let go of wanting to change this particular phrase. He then added the next phrase, "I really haven't time for a long story," and released on that, too. He decided it could have been leading into any number of things, some of which might not have been disadvantageous.

The next step was to add Gary's own name to Chambers' phrase, just as he had actually said it: "I really haven't time for a long story, Mr. Stevens." Could Gary let go of wanting to change the fact that Chambers' had added the words, "Mr. Stevens?" This he did easily.

Now came Chambers' statement, "I have some questions." To his own surprise, while this had formerly been a sticking point for him, Gary was now able to let go easily of wanting to change the fact that Chambers had said this. He guessed that somewhere along the way he might already have let go of wanting to change it automatically. When a person releases on one part of a situation, the other parts of the situation may be released on automatically at the same time.

Now we could go directly to the question that had most upset Gary. After asking several questions to which Gary did know the answers, Chambers had then asked about the projected delivery schedule for orders for the fall, and Gary did not know.

Because he found it difficult to release on this, I decided to use the exaggeration tactic at this point, and I asked Gary to exaggerate Chambers' voice in his mind. He was to pretend that he heard a loudspeaker amplifying Chambers' voice asking about the delivery schedule, and to repeat this sentence over and over in his mind. I then asked Gary to "keep that fight going— keep thinking the phrase 'delivery schedule,' and keep *wanting to change those words . . .*"

As Gary engaged in this task, it was apparent that he was going through an inner struggle. Finally, after about a minute of this exaggeration, he broke into a smile. The phrase was losing its effect on him. Now it was like hearing a phonograph record played over and over again; pretty soon you stop paying attention to the words.

Gary had now released on many aspects of the original phone call, so we were ready to go straight to the last part of the sentence, "for the fall." By this time, he felt that the whole incident wasn't worth bothering about and that there was no use knocking himself out over it. We then put the sentence together and found it was surprisingly easy for him to let go of wanting to change the fact that Chambers had said to him, "What is your projected delivery schedule for orders for the fall?"

Gary was now beginning to feel that it didn't make much difference what questions Chambers had asked; there were a lot of things he wouldn't have known. It also occurred to him that perhaps Chambers hadn't really expected him to know them. It was possible that Chambers might simply have needed to know that information and not been trying to examine Gary to find out whether he could come up with immediate answers. If that were the case, then all was not lost because Gary still had time to research the information and get back to Chambers. Gary's monitor had now opened up. He was processing the situation differently. The divide-the-divide tactic had worked.

Often we can accept a very small portion of even a difficult situation. What upsets us is not the details, but the total picture of what is happening as we conceive of it in our minds. Picking out some of the unimportant details and releasing on them can add up to releasing on the whole situation. By the time Gary had finished releasing on the details, the charge had been taken off the incident and his adjustment to his work problem had changed. Now he was able to proceed in a practical manner to acquire the needed information and to get back to Chambers, who, as it turned out, proved to be interested in hearing more about his proposal.

Work Problem 4

Pam was part of a secretarial pool in her office and, therefore, had many opportunities to compare herself unfavorably with other women. She was self-conscious about her weight problem and often found herself counting the times the men in the office talked to the other secretaries instead of to her, telling herself that the other women in the room were more attractive than she was.

This concern was actually unrealistic. Pam was a pretty woman, only slightly on the heavy side, who was popular with both her male coworkers and the other women in the office. But none of this seemed to register with her. She felt as though she were insignificant when others received attention.

Since Pam was undergoing psychotherapy for her emotional problems, along with her regular treatment I taught her to release and suggested that she apply the technique as quickly as possible to her difficulties at the office. She was a rapid learner and caught on readily to the method. The first day after learning, she had occasion to try Releasing on her own.

On her way to work in the morning, she imagined her boss stopping to chat with the secretary at the next desk while ignoring her. Because she had such strong feelings about this, it was difficult for her to let go of wanting her boss's approval, but soon she was able to let go of 10 percent and then 20 percent of this *wanting*. After a few more releases, she let go of most of this, and the situation now appeared different. It occurred to her that although her boss might find other women in the office interesting or attractive, this did not necessarily mean that he didn't value Pam.

Since her monitor had now opened, she was in a better mood when she arrived at the office. This turned out to be fortunate. One of the secretaries had come to work with a beautiful tan, wearing a striking new outfit which her model-like figure showed off to great advantage. Pam felt fat and clumsy by comparison, a feeling which was so overwhelming to her that she didn't think of releasing at the time. When she did remember to release, she found this too difficult to do in the presence of the other woman, so she retreated to the ladies' room.

Standing in front of the mirror in solitude, she was able to let go of wanting to control how the other secretary looked. She was then able to let go of wanting to change the other woman's clothes, her slim figure, and her tan. As she released on each of these details in turn, Pam could feel the muscles of her neck and jaw loosening. When she went back into the office, a thought occurred to her. If this other woman could dress so attractively and acquire a lovely tan and become slim, then Pam, *too*, could do these things. The slim secretary now seemed a role model for her. As she thought about facing competition with the other women, it occurred to Pam that perhaps she could handle her feelings better by dieting than by grabbing food to console herself. This insight was the start of a successful plan to reduce.

As the day proceeded, Pam found more opportunities to release. She let go of wanting to control the way one of the executives in the office complimented another office worker. She let go of wanting to change the fact that one woman in the office reported that she had become engaged. She also let go of wanting to control her boss's bad mood.

As she became accustomed to Releasing, Pam found it increasingly easy to do. If she happened to be immersed in work when some incident startled her unexpectedly, however, she might not think about Releasing unless she reminded herself. To forestall this problem, she printed a capital "R" on an index card and propped it up on her desk. Now, every time she turned towards her desk, she saw the "R" which served as a signal to her to release.

Soon she didn't wait for an unpleasant situation to come up but simply released whenever the "R" caught her eye. This led her to release on wanting to change the way her papers were scattered over the desk, on wanting to control the chatter in the room, on wanting to change the tightness of her new shoes, or on whatever else was troublesome.

Pam later claimed that this frequent releasing on minor matters probably did more for her than anything else. As she released on small items throughout the day, she would get into a Releasing mood. After that, Releasing would become an automatic response to every situation that required it.

The use of the Releasing strategy resulted in a significant step forward for Pam. From this point on, she was able to work more diligently in her psychotherapy and was eventually able to get matters under much better control as far as her work and social life were concerned. She also lost a good deal of weight because she found herself able to let go of wanting to change the slimness and attractiveness of the *others* around her.

Work Problem 5

Edith had completed an important project well ahead of her department's schedule and had done it more thoroughly than required. She had worked exceptionally hard because she had been led to expect a promotion.

As it turned out, this was not to be the case. Despite her outstanding work, the company announced a shakeup in her department and placed a job freeze on all concerned. Edith's position would be redefined, but she would not advance, either in salary or in prestige. In fact, she would probably be given more responsibility with no additional compensation.

Bewildered at what had happened, Edith had immediately requested a reevaluation from the vice-president in charge of her department. She was abruptly told by him that this was the way it was going to be, that everyone would have to adjust. The door had been shut in her face, and she was left with a conviction that her company's refusal to listen to her side of the story was grossly unfair.

When she attended a Releasing workshop shortly thereafter, the feeling of unfairness still rankled within her and she wanted to release on it. Other members of the workshop agreed that having a company keep its promise to an employee is desirable but pointed out that Edith still had herself to deal with. Could she let go of wanting the company to be *fair*?

This question startled her, and at first she was unable to conceive of releasing on "fairness." Soon, however, she was able to release on small bits of it at a time (to accept just 1 percent of the "unfairness"), and within a few moments she felt herself let go completely of wanting her company to be "fair."

When she did this, she felt deeply relieved. She sighed perceptibly after she experienced the release and said, "I think I've been looking for something that simply wasn't there."

Now, as she remembered the scene where she had discussed the reorganization with the vice-president, she felt differently about it. This time she was primarily interested in setting out to find another position as rapidly as she could. Her thoughts were turning to the future, rather than trying to repair an inequity in the past.

Something had clicked in Edith when she had been asked to let go of wanting the company to be "fair." She had then realized that its behavior simply reflected the way it operated. Having put the fairness issue to rest, she realized that it was not she alone who was not appreciated, but that everybody in the company was not appreciated at the present time. The company itself was in trouble. She had seen the handwriting on the wall some months ago but had thought she could beat the game by doing a superb job and gaining recognition. Now it occurred to her that the company's troubles were bigger than she was and that she couldn't win. However, as she surveyed the situation with her monitor fully open, she realized that some other company would be able to use her skills and that the project she had just completed had not been a loss. She would now be able to leave with excellent recommendations.

Work Problem 6

Problems at work do not always involve only one's own destinies. They may be interwoven intricately with the destinies of others for whom one is responsible.

Tom found himself in conflict with his boss over the treatment of a group of employees whom he supervised. His firm had introduced a new computer system, a complicated system which Tom and the project manager had discussed in detail. In order to work out procedures if the system were to crash, they had made plans to conduct a drill.

The chief responsibility for this drill fell to Tom, and he sat down with his employees to talk through what they could do in the event of such an electronic failure. Before the discussion got under way, however, the project manager burst into the room and, simulating an emergency, called out, "The system has crashed! What are you people going to do?"

Tom protested that he hadn't yet had a chance to rehearse these people and that they couldn't possibly know what to do. His boss paid no attention. The employees were held to account for their actions in the simulated drill. Tom was furious. In his opinion, asking the employees what they would do when they had not yet received the proper instructions was like teaching children to swim by throwing them into deep water. He felt he should have been allowed to run the drill the way he had planned, particularly since his boss had originally agreed to such a procedure.

Tom's temper flared up and he came close to walking out. Days later, he found himself still inwardly battling his boss and wanting to change how the boss had behaved.

As he set about releasing on this during a workshop, he was reluctant to let go of wanting to change his boss's behavior. His feeling was that if he did that, he could not be an effective intermediary for his employees, whom he liked and who were really good workers.

I explained to Tom that he was not being asked to let go of the *goal* of changing his boss's behavior at all—that seemed reasonable. What I was suggesting was that he let go of his *feelings* —the feelings or urgency and desperation.

When this became clear, Tom was able to proceed. By using several unlocking tactics, he was able to let go of wanting to change his boss's behavior. When he thought back over the situation, he could now view it differently. As he imagined his boss's voice asking his employees what they were going to do about the simulated emergency, he found himself half smiling as it occurred to him that if he had in fact remained silent, his boss would have made an even greater fool of himself. The boss's actions would have spoken for themselves. The fact that it was a poor idea to rush the drill would have become obvious.

While Tom had released on wanting to control his boss, he didn't relinquish his stand with respect to the employees' rights. He still knew what he thought should be done for those people and now felt that he could get his point across more effectively.

When he returned to the plant the next day, Tom confronted his boss in a different manner than before. The project manager was bewildered because he no longer knew where he stood with Tom. Tom, on the other hand, knew exactly what he felt. The result was that within a relatively short while, Tom had convinced the boss that it would be wiser to proceed in a different way in the future.

When learning Releasing, some people mistakenly believe that releasing on an argument means giving up on it. Actually, Releasing increases your options and allows you to recognize further possibilities for effective action. It can also give you the confidence to put these possibilities into action.

Releasing can be used to improve one's work life in a variety of ways. It can create a more balanced attitude toward the inevitable disappointments of business life, neutralize the rejections that come with attempts to market products or services, and greatly increase one's flexibility. It can also help people handle anxiety associated with a threat to job security, defuse interoffice conflicts, and relieve unproductive worry about one's performance.

These are but some of the ways that Releasing can improve work life. In the following chapter, we will look at another type of work problem where releasing is useful—career planning and the difficulties it poses in terms of life decisions and the marketing of *oneself*.

Chapter 14

RELEASING FOR CAREERS

Special work problems exist for people who offer their services as independent contractors. They may, for example, find themselves having to market their own work. Problems of selling oneself are encountered by such diverse groups as building contractors, attorneys, performers, physicians, writers, and others.

Long-range career planning is not confined solely to independent contractors, however. It is a problem for many people within business and industry who attempt to plan for their own advancement. The following accounts are of people who handled career problems by releasing on them.

Career Problem 1

Burt's ambitions extended well beyond the company for which he worked, and he viewed his current position as merely a stepping-stone for a career which he hoped would take him into the top levels of management at a large company. This was not entirely an unrealistic ambition on his part since he was a capable and intelligent executive, but his very ambition seemed to be a stumbling block to constructive planning.

Burt had set arbitrary limits on the amount of time he wanted to spend at any particular company. While a decision on how long to remain in a given position can serve as a useful guideline, to Burt such ideas were not guidelines but *rules*. His ambitious planning had taken on an inflexibility that hindered his freedom of choice.

After having worked for five years at his particular company, Burt's timetable now dictated that he should move on. The issue was confusing him, however, because at the moment many interesting opportunities were opening up at his present company. The business was expanding rapidly, and it looked as though Burt might carve out a niche for himself there which could be both interesting and engage more of his capabilities than he was using at present. Such a change might be valuable to him in the long run and result in advancement within this particular corporation, rather than advancement through changing companies.

At this point, Burt found himself torn between his own carefully laid plans and the change in circumstances. Because of his preoccupation with advancing more rapidly, he lacked the flexibility necessary to consider both sides of the question objectively. The result was physical and emotional stress. Burt found himself suffering from unusual restlessness, insomnia, and a tendency to smoke much more than was his habit. His wife complained that he tended to shut her out as well as his friends, and, indeed, he seemed to be retreating into solitary contemplation of his dilemma.

Fortunately, Burt and his wife attended a Releasing workshop at this time. When I inquired which members of the group were facing decisions that they would like to work on, Burt indicated that he had a difficult career decision to make. He felt he was a good candidate for the "decision-making strategy" which I was about to demonstrate.

This strategy is for those who find themselves torn between two courses of action. The practice of listing advantages and disadvantages of an upcoming decision in two opposing columns, then comparing them, is, of course, a familiar one. It is useful to a point but can leave us caught with many of the confusions that may have baffled us in the first place. Categorical labeling is not the most useful device when we want to clarify thinking.

The Releasing "decision-making strategy" makes use of listing advantages and disadvantages, but with a difference. When people list each advantage and disadvantage, they release on wanting to *change* (or "control," as the case may be) that advantage or disadvantage, or on wanting approval with respect to the advantage, thus neutralizing the overpush *in both directions*.

To get Burt started on this strategy, I asked him to state one possible way he could resolve his job decision. He selected leaving his company to seek a better position, and I wrote that down at the top of the blackboard.

I then asked him to list one *advantage* of leaving his company. The first one that came to his mind was that he was at the perfect age to make the switch. On further questioning, he identified this as a control issue—he wanted to control his career so that it would work out exactly the way he had planned.

When I asked him to let go of wanting to control at exactly *which point* he would leave the company, Burt had difficulty releasing and found he needed to use an unlocking tactic. For him, the most effective one appeared to be exaggeration. He allowed himself to *want* to control the exact age when he made the switch, and then to do so more and more *strongly*. He really got into the spirit of this exaggeration and finally got down to wanting to control the very day, hour, and minute when he would make the switch! At this point, of course, the whole thing suddenly seemed ridiculous! With a broad smile, Burt then let go of the whole issue of wanting to control *when* a change would take place. The age factor seemed secondary and unimportant now.

The next step was for Burt to identify a *disadvantage* of leaving his company right now. He readily answered that he might be depriving himself of an important opportunity if he did this.

Again, the strategy was to let go of wanting to control whether or not he got that important opportunity. The key word here was *control*. He could reasonably hope for the opportunity all he wanted but was simply to drop the *overpush*. Using the exaggeration tactic which worked so well for him, Burt was able to release on wanting to control whether or not he got that opportunity. As he did so, he felt himself ease up.

He then listed another advantage of leaving—he was likely to get a higher salary. He let go of wanting to control whether or not he increased his salary.

Next, he identified another disadvantage of leaving—he enjoyed his friends at this company. He let go of wanting to control whether or not he would remain near his friends.

Following the simple rules of the decision-making strategy, Burt moved back and forth between advantages and disadvantages, releasing on each side of the issue in turn until he had completed a long list. As he released on both options, he felt his sense of urgency lighten. By the time he got down to the bottom of the page, to his surprise he was beginning to feel quite easy about the whole situation. He no longer felt that so much was riding on his decision. For the first time, he felt free to decide either way. The over-intensity with which he had invested both sides of the argument was neutralized.

When Burt took his decision-making chart home, he was able to do more releasing and as a result was able to arrive at a solid decision. He chose to stay on at the company for the next couple of years to find out what future there might be for him in light of new developments. His decision on this was not a dramatic event, but a quiet process. He took a good look at the situation and, on balance, made what he considered the most practical choice. He felt at ease about what he had decided, was sleeping much better, and his compulsion to smoke heavily was gone.

A sample decision-making chart is shown on page 167. The letters "C" and "A" stand for "Control" and "Approval." Place an appropriate check in the control or approval column (or in both) for each advantage and disadvantage; then release accordingly.

Career Problem 2

Marjorie's legal career was building a bit too slowly, and she had hit on the idea of obtaining speaking engagements at local women's organizations in order to obtain wider exposure in the community.

Recently she had been asked to speak at a women's club some miles distant from her home. At the end of an hour-long drive,

The Decision-Making Strategy

1. Write at the top of the page an option which you are considering (for example, "Leave my job now," or "Not leave my job now").

2. Divide the page into two columns: "Advantages" and "Disadvantages." Under the Advantages column, list the first advantage that comes to your mind. Find out whether it relates to wanting approval or wanting to control, or both. Release.

3. Under the Disadvantage column, list a disadvantage. Identify whether it relates to wanting approval or wanting to control. Release.

4. Alternately list an advantage and then a disadvantage, and release on each in turn until you have completed your list.

5. If at some point you can't think of an advantage or disadvantage, draw a line across that space and proceed to the next column.

6. Keep going until you can no longer think of any advantages or disadvantages.

7. If you need to work further on this decision, switch the wording of your option to its opposite (if it is stated in the positive, now state it in the negative, or vice versa) and repeat the whole process.

8. When you are finished, engage in some unrelated activity. Within a short time, you should be able to make a balanced decision without emotional stress.

she arrived to find the meeting house locked. She was about to leave when a woman drove up in a car and informed her that she was sorry to have to tell Marjorie that the meeting had been postponed.

Upset, but keeping a tight control over herself (she didn't want to jeopardize her relationship with this particular community group), Marjorie discussed the situation and

OPTION:_____

ADVANTAGES		C	A	DISADVANTAGES		C	A
1.				1.			
2.				2.			
3.				3.			
4.				4.			
5.				5.			
etc.				etc.			

arranged for the woman to phone her between 2:00 and 3:00 P.M. the following Friday to let her know when the meeting would be rescheduled.

On Friday, Marjorie waited in her office at the prearranged time, but there was no phone call. At exactly ten minutes past three, when Marjorie was in conference with a client, the woman phoned to say that she was sorry that she hadn't made the matter clear but that the meeting had been permanently canceled. Marjorie thanked her abruptly and hung up. The woman called back and asked why she had hung up. Marjorie explained that she felt disappointed and again ended the phone call.

What was still upsetting Marjorie when she arrived at the Releasing workshop a week later was the fact that she had not expressed her true feelings at the inconsiderate behavior of this group. In helping Marjorie work on this problem, I asked her to go first to the original occasion of the trouble. In her imagination she moved backward in time to the moment when she first arrived at the meeting house, ready to deliver her speech.

She could imagine this vividly—the locked door, the absence of people, the woman driving up and commenting offhandedly that there was to be no meeting that day. As she described this, it became quite clear to Marjorie that she had felt very angry. She also would have liked to have handled the situation differently by having checked in advance and not gone out needlessly that afternoon.

We started with her wish to have confirmed the engagement before setting out. I suggested that Marjorie let go of wanting to change the fact that she *hadn't* confirmed.

This release came easily to her. As she looked back at the situation after having released, she realized that when she had been driving there, she had experienced a nagging feeling in the pit of her stomach that maybe she should have double-checked on the appointment. She hadn't paid any attention to that feeling. The next time she had such a feeling she *would* pay attention to it—perhaps stop and make a quick phone call to make sure of the engagement. She had learned something from this experience. As so often happens with Releasing, Marjorie now saw a positive use for the situation that she hadn't noticed before.

She next released on the follow-up telephone call on Friday afternoon. This had annoyed Marjorie, but she was able to let go of *1 percent* of wanting to change the situation. After this, when she thought about the event, she saw it very differently, now picturing this woman and herself caught in a comedy of errors that neither of them knew how to handle.

As she thought back over it, Marjorie commenced to laugh, and her laughter grew until her shoulders heaved and her face was suffused with color. Releasing doesn't always bring laughter, but when it does, you can be certain that you have released it! Bit by bit, Marjorie had let go of the intensity with which she had invested this situation. Now it was neutralized.

Career Problem 3

Soon after she had learned Releasing, Phyllis faced a disappointment. As an ambitious but unrecognized actress, she was scheduled to give a series of dramatic readings before a national women's organization. This was a major opportunity for her, and she had selected an excellent photograph of herself for the group to use in its brochure. Excited at the prospect of the publicity this would bring, it was a shock to Phyllis to discover, upon receiving the brochure in the mail, that the organization had printed the wrong photograph of her! Instead of the attractive publicity picture, they had used an old flashbulb photo which they had had in their files. It was faded and unclear, and Phyllis's mouth was wide open in a silly expression. The publicity photo which she had sent in had been lost and the unflattering flashbulb photo dug out by the secretary. The editor had assumed it was the correct photograph.

Phyllis had had high hopes for a successful performance under the auspices of this organization. On viewing the brochure, she felt deeply frustrated and throughout the rest of the day was totally preoccupied with this unfortunate occurrence.

Her thoughts consisted mainly of trying to set straight the situation in her mind by imagining herself having handled it differently. She was caught up in an elaborate attempt to rewrite history. With monotonous regularity, she found herself repeating in her mind exactly what she had said to the secretary on the phone and then imagined changing what she had said so that this time there would be no mistake.

The problem with Phyllis's mental rehearsal was that she was rehearsing an event in the *past*! There was absolutely nothing that could be done about the mistake now—the brochures had already been mailed. But although she knew this, she couldn't stop alternating between going back and trying to change the past and a wild present-time fantasy of grabbing the brochure out of the mailbox of each recipient!

Although her preoccupation with this matter receded during the day as she busied herself with auditions, in the evening her circular thinking was back full force.

Usually successful at releasing, Phyllis decided to tackle the issue. When she tried to release on wanting the approval of all those people who would see the brochure, she found strong feelings getting in the way. She was very angry. When she then released on wanting to change or justify her anger, allowing it to exist raw and unadulterated, another feeling surfaced. It was embarrassment. She was humiliated at being presented in that unflattering light.

When she let go of wanting to change her feeling of

humiliation, Phyllis now experienced a sense of inner quiet. She found herself respecting her own feelings, even the feeling of humiliation. "It's a part of me, after all, a feeling I have a right to." Images from the past now flashed before her eyes—pictures of herself as a little girl, embarrassed and trying to hide the embarrassment. When she realized that she had no need to hide that feeling now, her compulsive thoughts of changing the situation dissolved.

There were other layers of the problem to be handled, however. When she awoke the next morning, she discovered to her dismay that her circular thinking about the brochure was back in full force. She thought she had released on that!

Phyllis's monitor was so shut down that it would take several bouts of releasing before the issue could be cleared up. She now found herself angry at the secretary's "stupidity" but knew this was unproductive and decided to release on it. Once again she let go of wanting to change or justify her anger. She allowed it to exist as a strong feeling throughout her body. The release she obtained this time was profound.

Phyllis had experienced what I call the "jack-in-the-box" effect—a tendency for intense emotional reactions to recur and require further releasing. When the jack-in-the-box effect occurs, your second or third round of releasing is often more effective than the first. It is as though each subsequent Releasing session handles another layer of the original distress until finally a resolution of the problem is achieved.

After her second Releasing session, Phyllis's thoughts about undoing the original situation had vanished. In their place was a sense of being misunderstood. Her anger had faded. The incident with the publicity photo seemed far away, almost funny. She wasn't even certain now that the unflattering picture would cut the attendance at her performance, and if it did, the event could still be successful.

Actually, Phyllis had hit on her solution by trying a number of different approaches to Releasing, and then trying them again the following day under different circumstances. Her experience underlines the advisability of trying other Releasing tactics when the first few don't work until, finally, one does work.

Releasing can be useful in furthering a career and can help you cope with the many frustrations involved in marketing your own talents. It can handle the inevitable rejections which have to be faced, and facilitate sound career decisions. It can also assist in a number of other ways, including helping you handle a need to *overcontrol* your destiny.

Problems of being evaluated inevitably arise during career planning, as they did with Phyllis, but these are frequently seen in many other areas of life as well. They deserve a chapter of their own. We will now turn to the manner in which Releasing dissipates the anxiety so often involved when we are being evaluated.

Chapter 15

RELEASING WHEN BEING EVALUATED

Tests in grade school, college-entrance examinations, job interviews, on-job evaluations—the process of facing evaluations seems to dog our footsteps throughout life. For many people it can be so stressful that they fail to do their best when being evaluated. The following accounts are of people who had used Releasing to help themselves handle evaluations more successfully.

One of the most common examples of evaluation stress is the job interview. The unspoken requirement of selling oneself at such a time can make this experience unpleasant. The ability to sell oneself may have little to do with one's capacity to fulfil the tasks required on a job.

Evaluation Problem 1

Leslie suffered from extreme shyness and was unable to express herself in words likely to impress a prospective employer. She was, nevertheless, a skilled biochemist, and her combination of intelligence and excellence at her work was exactly what was needed by the pharmaceutical company where she was to be interviewed.

Aware that she was well qualified for the job, Leslie's problem was the interview. It promised to be especially difficult for her because she wanted this position so much. Getting the job would enable her to move to another city where she preferred to live and where there were exciting research opportunities. The fact that she wanted this job so much made the interview seem like a test which she must pass at all costs.

It was fortunate that Leslie attended a Releasing workshop at this time, where she had the opportunity to release on her anxiety about the job interview. As can be imagined, she had a strong wish to control how the interview turned out. This meant that she was trying to control a great many factors outside of her sphere of influence. Applicants for a job can do little more than establish rapport with the interviewer and present themselves to their best advantage. Factors that may determine the organization's eventual decision such as economic conditions, the qualifications of other applicants, seniority rights, or special attributes needed for the position are exempt from any influence which the interviewee can exert.

Leslie's wish for this job led her to feel that she *must* get it, and she placed the total responsibility for doing this on her own shoulders. It was therefore necessary for her to release first on her need to control the *outcome* of the interview. Hoping it would turn out well was a valid goal. She had to let go of the overpush—an excessive demand on herself to control what was not in her power to control.

She quickly discovered that for this she would need to use a divide-and-conquer tactic. She could let go of wanting to control such seemingly unimportant details as the type of room in which the interview might be conducted, the way in which the research director might dress, or whether or not she would have to wait a long time before being admitted to the director's office. As she let go of wanting to control these seemingly minor aspects of the interview, she felt herself get into a "Releasing mood." To her surprise, she was soon able to let go of the feeling of wanting to control the outcome of the interview itself. As soon as she had done this, she felt tension leaving her and a more balanced, "let's-see-what-happens" attitude emerge.

Next, she turned her attention to how she might be attempting to control *herself* in this situation. She wanted to make sure that she would come over well in the interview and that she would behave in a fashion particularly pleasing to herself. She would have to release on this aspect of the situation, too. Unfortunately, when we try to overcontrol our own behavior, we stand less chance of behaving flexibly. While the Releasing technique does not ask that we give up constructive planning, it does help us to let go of overcontrolling ourselves.

Leslie was able to let go of wanting to control a number of details about how she herself would be on the day of the interview—the degree of energy that she would wake up with on that morning, the way her eyes would look when she put on her makeup, the way her hair would be arranged, the manner in which she might shake hands with the research director, and so on.

After she had released on the details of how she would be that day, she unexpectedly found herself able to let go of wanting to control how she did in the actual interview. She could now coast with the idea that whatever was going to happen, would happen. As she accepted this, a weight seemed lifted off her shoulders.

For the next few days, as she prepared for her trip to the city where the interview was to take place, Leslie observed her own moods with great interest. When she discovered herself becoming anxious about the interview, she released. She let go of wanting the approval of the research director, of wanting her own approval, of wanting to change various details of the imagined interview and then released on a number of other issues involving control. She began to interpret each "worry" of hers as a signal to start another session of Releasing, with each new session putting her that much farther ahead with regard to the upcoming interview.

When she boarded the plane, she continued to release on a number of aspects of the interview, and as she let go of wanting to change each of these, she relaxed even more. The result was that when she came to the interview itself, most of the charge had already been taken off the situation. She had "gone through" and handled the major difficulties by releasing on them in advance. By this sequence of releasings, she was able to relax, free her monitor, and rid herself of uncertainty.

During the interview she actually felt at ease. For the first time in her entire work experience, she found herself able to sit and listen quietly to the questions of the interviewer instead of being preoccupied with thinking about what she was going to say next. Because she had let go of her desperate need to control the outcome of the interview, she was also able to take the risk of describing honestly and fully how she would handle the job that might be assigned to her. She presented herself in a more favorable light than in any of her former job interviews. The research director was impressed. Within a week she received word that she had been selected for the position.

The most important thing about the interview was that Leslie had discovered how to use Releasing for situations where she put unnecessary pressure on herself to make an impression. In the future she could use it to prepare herself for social events, parties and the like. Releasing was, for her, a new-found source of strength.

The On-Job Evaluation

On-job evaluations can sometimes give rise to even more anxiety than interviewing for a new position. A person may or may not get a particular job for which he or she interviews, but there are usually other interviews pending. An on-job evaluation, however, may mean the difference between a raise or a promotion, or their opposites. At times it can mean the difference between being retained on the job or dismissed. Survival anxiety may be involved in an on-job evaluation. Often it can block a person from performing at optimum level.

Evaluation Problem 2

Alan was relatively new to the school system, but his gift for making math exciting for even the most unmathematical students was remarkable. Despite this, he notoriously froze up whenever his supervisor entered the room. As soon as he saw the supervisor sitting in the corner, Alan's teaching became stilted, and his greatest asset, his ability to scan his students' faces and accurately assess their involvement, was gone. All that he saw now (out of the corner of his eye) was the supervisor. Because of this, under supervision he gave an adequate but uninspired performance.

When Alan attended a Releasing workshop with other teachers from his school, he expressed concern about his poor performance during evaluations and wanted to release in anticipation of his supervisor's next visit. He also wanted to learn how to release *during* the evaluation session itself.

It became apparent that approval was a paramount issue for Alan. Just as he was extremely sensitive to the ways in which he could obtain the approval of his students (which helped make him a charismatic teacher), his very ability to be sensitive to outside approval hamstrung him when his supervisor appeared. It was as though at such times he became a little boy evaluated by an all-powerful parent.

As he talked about his problem, Alan discovered that an effective way for him to release on his supervisor was to let go of wanting to change her reactions in any way, First he let go of wanting to change unimportant details about her—the color of her hair, the way she dressed, the way she was seated in her chair, the way she wrote in her notebook, the way her eyes looked up from the page and lowered again as she was evaluating him, and other things about her. By first breaking up this troublesome situation in his mind (dividing and conquering it), he was then able to release on wanting to change her total behavior. As soon as he did so, he found that he could let her "be the way she was." He also noticed that now, as he envisioned the scene, she no longer seemed to fill the whole room with her presence; she was merely a person sitting in the corner, doing her own thing. This left Alan free to relate to his pupils.

As a result of this anticipatory releasing, he was prepared to handle the challenge differently when, the following week, his supervisor entered his classroom unexpectedly. Although he experienced a momentary inner trembling, he remembered the Releasing strategy and let go of wanting to control where she was going to sit. Then he let go of wanting to change where she did sit. To his own surprise, this was all that he had to do to start a train of automatic releasing. He found himself continuing to release easily on his supervisor's presence without having to ask himself to do so. Soon he realized that he had no intention of letting her presence impede his teaching. Instead, he found himself in his usual lively give-and-take with the class. Alan was now home free.

After this, he was able to forget about his supervisor for extended periods of time. The result was an enthusiastic evaluation by the supervisor, who informed him that his teaching had "improved enormously" and that she was extremely pleased with his progress. Actually, Alan's progress had been in the way he handled the evaluation, not in his teaching. He now had a tool, Releasing, which would stand him in good stead for other evaluations in the future.

Facing Examinations

There are those who wonder whether it is wise to eliminate test anxiety. Suppose students were to release on wanting to control how well they did on an exam, or on how carefully they studied for it—wouldn't this lead to laziness and poor work? Some students believe that if they didn't experience anxiety before an exam, they couldn't get themselves to study for it. They therefore look upon exam anxiety as a necessity.

Actually, these students don't need that anxiety, either for proper studying or for doing well on the exam. They will find that excitement and a sense of being "keyed up" on the day of the exam is very useful, but such feelings need not include anxiety. While the notion that anxiety is necessary for good school work is a myth, it is understandable why so many people believe it. This is due to what I call the "trained-seal error."

Circus folk tell a tale about a trained seal named Oscar who used to perform remarkable tricks for which he was paid daily in the form of fresh fish. He was a renowned performer, the only seal who had ever learned to catch a tiny ball no larger than a golf ball on the tip of his nose and balance it there perfectly for a period of one minute. He could catch this ball after it had been tossed thirty feet into the air, a spectacular feat.

Oscar had a special procedure for doing this. In order to catch the ball as it was descending, he would tilt his head back and stare into a brilliant spotlight which hung from the ceiling of the circus tent. When he did this, he was able to catch sight of the ball, move so that he captured it with his nose, and manage to keep his head tilted back at the same time so that the ball remained in place. Throughout this delicate procedure, Oscar was almost blinded by the glare of the spotlight. As soon as he had finished his remarkable trick, the audience would break into applause and his trainer would pop three fresh fish into his mouth. Oscar was delighted with all this and considered his trick an excellent way of gaining both fame and food.

During all the years he performed, however, no one thought of asking Oscar what he was thinking while he was performing his trick. Finally, another seal who had more than an ordinary interest in food asked him how he was able to obtain so many fresh fish in one day. Oscar replied, "It's easy. You just look up into the blinding light, and if you can stand it long enough, a ball lands on your nose. Then you look at the blinding light again, and if you can stand it some more, the ball stays on your nose. Then they cheer and clap, and someone throws you three fresh fish."

The point of this story is that Oscar didn't know the extent of his own skill. Actually, he could have performed the trick just as well if the spotlight had been placed on the floor instead of over his head, or if it had been by his side, or if it hadn't been there at all. To do his trick, he would simply have had to learn to tilt his head back the same way and keep his eye on the little ball just as he had always done. But because the light had always glared into his eyes at the exact moment that he was catching the ball, he sincerely believed that the spotlight was responsible for his success!

The moral of the story is: *We don't always know what causes our triumphs!*

Many students believe that their anxiety and desperation have enabled them to study successfully for exams. What they don't realize is that they have been doing a lot of other things at the same time they were also experiencing anxiety and desperation. They have been doing such things as rereading portions of textbooks, reviewing class notes, making outlines, and memorizing essential material. These activities are very helpful in passing exams. Anxiety and desperation are not. In the students' experience, however, anxiety and desperation have, in the past, occurred along with these positive and constructive acts. Like Oscar, these students now mistakenly believe that the reward (passing the exams) has been brought about by something that actually had nothing to do with their success. They have passed their exams *in spite of*, not because of, their overpush and anxiety. They will do even better if they release on these negative feelings.

There are many situations in life which are accompanied by anxiety, pushing, and an exaggerated need to control. When these situations turn out well for us, and often they do so because much hard work has gone into ensuring that they will, it is easy to make the trained-seal error and believe that it was our anxiety and need to control which *caused* the success. When we release on these unnecessary ingredients, however, what is left are those actions which actually help us accomplish what we want, without taking their toll in terms of health and well-being. The result is that we are likely to do even better.

Evaluation Problem 3

Although classroom-evaluation problems usually center about issues of approval, these do not always involve the approval of other people. One's own self-esteem can be at stake.

Dirk was doing acceptable work in his college subjects but was disgusted with himself for what he felt to be a poor examination he had written. In his customary fashion, he had crammed all studying for the exam into the last few days and then found himself unable to cover the material to his own satisfaction. Because the subject was interesting to him, he knew that he could have handled it well if he had begun studying earlier and was unable to forgive himself for procrastinating.

Having learned Releasing in one of my classes at the university where I taught, Dirk decided to use it to cope with self-recrimination about this particular exam. He identified the basic issue as wanting his own approval, released on the approval issue, and then proceeded to let go of wanting to control *how* he had studied. In essence, this meant asking himself to stop "fighting himself."

He found at first that he could let go of only 1 percent of wanting to control whether or not he approved of the way he had studied. Then he could let go of 5 percent, 10 percent, and finally, of 80 percent of it. When he had done this, it occurred to him that his manner of studying for that exam was already past history. As he released further on the issue of wanting his own approval, the situation began to fade in Dirk's mind. As a result, his thinking changed. He now tended to see his behavior as simply "irresponsible" and felt more inclined to wait for the results of the exam before getting upset. Perhaps he hadn't done as badly as he had imagined. He had always passed exams, so it wasn't a question of having failed. His thoughts now turned to a physics exam coming up for which he felt he could get started studying now. This seemed to him a more constructive use of his energy than kicking himself because he hadn't studied sensibly for the previous exam. Releasing had opened his monitor. He was in shape to handle his next examination more effectively.

Evaluation Problem 4

Sometimes classroom-evaluation anxiety refers to an entire situation, rather than to a specific examination or interview. Such was the case with Grace, who felt uneasy about signing up for a course to prepare her for work which she wanted very much to enter.

It had been many years since Grace had last attended school; she had been busy raising a family. As she began to make plans for her continued education, she wondered what the other students taking the course would be like. When she did so, they seemed in her imagination to look and act more confident than she. She also imagined them as being a good deal younger than she.

These thoughts made Grace feel at a disadvantage, and she began to experience a "sick feeling" when she thought of attending the first class. At the time Grace attended a Releasing workshop, she had already signed up for the course which was to begin in two weeks. To help her release, I asked her to imagine in full detail what the first day of class would be like. How did she envision the classroom? The other students? Her professor?

Grace reported imagining the room as surprisingly like the classrooms she had known in grade school. It seemed large and austere, with an immense blackboard. The other students in the class were all young, competent, and full of energy. She noticed that most of them were women. The professor appeared to be an older man with white hair that stood up from his head and who talked rapidly, giving the class a lot of information at once. Grace felt clumsy and out of place in this picture. Again she experienced a shaky, sick feeling.

I asked if she could let go of wanting to change her feeling of shakiness and just let it "be there" for about thirty seconds. When she was able to do this, she felt steadier and could now imagine the student sitting next to her in class. According to Grace's description, her imagined classmate was an attractive, well-groomed young woman. She was alert, had bright eyes and "a lovely natural haircut" and seemed to know exactly what she was doing—when to write down what the professor said, when to just listen, how to handle the whole thing. She seemed, in short, to have everything under control, exactly the kind of control Grace wished she could have.

We then used the "divide-the-divide" tactic, imagining one detail of the scene at a time. Starting with the note pad that the young woman had in front of her (imagined of course)—could Grace let go of wanting to change the way the pages of that note pad lay open as it rested on the other student's lap?

Grace could easily let go of wanting to change the pages (this seemed to be a neutral thing), and as she did so, the notebook began to look rather pleasant to her. She was then able to let go of wanting to change the way the woman was holding her pencil and to let go of wanting to change the way her hair was arranged around her ears. These details were so unimportant that Grace had no difficulty releasing on them and so she was able to take the next step—letting go of wanting to change the way the young woman was looking at and listening to the professor.

When she had released on that, Grace commented that she now saw something different in the scene. She liked the way this young woman seemed to take in everything with a "steady gaze." She thought that perhaps she herself could learn something from how this other student behaved.

Next, she turned to the professor. Grace was able to let go of wanting to change the way his unruly white hair was combed. This actually made her laugh and feel more comfortable about him. "At least he isn't perfect." Next, she let go of wanting to change the fact that he looked over to her neighbor, the young woman she had been talking about before, and addressed several sentences directly to her. As she released on this, Grace felt that several sentences "really didn't make that much difference."

Now I suggested that she imagine the professor turning to the blackboard and writing there the outline of the course. He would be writing fast and putting a lot of information on the board which she was not sure she was grasping. Could she let go of wanting to change the wording of the *top line* that he was writing?

Grace was easily able to let go of wanting to change the top line. She was then able to let go of wanting to change the second line, and the third. The divide-the-divide tactic was working. When we got down to the fourth line, Grace volunteered that she could let go of wanting to change everything on the blackboard. "I just see that that's the way he does things," she commented.

Grace no longer seemed to feel any particular difficulty about whether or not she understood the material. She realized that it was simply information, and the thought occurred to her that she could copy it if she wanted to and try to figure out later what it meant. After all, presumably she would be assigned a textbook in which she could look up whatever she didn't understand. She could even ask the professor for clarification afterwards. She no longer saw information gathering as a problem.

We then moved on to her next difficulty. I asked her to look around at the imagined room and notice the other students. How did they seem to her at this point?

Actually, they seemed nicer now. She felt better about them. She could see they were absorbed in what they were doing, but it occurred to her that they, too, might not be understanding everything that was going on up there on the blackboard. What had changed was her perspective. These students seemed more human.

At this point, Grace experienced a feeling of excitement which she had not felt before about being in the class. For the first time, she was aware that she was going to learn how to handle classroom material in a way which she had not been able to do years ago. She now felt confident that by using common sense and watching what the other people in the class did, she could do as well.

Because most of the things she had complained about seemed already handled, I asked her whether there was anything about the situation that still bothered her.

Grace hesitated and then said, "Yes. My age. I still feel that I'm a little out of place because everyone else in the classroom is just out of college!"

Grace was ready to release on this final aspect of her back-to-the-classroom project. I asked her to think of her neighbor again, the one she had released on before. Could she let go of wanting to change the fact that this young woman had once been a little girl five years of age? Grace smiled. How could she say no to that?

I asked her if she could let go of wanting to change the fact that this young woman had once been fifteen years old. She released on that, too.

Could she let go of wanting to change the fact that the woman was now her present age and recently graduated from college? She could. "That's a given, a fact of the universe," she said.

"Could you let go of wanting to change the fact that *you* are the age you are?"

Grace found that she could let go of wanting to change that, too. When she did so, her perspective on her own age changed dramatically.

"When I let go of wanting to change my age, I can see that it's just there," she said, "like the trees are out there in the garden, or the floor is here under my feet. It just 'is.'"

After releasing on her age. Grace was silent for a moment and then reported a surprising fact. She was no longer imagining that all the women in her class were so young. A lot of them still seemed to be young, but she now pictured several other people her own age, and even some who she thought might be older than herself. At last she felt comfortable. Who they were didn't seem to have much bearing on how she was going to learn the material. She now felt that she would learn it through her own effort and that her age really had no bearing on how well she would do. To her surprise, Grace wished the class were starting sooner. She was eager for her new adventure.

Evaluation and the Creative Process

Evaluation is inherent in the creative process, but creativity can be hampered by the wish for approval from an audience, publisher, readership, or other parties who will ultimately judge the artistic product. In the case of those who create in solitude, this may involve seeking the approval of an unseen audience. For performers, a live audience represents evaluation of the creative product as it is being produced.

In addition to considerations of the marketplace, the artist must also contend with his own self-criticism. Constructive criticism of one's own work is essential. By such feedback to ourselves, we can shape a more effective, beautiful, or powerful creation than would otherwise be possible. Constructive criticism differs greatly from negative criticism, however. It is the latter which needs to be released on in order to free creative energies.

Evaluation Problem 5

Camilla was a gifted sculptress but once or twice a year found herself entering what she called a "blue period," a time when for a month or more her work seemed to her to be unsatisfactory and uninspired. At such times, she lost the creative excitement and sense of flow which resulted in work which she found exciting. During the course of her psychotherapy, I taught Camilla the Releasing technique, and she decided to apply it to the problem of her blue periods. Self-criticism was heavy at these times, so she started out by applying releasing directly to wanting her own approval on her current piece of work.

At first it was difficult for Camilla to find a way to let go of wanting her own approval. She could let go, however, of just the *feeling* of wanting that approval. Then she could let go for only one second at a time. By a series of four or five steps, she was eventually able to let go of struggling for her self-approval. When she did so, she saw the possibility of just "playing" with her sculptor's clay for a while. As she continued to release, she also saw that she needn't depict a particular model in any *one* way—there were a number of different possibilities available to her. She now felt that she could toy with them, deferring her artistic judgment until later, when she could select the approach which seemed most appropriate.

Camilla discovered that letting go of wanting her own approval was a key to handling her blue periods. As she became adept at releasing in this manner, the technique interrupted the vicious circle of self-criticism. Her inventiveness would return as she allowed herself to play at her work. This was a breakthrough. Releasing became an important resource which she could use whenever she felt herself slipping into self-doubt.

The criticism which inhibits creativity does not always stem from oneself. Performers face a particularly difficult task because they are always aware of their audience, even if it is unseen, as it is when they are making a film or recording. The performer knows that a particular audience contains both potential enthusiasts and potential critics. If awareness of the audience becomes concern about approval, it can seriously impede the performance.

Evaluation Problem 6

Gene, a promising violinist, experienced difficulty when his audience was composed largely of musicians whose approval he valued highly. He decided to use Releasing to lessen his overconcern about these professional audiences.

Since each person finds special ways of applying the Releasing technique, he found it easiest to release on wanting to *control* the approval of such an audience. For Gene, the key phrase was *controlling their approval*. He realized that he had been trying to force these important people in the music world to approve of his performance. When he stopped trying mentally to force them to approve, he freed himself to play with greater sensitivity and depth.

Gene's own particular brand of Releasing was a tool which he could use anytime he faced this problem. To make sure he would be able to release under the pressure of even a strenuous performance, I suggested that he anchor the feeling of Releasing so that he could recall it instantly when needed. This he did by using his thumb-pinkie touch signal before starting his rehearsal, and holding this signal for a few seconds at the same time that he released on wanting approval. This associated the feeling of releasing on his audience's approval with the act of touching his thumb to his pinkie. After that, when walking out on the concert stage, he would simply trigger this Releasing signal and the feeling of releasing on his audience's approval

---

Ways to Release on Evaluation Anxiety

1. Release on wanting to control the *outcome* of your evaluation.

2. Release on wanting to control your *own behavior* in the evaluation situation.

3. Release on wanting the approval of others (or on wanting to *control* their approval).

4. Release on wanting *your own* approval.

5. Anchor your release by touching some specific spot on your skin (preferably an unobtrusive one) at the moment you feel a *full release*. When you need to release at the time of an evaluation (performance, etc.), reactivate your release by simultaneously repeating the releasing phrase and touching that exact spot.

would sweep over him again, freeing him for his performance. Releasing is a useful way to relieve the pressures of an evaluation situation. It neutralizes the stifling effects of an excessive need for approval and allows one to become flexible and resilient. It prevents the need to overcontrol oneself or the outcome of a situation. The result is often a better evaluation, along with a reduction in debilitating anxiety.

At this point, in the book, you have read about a number of actual cases where Releasing has been helpful. I do not intend to suggest, however, nor do I believe, that the Releasing method is sufficient to deal with *all* problem situations. It may not solve a particular difficulty, especially if it involves deep-seated personality problems. In most instances, however, it will be helpful even when other therapeutic interventions are employed. Releasing combines excellently with counseling and psychotherapy.

We will now turn to an area where the Releasing technique can make a difference between being deeply depressed or coping constructively, usefully, and humanely. This is the application of the method to issues of physical distress: the adjustment to illness, pain, or problems created by death and dying.

Chapter 16

RELEASING FOR PAIN, ILLNESS, OR DEATH

Critical situations such as illnesses, natural catastrophes, or death can cause deep feelings of helplessness. At such times, Releasing can help us regain mastery and thereby enable us to be more helpful to ourselves and to others.

Releasing on Pain

While Releasing does not ordinarily eliminate severe pain caused by serious physical conditions, it may be helpful in modifying one's attitude toward pain so that the intensity with which a person experiences it is markedly reduced. In the case of minor pains, Releasing often causes them to disappear entirely.

The methods below can be applied to states of tension as well as pain, the same approach working for both.

To release on pain, think to yourself or say out loud:

"Could I let go of wanting to change my *awareness* of the pain?"

Since you aren't aiming at changing the pain *itself* (something which may seem impossible to you), you are "home free" with this method. We can always deal with our awareness of something. Letting go of wanting to change our awareness of pain is as easy as allowing a pin to drop. As a result, you can "flow with" the pain without fighting against it, an essential step in coping with it.

Releasing on the Feelings That Accompany Pain

It is also useful to release on wanting to change the emotions of fear or anger which can be associated with pain. While it is natural when hurt to become either frightened or angry (or both), unfortunately, these emotions serve to tense our muscles and increase the adrenaline flowing throughout our systems, thereby markedly increasing the pain. When we let go of wanting to change our anxiety or our resentment about pain, the pain often lessens noticeably.

Releasing on Pain By Exaggeration

Strange as it may seem, if you can exaggerate your feelings of pain, you can probably lessen them. Being able to exaggerate the pain means that you have acquired control over it. To use the exaggeration tactic, turn your attention to the pain and consciously try to make it worse. You will discover that your perception of the pain will have changed. This will allow you to deal with it quite differently.

Wordless Releasing

Another way to release on pain is to forgo questioning oneself at all but, instead, wordlessly place your attention on the pain without making any attempt to fight it or make it disappear. Some people describe this process as allowing themselves to "love the pain." Surprising as this may sound, such a nonstruggling attitude can be extremely helpful. If you flow with the pain, it can lose its power over you.

Dividing and Conquering

You can also use the divide-the-conquer tactic to deal with pain. To do this, mentally divide up the pain into a number of small areas and release on each of these in turn.

A member of a Releasing workshop who experienced an intense arthritic pain in her arm discovered she could release on this pain by starting with a circle of about a half-inch in diameter at the tip of her elbow. She could let go of wanting to change her awareness of just this small area. Next, she would move on to a series of discrete points located elsewhere on her arm and release on each of those in the same way. She found it much easier to do this than to release on the entire pain at once. After releasing on these small areas, the overall pain seemed to "dim out" and she scarcely noticed it.

The Dispersal Tactic

One of the most effective of all Releasing strategies for use with pain is a maneuver I call the *dispersal tactic* because it involves systematically removing your attention from the pain.

When we are in pain, our attention becomes focused on the area of trouble. Even if we are paying attention to something else, in the back of our minds we are keeping track of just what the pain is doing at every moment.

No doubt this ability to focus intensively on a site of pain has survival value. If we were wounded and failed to focus on our wound intensively, we might not stop to take care of it. Under certain circumstances, such neglect could cost us our lives. However, if we are already taking care of the injury or illness and there is nothing else to be done about it, the tendency to remain acutely aware of it no longer has any survival value. Now our focusing on the area of pain becomes a problem in its own right. In this case, the dispersal tactic is useful. Here is how to use this maneuver.

When you feel an acute physical discomfort, direct your attention to another area of your body as distant as possible from the site of pain. Notice what kinds of sensations you feel in that new area (however faint and indistinct they are), and then let go of wanting to change *those* sensations. For example, if you feel a pain in your shoulder, you might release on any sensation you located in your foot or in your hand. If you can't identify any sensation in a distant area of your body, then imagine one and let go of wanting to change that; it will work just as well. Continue releasing on sensations in other areas of your body unrelated to the original source of pain or discomfort until the original pain lessens. This is often all you need to do to obtain a remarkable difference in your perception of the pain, or to have it disappear altogether.

It is a good idea when using Releasing to handle pain to be as flexible as possible. Be experimental, try out all approaches, and then try them again in the future if you need to. Some of these approaches will be much more effective for you than others. When you find the right one, it can be invaluable.

Just as with emotions, pain increases as we fight it and decreases as we allow it to "be."

Illness 1

Jim suffered from chronic low-back pain which could incapacitate him for days and lead to lost work time and emotional stress. Uncertain of when the back problem might reassert itself, he was always in fear of immobilization. Though he was not suffering from back pain during the Releasing workshop he attended, when he learned the technique, he filed it away for future use.

It was not long before he had a chance to put Releasing to the test. Leaning over to tie his shoes, he triggered a severe recurrence of his back problem, which led to his remaining flat on his back for several weeks. At this time, though his pain was severe, Jim gave himself relief by Releasing.

It seemed sensible to Jim to ask if he could let go of wanting to change the *awareness* of pain (but not the pain *itself*). Each time he did this, he was able to release more of his sharp consciousness of the pain. As a result, there would be an immediate relaxation of the muscle spasm in the afflicted area. This process worked excellently. While Releasing didn't prevent the pain from reappearing when he shifted position, he found he could release again and bring relief once more.

Jim used Releasing as a means to control the emotional intensity of the pain and to relax the area of trouble sufficiently to get some much-needed rest. It permitted him to dispense with muscle relaxants much of the time and, in his opinion, allowed his back condition to heal much faster. Releasing seemed to remove his attention from the pain so that the healing forces in his body could take over and do their job.

What happened with Jim is not surprising in light of what we know about the distinction between our mental awareness of pain (which results in the sensation of pain) and the pain *experience* itself—the sensation can be different from the emotional experience that accompanies it. In his book on the control of pain,* Dr. David Bresler, director of the UCLA Pain Control Unit, points out that a soldier seriously wounded in battle may know that he is injured but may not be caught up in the total-awareness state which is known as "pain" (and which can be agonizingly difficult to bear). He may be so relieved to be going home alive that this emotion overrides the all-enveloping and debilitating experience of total pain. Had he, on the other hand, experienced the total pain, it could have impeded the healthy healing response.

By releasing on the awareness of pain, we let go of our *involvement* in the symptoms. This makes the pain a shallower, more localized experience, which in turn relaxes muscle tension around the injured area, increases blood flow to that area, and affects other crucial physiological variables which promote healing.

There are a number of ways to lessen pain with releasing. Each person finds the one that works best for him or her. It is advisable, if you are suffering from pain, to try *each one* of the releasing tactics suggested here until you find the right one for you. It is also useful to keep in mind that what may work for you one day will not necessarily work for you at another time—our

---

* For a most helpful discussion of pain, see David E. Bresler, *Free Yourself from Pain* (New York: Simon & Schuster, 1979).

psychological and physical state may be markedly different from day to day, week to week, and month to month.

Illness 2

Harriet had suffered a series of painful accidents over a period of a year, and her mounting resentment at this predicament made it difficult for her to cope with the residual pain. She felt as though she were losing a never-ending battle.

When she learned the Releasing technique, she started by releasing on her anger at the pain. When she was able to let go of wanting to change or justify the anger, it receded enough for her to recognize her underlying fear that she would never again be free of pain. She found it was possible to let go of this fear only in small steps. First she let go of 1 percent of wanting to change her fear of being in pain; then she let go of 2 percent, then 5 percent of the *wanting*, and then continued releasing until she found herself able to let go of 100 percent.

At this point, she was less threatened and ready to let go of wanting to change the experience of pain itself. She chose to do this by means of the *dispersal tactic*—releasing on wanting to change a discomfort in *another part of the body* (see page 190). Since she had already released on her *feelings* (the emotional overload), releasing on the pain itself (the *sensation*) was easier and more effective than it would have been had she started by releasing directly on the sensation itself. Harriet was able to get considerable relief from the *dispersal tactic*. Combining it with releasing on the emotions surrounding her pain made an effective program of pain control.

Illness 3

Marie, who was attending a Releasing workshop, complained of a headache between her eyes, and I asked her to turn her attention to her right wrist and notice any sensations she could detect there. From her description, I assumed she had no pain in her wrist. I was applying the dispersal tactic.

After thinking for a moment, she replied that she wasn't sure that she felt anything special there but that perhaps there was "a little warmth" in her wrist. Noticing any kind of sensation would do (even the vaguest one), so warmth was fine. I asked her to let go of wanting to change it. She found this easy to do because, as she pointed out, she really didn't want to change it in the first place!

I then asked her to locate a sensation in her left knee. Again after thinking about it, she reported noticing a slight tension there. I asked her to let go of wanting to change this slight tension. Again, she had no problem because this seemed unimportant to her.

At this point, to her surprise, Marie found that her headache was gone. The success of the dispersal tactic relies on the fact that when one part of us is in pain, that part usually takes center stage. It is easy to forget that there is anything more to our body than just pain. The dispersal tactic increases awareness of sensations in other areas and restores a more appropriate perspective.

This tactic can also be useful for counteracting tension. Illogical as it may seem, if you are suffering from muscle tension, one way to release on it is to select a part of your body that cannot *possibly* tense up (such as a fingernail, toenail, your bones, etc.) and release on wanting to change the "tension" there.

When a workshop member complained of tension in his shoulders and neck, I suggested that he let go of wanting to change the "tension" in one of his fingernails—the thumbnail on his right hand. I explained to him that of course this didn't make sense in any logical manner, since I would not expect that a thumbnail could have tension. However, I asked him to suspend all judgment at the moment and see if he could let go of the tension in his thumbnail by a leap of his imagination.

He smiled indulgently at me but tried to do as I asked. In spite of the fact that he was letting go of something that didn't exist (he knew he didn't have tension in his fingernail), he was able to imagine letting go of that nonexistent tension. When he did so, he felt himself release. His shoulders and neck now felt much easier.

Since it seems to have no logic and requires an act of imagination, this tactic may not appeal to all people. If it doesn't suit you, don't use it. However, it is useful to recognize that it is not always necessary to know *why* something works in Releasing in order for it to work. If it works, it can be valuable for you. Releasing an imaginary tension in an area where it is not possible to have muscle tension (as in a thumbnail) may be an effective strategy because it serves to remind us that there are parts of our bodies that *never* tense up. Or it may work for some entirely different reason. I can vouch for the fact that it *has* worked for many people, and suggest that you try it and judge it on its merits.

Releasing on Your Own Illness

An illness has many different components which can affect us— pain can be one of these, but malaise, weakness, nausea, dizziness, or any number of other symptoms can present problems of their own. It is useful to apply the divide-and-conquer tactic when releasing on an illness, releasing separately on each of the discomforts you feel.

Releasing only once may not be sufficient to effect significant change in an ongoing illness. For this situation, you may have to "let go" repeatedly. Each time you release, you will be allowing your body to fight the illness in its *own* way without interference from your overpush. You will also not be blocked by anxiety or anger—factors which can inhibit healing.

At this point, you may raise an objection. Isn't it "good" to fight an illness? The will to live is an essential ingredient in healing. Why shouldn't someone be angry at an illness that is debilitating? Won't this anger lead to determination to conquer the illness?

At first glance, this objection sounds reasonable because both the will to live and the natural fight-back of the body are necessary for healing. But both these forces are *fostered* by Releasing, not retarded by it. Illness is not fought successfully by figuratively "punching the illness in the nose," but by creating a feeling of well-being, a sense of being on the way toward recovery—exactly the attitudes encouraged by Releasing.

When we become ill, our bodies are threatened. Understandably, we want to do everything we can to combat the symptoms and take steps to make ourselves feel better. But if we take these steps as though we were desperately battling an unseen enemy, our urgency will only increase the hold of the illness upon us. This is true even in the event of a life-threatening illness. A bitter struggle against the illness weakens us, leaving us more vulnerable to disease. A constructive effort to get well allows our life force to flow again unimpeded. This process involves letting go of our *frantic* effort to change the illness and allowing healing to "happen."

Just as strong emotions can cause our monitor to close down in an emergency, battling fiercely to subdue our own illness can close down the healing forces of the body. When our monitor opens up, our body's health-building options open up as well.

To release on an illness, think to yourself, or say out loud:

"It would be good not to have this illness—but could I let go of *struggling* to change it? . . . Could I just let it 'be' for a little while?"

Allow your symptoms (the illness) just to "be there" for about thirty seconds. This will release your energies from their unproductive struggle and free them to rebuild your ailing body. Freedom and wholeness are the best antidotes to disease. They are the forces that are liberated when we release. Therefore, it is useful to release as frequently as comfortable when you are ill.

Releasing on Another's Illness

For many people, the illness of someone who is close to them is as painful, it not more so, than their own illness. To watch someone we love go through a serious illness is extremely difficult. Releasing can do much to help us handle such a situation with equanimity, with the result that we can then be more effective in helping the person who is ill.

There are several principles to keep in mind when releasing on another's illness. While some people find it possible to let go of wanting to change the fact that the person they care about is ill (because they understand that the question: "Could I let go of wanting him or her to be well?" is part of the Releasing process and therefore don't take it literally), others find the question impossible to answer affirmatively. If this is the case, the situation can still be released on by changing the wording of the Releasing question so that it is compatible with your present frame of mind. If you cannot readily release on wanting to change or "control" another person's illness because you want so much for them to recover, then think to yourself, or say out loud:

"Could I let go of *mentally pushing* to change the illness?"

When the situation is critical, *mentally pushing* is an easier concept for some people than *wanting* because it doesn't involve asking yourself to let go of wanting the other person to get well. If we can let go of *mentally pushing*, we become calmer. This calmness is quickly transferred to the person who is ill. Because our monitor has been opened by Releasing, we are now likely to think of more things to do which are helpful.

Another useful question under these circumstances is:

"Could I accept *1 percent* of the illness (pain, etc.)?"

It is usually possible to accept this very small portion of another's illness, and when you do, you will be able to behave more supportively and constructively with this person.

Releasing on Our Competency to Help

Concern about whether we are doing all that we can to help someone who is ill—if this causes worry and guilt for not "doing enough"—can make us less helpful to that person. If you find yourself under pressure to be a better nurse or helper, think to yourself, or say out loud:

> **"Could I let go of wanting to be a *perfect* (nurse, helper, etc.)?"**

This phrase helps to remove any residual feelings of guilt. When we use it, we no longer struggle to attain the impossible. Releasing lifts a burden from our shoulders so that now we can *really* be a good nurse, helper, or whatever.

Illness 4

Rita stood helplessly by when her son was brought into intensive care after his motorcycle accident. All she could do was watch the machines monitoring his vital signs while the nurses hurriedly attended him. He seemed to be in a coma, although she secretly suspected that he knew of her presence by the bed.

As she stood there, Rita kept frantically asking herself, "What can I do about this? What can be done?" Then, since she had learned Releasing, she decided to use it to quiet down these racing thoughts. Intuitively, she sensed that Releasing might help her to help her son Craig.

She remembered to use the special phrasing which I had presented as the preferred one for emergencies. She could not ask herself to let go of wanting to change the fact that Craig had been injured—she wanted him to be well too desperately. Instead, she asked herself whether she could let go of her "mental pushing" to save Craig—those obsessive thoughts that revolved in her head.

To her relief, she was able to let go of the feeling of mental pushing. As she did so, she felt herself quiet down.

The frantic circular thinking dropped away, and she now seemed to sense a kind of inner silence. The silence allowed her to look outside of herself in a more sensitive manner.

With surprising calm, she now watched her son as he lay in his bed. As she did so, she noticed once again that every muscle in his body was taut, drawn as tight as a violin string about to snap. She also noticed that his face was heavily flushed and his breathing rapid, almost gasping. She had seen all of this before, but noticing these things had simply led her deeper into helpless circular worrying. But as she saw these troubled signs now, in her present state of relative inner stillness, a new thought occurred to her.

She remembered a lecture she had once attended, in which the lecturer described a way he had assisted a critically ill friend by gently leading his breathing. He had done this by first allowing his hands to keep pace with the strenuous breathing pattern of the person who was ill, and then changing his own hand rhythm to influence his friend to breathe more comfortably.

Rita found herself placing one hand lightly on her son's chest and allowing the fingers of that hand to gently contract and expand in rhythm with his rapid breathing. Almost imperceptibly, she was able to get her hand into a perfect beat with his breathing, allowing it to pulsate in harmony with it. Then, after a little while, she found herself gradually reducing the speed with which her own fingers opened and closed. As she did so, Craig, who was now breathing in rhythm with her hand, imperceptibly began to slow his rate of breathing as well. As he did this, little by little his musculature began to relax. First the muscles in his arms, and then those of his hands and face began to take on an easier, more restful appearance.

Rita gently continued with her therapy, absorbed in what her son was going through, feeling completely in harmony with him. It was a harmony she had not felt since he was an infant in her arms. It was as if the two of them were one at this moment. She felt that because of this she might be able to lead him out of danger.

Within about fifteen minutes, Craig did, in fact, seem to be pulling out of danger. His breathing was now much quieter. His face was no longer flushed; his body muscles were more relaxed. At this point, Rita knew that whatever was being done for him medically could now be accepted by his body in a more constructive way. The immediate crisis was over. The way had been paved for healing.

Letting go of our mental pushing in an emergency is a powerful technique which can be used for one's *own* illnesses as well as those of others. Often, it is only our mental pushing that gets between ourselves and constructive handling of our state during an illness or accident. When we remove this overpush, healing can take place.

Releasing on Handicaps

I am often asked what effect Releasing has on the determination needed to overcome handicaps or to learn new skills such as are taught in physical rehabilitation programs. Willpower and the ability to keep going against many odds are important qualities for disabled people. At first glance, it might seem undesirable for handicapped people to let go of their insistent wanting to get well.

Actually, such a conclusion is based on a misunderstanding of Releasing. Disabled and handicapped people make excellent use of this technique because determination, willpower, persistence, and the ability to forge ahead despite difficulties are increased by opening up one's monitor.

While genuine willpower is strengthened, the desperation and overpush drop away, a distinct advantage for any rehabilitation program.

This may be easier to understand if we distinguish between "determination" and "desperation." The two are not the same. When we have the willpower needed to overcome hardships, our monitor is open and we exert a directed push. When we experience blind insistence on overcoming a hardship or disability, we struggle with it in a manner that involves rage, fear, despair, and other negative emotions. Our monitor then closes down, which can lead to ineffective action. The Releasing technique allows the person to let go of her desperation about a disability, so that genuine determination and willpower can take over and help her do the job that really needs to be done.

Releasing on Death and Dying

At some time, all of us face the inevitability of losing someone we love, through death. In this difficult situation, Releasing can be of immense help. In addition to the standard unlocking tactics, there are some special strategies that can be used to release on the fact that someone has died (or is threatened by death).

Releasing on Our Sense of Helplessness

A helpful way to release on the threat of death is to think to yourself, or say out loud:

"Could I let go of wanting to change my feeling of helplessness?"

Feelings of helplessness can cause great distress in times of bereavement. It is only if we can stop fighting against the helplessness that it lessens its hold over us. When we release on our feeling of helplessness, we can move ahead quietly in ways that are more meaningful for ourselves and those around us.

Releasing by Acceptance

Another way of handling the inevitability of death is to change the wording of the Releasing question so that, instead of asking yourself whether you can let go of wanting to change the situation (which is impossible), you ask yourself:

"Can I accept the fact that (so-and-so) has died (is dying)?"

Or if that is too difficult:

"Can I accept 1 *percent* of this fact?"

Acceptance can bring peace.

This concept can create a problem, however, if you confuse "acceptance" with "resignation." Resignation implies giving up in despair, relinquishing our freedom. Acceptance implies an active, free, forward-thinking attitude. Resignation closes down the monitor, forcing us to act as automatons. Acceptance opens up the monitor and allows us to act with awareness, sensitivity, and humanity.

The phrase, "Can I accept" is one of the most effective ways of opening the monitor when we are suffering from heavy emotional burdens. Asking yourself this question releases you from having to fight the inevitable.

When we are fighting the inevitable, we are not taking steps to change what can be changed. When we release this fight, we can move forward again.

Releasing on Understanding

There is one final question that can be helpful when confronting the finality of death or any other unalterable fact. This is to think to yourself, or say out loud:

"It would be useful to understand why this should happen—but could I let go of *wanting* to understand?"

Why *was he or she born handicapped?*
Why *does he or she have to suffer?*
Why *did he or she have to die?*

Such "whys" have echoed throughout human history. When a "why" translates itself into productive ways of changing the human situation so that suffering is lessened, then it makes an important contribution to human life. But when the "why" is used to torture oneself and others, then it is destructive. Letting go of the kind of "why" which goes nowhere can free one's energies to cope, to build, and to heal.

To release on wanting to "understand" or to release on wanting life to be "just," or "fair," are among the most healing moves you can make when facing the inevitable. This does not mean, however, that you should not stay in touch with your own deep feelings at such a time, even your feelings of outrage. These have a legitimate place. What it does mean is that you can relieve yourself of having to ask questions that will only diminish your resources. Releasing on "understanding," or releasing on fighting against the inevitable, opens the way for healthy sorrow and genuine regret. It is a way to help yourself put together the pieces, sense again your own internal strength, and become aware of that which is positive and ongoing in life. Releasing is a device which provides a way for human beings to cope more calmly and constructively with a universe which often does not go the way we wish and rarely has the good grace to explain why.

Illness 5

Carl found his father's terminal illness deeply disturbing. During the elderly man's final days, his son spent much of his time at the hospital with him. Despite this, he felt futile, awkward, and unable to be of any real help.

This reaction had a long history. Carl had always felt uncomfortable in his father's presence; the two had been distant for as long as he could remember. Now, during the last days of his father's life, it seemed to Carl that this was his last chance to make up for lost time. He wanted desperately to establish some sort of connection with this man who had been so absorbed in his own career during Carl's early life that he had had little chance to get to know his only son. However, any attempts on Carl's part to establish a close tie now were clouded by the old man's illness, with its attendant fears and confusions. Carl did not know how to act.

Three weeks before his father was taken to the hospital in critical condition, Carl had attended a Releasing workshop where he had absorbed much of what was going on, although he had participated only minimally. The week following the second meeting of the workshop, he found himself releasing on a number of problems in business life and at home, and it greatly lightened the load he was carrying. When his father was taken to the hospital, however, Carl's monitor had shut down temporarily and he forgot about Releasing. It was not until three days later, as he sat in the hospital room watching the frail man who had once seemed like a tower of strength seemingly waste away, that Carl remembered that Releasing can be helpful in life crises.

At a loss to know how to get started, Carl decided that what he was experiencing were regrets about the past—in Releasing terms, a strong need to "rewrite history." He wanted desperately to have had a different relationship with his father. This led him to let go of wanting to change the fact that he and his father had never been close.

When he was able to let go *even a little bit* of wanting to change that unfortunate history, he then felt a welling-up of deep sadness. He next let go of wanting to change his sadness, and just "let it be." This meant that for a period of five or ten minutes Carl sat quietly in his father's hospital room, experiencing his own sadness without trying to change it. Alone with his father, he watched the monitoring instruments ticking away, the nurse tiptoeing in and out of the room, and the breathing of the frail body that seemed like a shell of the man he had formerly known.

As he allowed his sense of sadness simply to be, without trying to fight it or push it away, Carl began to sense a quietness within, a peace, as though the sadness itself were in some way nurturing and helping him. It was as though allowing the sadness to "be" was something that had needed to be done.

Now Carl's sadness seemed appropriate. It was nonthreatening. Several times during this interval he released on wanting to change the sadness, and each time he did so, he found the feeling gradually subsiding and a sense of acceptance beginning to come in its stead. It was an acceptance of the unfortunate rift which had separated the two of them.

At this point, Carl was able to ask himself if he could let go of wanting to change the fact that he and his father had rarely contacted each other in the past. He now found himself able to do this. At exactly that moment, he felt himself let go of his struggle to change the facts. When he did so, he saw the ailing man on the bed before him as a frightened person. He could now see his father as another human being, rather than as the father he had wanted him to be.

This was a new experience for Carl. It freed him to approach the bed and ask his father, in quite a different voice than he had used before, whether there was something he could do for him. To his surprise, his father, evidently responding to the change in Carl's voice, answered by telling him there was something that he could do. Opening his eyes for the first time that day and focusing them upon Carl, he told him certain things he wanted attended to with respect to his will. He appeared both relieved and grateful that his son was able to help him with this.

Carl, in turn, experienced a sense of comfort at being able to be useful to his father. He went to attend to these matters; got them well in hand; and, as he proceeded through the rest of that day, continued to release.

Carl now felt ready to let go of wanting to change the fact of his father's impending death. He also let go of wanting to control exactly *how* his father would die and released a number of times on wanting his father's approval. This brought him even more relief and enabled him to go about handling his father's affairs without worrying about whether his father would ever become conscious again to know or approve of what he had done. Carl also found himself able to be constructive in new ways as he continued to release and his monitor continued to open up further. Ideas came to him of how he could contact certain family members and have them rally around to help his father. His organizing capacity took over.

When later that evening his father died quietly, Carl found himself reviewing all that he had known about him and finding some surprising values in his father that he had not recognized before. Knowing that he would not have an opportunity to observe these qualities again left him feeling at a loss, but these natural feelings of grief and strangeness were greatly helped by more releasing. Carl simply asked himself if he could *accept* his father's death and then let go of wanting to change the fact that he would never see this man again. The word *accept* was helpful to him because it didn't seem to deny his feelings of regret or loss. He recognized his grief as natural and, in fact, released on wanting to change it.

Although Releasing helped Carl go peacefully through the period of disorientation which often follows death, he soon found himself experiencing strong feelings of personal vulnerability. He felt much older since his father had died and envisioned his own life stretching out before him to its inevitable conclusion. This disturbed him.

Quietly, Carl now asked himself if he could let go of wanting to control how long his own life would be and how he himself would die. Into the spirit of Releasing by now, Carl found this quite possible to do. As he released on wanting to control his own fate, he felt himself flow along with the tide of his life in a way that brought back a sense of vitality and meaning. He no longer needed to fight against the fact that life would someday end for him, as for all of us. Rather, he was able to accept this fact. This attitude lent a sense of poignancy and reality to the present moment, and vitality to the way he felt about it.

As so often happens with the Releasing technique, when we let go of wanting to change something negative, its power over us diminishes and we end up with more positive feelings. As Carl stood by his father's grave and watched the sod shoveled in and the blanket of flowers rolled out, he let go of wanting to change the reality of death. The relief this brought him was then expressed in a feeling of sadness mingled with tenderness toward the living things about him. He was aware now of the flowers on and near the grave and of their stems bending in the breeze, of the fresh smell of new-mown grass along the cemetery plots, and of his own and several other family members' children who stood quietly nearby, symbols of life and its ongoingness.

The acceptance of death which Carl obtained from his releasing was profound. He had released on wanting to change his father, he had accepted his father as he was, and now he was able to accept the loss of his father. Releasing had helped the natural healing forces within Carl to rally, and his strengths to take over in an appropriate way. It had brought both him and his family through their life crisis with a sense of meaning.

*

Releasing is helpful in times of despair, pain, illness, or bewilderment. It is a tool which we may employ to lighten our burdens and make them more manageable. Releasing during life crises enables us to use our strengths to best advantage and make those changes that can be made with both ease and grace.

Just as Releasing is valuable during painful times, it is also useful in situations that are intrinsically enjoyable. The most pleasant activity can be marred by *pushing* oneself to do it. In the following chapter we will look at ways in which some people have used Releasing to increase their relaxation and enjoyment during times of play.

Chapter 17

RELEASING WHILE AT PLAY

Children are not the only ones who like to play. As adults, we eagerly await vacations and fight to find time for absorbing hobbies or in reading a new book. We seek out entertainment of all sorts, and many of us take up sports with tireless enthusiasm. Our play activities are among our most valued moments and contribute immeasurably to both our mental and physical health.

The value of play can be spoiled for us, however, by worry about our own competence, or by guilt about our right to enjoy ourselves. Releasing can be of immense value when we are at play, making our leisure activities more fun.

Releasing at Sports

It may be difficult for some people to imagine that letting go of the excess effort involved in a sports activity can result in improved performance in that sport. There is, however, mounting evidence that being "pitched high" in terms of wanting to do well may seriously impair an athlete's performance, particularly if he is engaged in a complex task which requires attention to be divided among many factors at once.

According to Dr. Robert Nideffer, a specialist in the problems which beset athletes, it is only when people are asked to perform simple tasks which require a sharp narrowing down of attention that arousal and anxiety may help at all. Anxiety does narrow the attention and thus *sometimes* helps to improve performance. Even with the simplest tasks, however, experiencing more than just a moderate amount of anxiety causes performance to deteriorate rapidly. When a person becomes extremely anxious, she tends to fall apart, and if the athlete faces a complex task (as is the case in most games of skill), athletic performance deteriorates rapidly in the face of even small increases in anxiety or tension.

To examine the effects of arousal (being high-pitched) on athletes' performances, Dr. Nideffer conducted a study of divers on the University of Rochester men's swimming team. His aim was to examine the divers' ability to perform under different levels of arousal* and anxiety.

One of the physiological changes associated with increased arousal is an increase in perspiration, as many anxious persons have noticed to their dismay. This fact is often utilized in psychological research, because as perspiration increases, it becomes correspondingly easier to pass fine electric currents through the skin. Then, by measuring the changes in the individual's skin conductance (this is usually done on the palms of the hands), it becomes possible to estimate the changes in arousal level. This is the same principle used in the so-called "lie-detector test." Nideffer, therefore, measured arousal by monitoring the divers' skin-conductance levels.

He and his fellow researchers also measured the level of perceived anxiety (technically known as "state" anxiety) by means of a paper-and-pencil test, conducting all measures immediately prior to each meet in which the University of Rochester divers competed during a complete season. The results were taken as indications of a diver's levels of arousal and anxiety for that meet. It was then a simple matter to examine the relationship between the divers' level of arousal and anxiety

---

* Nideffer uses the word *arousal* to refer to a tense, hyperalert state, *not* to refer to sexual arousal or to a nonsleeping state. His findings are reported in Robert M. Nideffer, *The Inner Athlete* (New York: Thomas Y. Crowell, 1976).

and their performance on the dives. It was also possible to see whether there was any relationship between the complexity of the dive and how greatly arousal had affected that *particular* dive.

The results of the study were striking. The researchers found that, independent of the complexity or difficulty of the dive which was being engaged in, the *lower* the level of arousal in the diver and the *lower* his level of felt anxiety, the *better* his performance. In addition, they found that complex "optional" dives were somewhat more affected by increases in arousal and anxiety than the relatively simple required dives. This supported Nideffer's supposition that truly complex athletic tasks are more readily affected adversely by an increase in anxiety or arousal.

If these important findings show adverse effects from being anxious and tense when engaging in athletics, why then do so many people fail to recognize the advantages of a relaxed, nonanxious state during athletic competition?

Possibly this is because they fail to make a distinction between the excitement and enthusiasm felt when looking forward to an athletic competition—and the inhibiting effects of fear and anxiety about that competition. Positive expectation and excitement, the exhilarating tingle of anticipation which the athletic performer feels when he hopes or expects to win, are what good coaches try for when they want to get their team "psyched up." Some coaches, however, mistakenly think that being psyched up is equivalent to having a high tension level. This is a serious mistake.

In yet another study conducted at the University of Rochester, Nideffer measured the level of swimmers' arousal by measuring their skin conductance just before each meet during a swimming season. Once again, with the swimmers as with the divers, the investigators discovered that the more aroused the swimmer was before the meet, the more poorly he performed. In fact, if the swim-team members when they were least aroused could have swum against *themselves* when they were most aroused, they would have cut an average of 3.3 seconds off their swim times. This means that if a swimmer swam a 54-second 100-yard freestyle with a high level of arousal, he could swim a 50.7-second 100-yard freestyle with a low level. In fact, this finding of improved performance was so consistent with swimmers that, according to the researchers, the scores for a dual-meet would have been 77–10—that is, swimming at low-arousal, the swimmers would have beaten *themselves* at high-arousal by a score of 77–10.

Nideffer also discovered that in those meets where the swimmers were least aroused (most relaxed and thus most likely to do well), their coach had thought that they were most "psyched up." This seemed to be because when they were least aroused, the team members were talkative; but when they were actually more physiologically aroused (as measured by their skin conductance), then the swimmers became quiet, tense, and tended to keep to themselves. In fact, when the swimmers were most anxious, according to the paper-and-pencil tests, the researchers discovered that many of them had convinced themselves before the meet had ever started that they could not possibly win.

It is essential to keep in mind this distinction between having a positive enthusiastic attitude on the one hand and being physiologically aroused and anxious on the other. It is all too easy to assume that if adrenaline is flowing and the athlete is physiologically pitched high, then he has a "winning" attitude. The evidence, however, runs contrary to this. As soon as people engaging in sports realize this, they will begin to perform better.

Releasing is a powerful strategy for reducing arousal and "performance anxiety," and an excellent means of lowering tension during an athletic event, allowing the natural ability of the well-trained performer to take over. For this reason, Releasing can result in striking improvement in performance even when the Releasing strategy may not be directed to performance at all. It may, instead, be directed to letting go of the *overpush* to win the game, to play superbly, to be outstanding, to gain approval, or to any number of other troublesome feelings. Because of its effectiveness in cutting down on the factors that lead to "choking" (inhibited performance during a sport), Releasing is being used as an important aid by many people engaged in athletics.

Sportsperson 1

It is generally recognized that increased confidence improves athletic performance. By releasing on fears of failure, athletes can increase their self-confidence and, consequently, their performance. Marianne, an enthusiastic jogger, used Releasing while running in an event, a 10K (10 kilometers or 6.2 miles) Memorial Day Race, which she had entered along with her husband and a female friend with whom she ran regularly each morning. There were about thirty people in the race, quite a few of them runners Marianne had seen before at other races and knew were "good runners." Since her husband always ran faster than she did, she expected him to outdistance her quickly, but her friend had told her that she would run along slowly with Marianne for the first three miles and probably pick up speed on the second three, if she felt "good."

For several days prior to the race, Marianne had experienced anxiety about where she would place, and on the morning of the race she found her "insides shaking" from both excitement and anxiety. An experienced Releaser, Marianne immediately let go of wanting to change the fact that she was nervous about the race (which was the longest one she had ever run) and thereafter lost her nervousness.

When the participants began to run, it seemed to her that everyone took off so fast that it was going to be impossible for her friend and herself to catch up with them. As they went along, the two women decided that they would catch up to the others later in the race because everyone was "probably having a fast start and would slow down." To their dismay, however, this never happened. The others were "just fantastic runners."

Marianne's husband "ran off with another woman," and she didn't see him again until he (and the woman) had finished the race. This didn't bother her because she already knew that he was considerably faster than she was. According to Marianne, the hard part came about two miles into the race when her partner, who had just said that she couldn't catch her breath, began to run ahead of her—at first a few steps, then a block, and finally so far ahead that Marianne couldn't see her. She couldn't believe that this was the same person who had always run "nice and easy" with her every morning. At this point, she felt she would be the last one in and was experiencing feelings of humiliation (even though there were about four persons behind her throughout the race).

For a moment, she thought of "running home and forgetting it" but then decided that she would rather come in last than give up. At that point, she decided to release on the overpush—trying to run faster than was physically possible for her—and she also let go of wanting the approval of others for a good finishing time.

Eventually, Marianne was able, through her Releasing, to set her own pace. She decided to run at this pace and come in "nice and easy." When she came close to the finish line, her husband met her and ran in with her. As he did so, he mentioned to her that she could pick up speed if she wanted to, and she found herself replying easily that she didn't have to prove anything and would go in at her own pace.

When she finally crossed the finish line, Marianne had a chance to talk with those people she considered exceptional runners and told them that her finishing time was "terrific for me" because she had never before maintained ten minutes a mile for a distance of six miles. The other runners commented that she had run an extremely good race, considering the short time she had been running.

Releasing had permitted Marianne to avoid becoming embarrassed or humiliated at being one of the last to come in—feelings which would actually have been unrealistic because she was running with a field of runners totally out of her class. It also enabled her to decide that her friend who came in way ahead of her was "just a better runner" and that this did not reflect on her own achievement.

Many people have reported that they play better tennis, golf, or squash after having learned to release. This has occurred regardless of whether they were consciously using Releasing during the sport itself. For these people, Releasing has become such a regular part of their lives that they seem automatically to let go of the overpush which formerly interfered with their sports activities. The result is better performance all around.

Sportsperson 2

Ralph, an avid tennis player, reports that his game is much more consistent since he learned Releasing. He attributes much of this to spontaneous releasing, which he feels occurs "subliminally" while he plays a game. At times, however, he releases consciously during the game. Formerly, he would find it upsetting to miss an easy shot. Since he is an extremely good player, missing the easy shots would inevitably make him angry, with the result that he would be apt to blow the next couple of points as well.

Now when he misses an easy shot, he lets go of wanting to change this fact, which in turn dissolves the distressed feeling and gives him a fresh start on the following shots. The result is greater consistency in his game.

When playing a match, Ralph has also found it useful to let go of wanting approval for "winning the match." This has enabled him to concentrate on playing the game, rather than being preoccupied with wanting to win.

These strategies could be applied equally well to other sports. For example, the president of an insurance company has reported lowering his golf score several strokes by releasing before each shot. He let go of wanting to be a "competent golfer."

Even athletes who generally play well under pressure are not exempt from "choking." John McEnroe, the tennis star, occasionally puts his hand to his throat after missing a crucial shot to indicate that he has "choked." Once athletes become accustomed to releasing on their game or a particular skill, a Releasing attitude may become an automatic response to engaging in their chosen sport and serves to counteract "choking." To help this along, many athletes find it useful to first establish a thumb-pinkie signal for Releasing and later on transfer this to a mental signal such as the word *release*.

This is easily done. Once you have a well-established signal for Releasing (such as the thumb-pinkie), you can convert it into a mental signal by thinking (or saying out loud) the word *release* at the *exact moment* you trigger your physical signal for Releasing. If you do this twenty times in a row (think *release* at the precise moment you touch thumb to pinkie), you will soon link the word to that easy feeling of letting go.

Eventually you will be able to get a strong sense of releasing by simply thinking the word *release* and can drop the gesture—an obvious advantage for athletes and others who need to release rapidly while in full action.

Releasing can of course be used for team sports too. I had the opportunity to train the Princeton University Women's Swimming Team in this method. Team members learned how to release before and during inter-collegiate swim meets. Despite the fact that these women had a strong wish to win (an excellent *goal* which they were encouraged to *hold on to*), when they let go of wanting to control what kind of swim times they would make, how their teammates would do, what the behavior of the competing team would be, and how their own bodies would react to the challenge, Releasing resulted in many of them being able to be at their very best as far as performance was concerned while simultaneously experiencing more than their usual amount of relaxation and confidence. The releasers also tended to be more at ease *between* meets.

Releasing with Hobbies

A hobby, by definition, is something which should be play rather than work. If competition or prestige becomes heavily involved, then the hobby becomes work. It is, of course, legitimate to turn a hobby into work, provided the person involved doesn't mistake the activity as being any longer a hobby.

The essential value of a hobby lies in its freedom. It can evoke in us the wonder and absorption of a child. The fun that comes when the main point of an activity is the activity *itself* is the whole point of having a hobby in the first place and the reason that it can be such a beneficial addition to our lives. This spontaneity can be seriously interfered with by introducing striving for a goal into what was once enjoyed for its own sake.

Hobby 1

Ed was a topnotch amateur photographer who found to his dismay that after he had won first prize in a photography contest at his local yacht club, his enjoyment of his hobby of photography suffered seriously. Until that time, Ed's camera work had been a source of delight to him. He had carried his single-lens reflex wherever he went; whipped it out whenever he saw an interesting scene; and played at capturing a particular visual experience in a way that would be original, creative, humorous, or telling in its starkness. He had a natural eye for photography, and his collections of color slides from his travels were of such high quality that friends and acquaintances eagerly sought the opportunity to view them.

Over the course of one summer, Ed took a number of photographs of people working on their own boats and was persuaded by a friend to enter them in a contest at the local yacht club. His photographs of boat life were true character studies, depicting people's intense (sometimes overintense) involvement with their own boats, their struggles with the exigences of sailing, and their moments of delight in the experience when it was going well. As a group, these photographs made up a pictorial saga of the sailing experience which was impressive and personally meaningful to many members of the club. The first prize in photography was clearly deserved by Ed, and with it went a small trophy, a pleasant after-dinner speech, and many compliments on his photos.

The problem didn't arise at the time Ed received this award, but soon after the award dinner, Ed found that his hobby was now seeming more like work than fun. He now felt that he must live up to the reputation which he had obtained through the award. Each time he began to take a new photograph, he found himself trying to duplicate the originality and humor of some of the photos which he had taken for the first exhibit.

The result was that Ed's camera was no longer giving him the same pleasure as it had previously. To add to this problem, the photographs also seemed to have lost a certain quality. Although they were still technically fine, there was a studied note to them which had been absent before. The candid quality of his photos had been one of their greatest assets, but now the more Ed tried to do well, the less well he seemed to do. He did manage to win another local contest, but that was little consolation to him because he felt he was losing his touch.

At a Releasing workshop, Ed decided to release on his photography. First, he let go of wanting to control how any particular photograph would turn out. Next, he let go of wanting approval for his photographs. Finally, he let go of wanting to control how his subjects might pose and the fact that he couldn't get a particular shot which he might want. He then trained himself to release every time he picked up his camera and to release on every aspect of his photography that came to his mind.

The interfering standards which Ed had interposed between himself and his once-enjoyable hobby began to dissolve with Releasing. As he released on wanting to control how his photos would turn out, he found that he was once again able to *play* at taking pictures. He no longer thought about photography contests. Photography, as a hobby, was his once more.

Releasing on Vacations

For many people, a vacation is the ultimate play experience. Often they wait for it in exquisite anticipation for a full year.

Precisely because it is so longed for, a vacation, with its many hopes and expectations to fulfill, can defeat its own purpose. You may have seen friends return from holidays exhausted by their strenuous efforts to enjoy themselves. A rest from cares and routine cannot be too planned, or it ceases to be a rest and instead becomes a different sort of routine. Releasing can be particularly helpful to vacationers, taking them off the hook and allowing them to "do nothing," with pleasure.

When Lewis' family finally agreed to camp out in Maine for a vacation, he experienced a surge of excitement. It had been years since he and his wife had traveled cross-country with their pup-tent, and he expected that a vacation of this sort would bring back their days of freedom in the Northeast, times when the two of them, on far less money than they had now, had seemingly found many more opportunities to enjoy themselves. As Lewis was buying the new tent to accommodate their two teenagers as well as himself and his wife, he laid careful plans for this vacation.

No sooner had the family set out for the mountains, however, than they ran into torrential rains, which meant an extended stayover at a highway motel before they could move on. Though his wife and children took this quite well, Lewis felt restless and depressed. This was not the way he had envisioned things. As the family sat at Howard Johnson's, munching snacks and watching the rain splash across the windowpanes, he felt compelled to make the most of even this unfortunate circumstance. Keenly aware that he had only fourteen days to enjoy his vacation, he was at a loss as to how to do this by sitting around in a second-rate motel on a rainy evening. His plans had been to arrive at campsite before nightfall.

It was at this point that Lewis, who had learned Releasing at a workshop about a month previously, decided to let go of wanting to control the weather. After that, he let go of wanting to control exactly when they would arrive at the campsite. Then he was able to "accept 1 percent" of the appearance of the second-rate motel—at least, he thought, it had a pleasant view from the window. As soon as he had released on these various aspects of the situation, his mood lightened. He now found himself relaxing as he watched the rain, and a sense of the ridiculousness of all this began to come over him. He began to feel delight in seeing his entire family together ("For once!" he thought), with all of them facing a deluge from nature which was stopping them in their tracks.

As he responded to this changed feeling in himself, Lewis took advantage of what he called the "state of seige" to question his son and daughter about their friends and summer plans. As he did this, he found the family getting into a discussion of a sort that they had not had for quite a while—one of his children was away at college and the other one busy most of the time with high-school activities and a job.

The next day, however, Lewis had to do some more releasing. When they reached the campsite, he was once again determined to have a good time "just the way we used to." This led to trouble. Lewis was now twenty-five years older than when he and his wife had traveled across the country, and now he had a bad back. This meant he had to ask his son to give him a hand with a great many things for which he had needed no help at all in the earlier days, and he also discovered that his son was able to repair the car more efficiently than he could.

After letting go of wanting to change the fact that he couldn't handle things the way he had some years ago, Lewis finally decided to take the bull by the horns and let go of wanting to change his age. When he did this, he felt immediate relief.

The next bout of releasing came that night as they sat around the campfire. It suddenly occurred to him at this time that he was pushing the family a bit too hard to have fun on the vacation. Again he decided to do some direct releasing. Leaning back, his eyes squinting as he watched the fire and the slightly dried-out hamburgers, he thought to himself, "Could I let go of wanting to enjoy myself?"

This question startled him, which, of course, made it unusually effective. As soon as he had let go of *wanting* to enjoy himself, his perspective changed radically. He now saw the vacation for what it really was and realized that it was going to proceed in the way that *it* proceeded. He began to remember how, even in the past, many aspects of his vacationing had not been ideal and that when enjoyment had come, it had frequently come unexpectedly.

As he released more on wanting to enjoy himself, he realized that enjoyment can't be planned. One can plan for the practical aspects of a trip and set up the probabilities that fun may occur. But whether or not a vacation is fun is really "up to the gods." Letting go of the need to make this vacation "great" or a "memorable experience" freed Lewis to begin to experience what was happening around him.

For the first time since they had set out on the trip, he could now lounge around without guilt and, to his surprise, discovered that lounging was exactly what he wanted to do! He was, he realized, "damned tired" from his year of working, and the last thing he wanted to do was to expend energy until he had recouped his strength. The result was several days of luxurious relaxing for Lewis: times of lying around the campsite, reading books he wanted to read, taking short strolls or flopping in a dinghy while he pretended to fish. This seemed all he could muster energy to do.

As he released more, the vacation began to feel as though it were exactly what he needed. By the same token, the family, no longer pressured by him to hop to and make everything "go," was also relaxing, all doing whatever they felt like. If the kids wanted to go to the nearest town or hike into the mountains on their own, they did. If his wife wanted to drive to town and shop all day, she did. When they all gathered in the evening, everyone was now in good humor, friendly, and at ease.

As the days passed, Lewis became somewhat more energetic, did more interesting things that he liked to do, and kept releasing on "wanting to have a good vacation." The result was a delightful vacation; not exactly what he had expected, but exactly what he and the family needed. Letting go of his pressure to overcontrol, Lewis had allowed the vacation to happen.

All too often, trips and other enjoyable experiences lose their spontaneity—become heavy and not much fun—because they are overplanned. This knocks out the surprise element and takes the spice out of an undertaking. Releasing on a vacation in advance, as well as during the vacation itself, restores its freedom.

It is, therefore, useful to release in advance on wanting to "enjoy yourself," on wanting to have a "good vacation," or on any other form of mental pushing that may emerge as you approach a holiday. A holiday becomes a vacation only if it is free from inner as well as outer pressures.

Releasing contributes to adult play activities in a variety of ways. We have already discussed how it can free one to be more spontaneous and playful in sexual experiences, and how it can liberate the creative process so that joy reenters the act of creating. In a similar way, it can release previously constricted energy in sports activities by eliminating the inhibiting overpush, can remove extraneous considerations of approval or control from hobbies, and can create the unpressured relaxation necessary for true vacations.

The Releasing technique, therefore, contributes to our basic enjoyment of life. In part 3, we will consider how it can be used in a more specific sense to expand your fundamental capacity for enjoyment, and turn to the practical details which can make Releasing a more successful part of your everyday life.

Part 3

ACQUIRING A RELEASING ATTITUDE

Part 3 of this book is designed to help you establish the Releasing program as a regular and important part of your life. Releasing is a powerful tool—the more you use it, the more you benefit. In this section, you will be given a number of strategies for making Releasing easier, more pleasant, and more effective.

The point of this part of the book is not to give you the final word on your Releasing practice, however. That can come only from you. This section is intended to start a process which you yourself will develop. After reading it, you may think of ingenious new ways to ensure your continued releasing on a regular basis, or creative new ways to release. If this is the case, you will have used this book to your very best advantage.

I suggest you coast along when reading these last few pages, release on wanting to learn Releasing too quickly, and allow yourself to absorb the suggestions given in an effortless manner. This will allow you to put together a successful program to suit your individual needs.

Chapter 18

HELPFUL HINTS

In part 2 of this book, you read about people who used Releasing to deal with pressing situations or even with major stresses in their lives. Obviously, life crises or continuing pressure from unresolved problems can cause debilitating reactions. Clinical research suggests, however, that an accumulation of *small* stresses can often undermine health as much as can an occasional major stress or traumatic event. Such minor stresses are apt to be the rule rather than the exception for many of us, and their proper handling is extremely important.

During the course of a single day, many small things can go wrong. Your shoelace breaks when you're in a hurry. Someone cuts you off on the highway. The candy machine steals your money. You miss your bus (train, plane). You discover you are going to be late for an appointment and have no way of notifying the other person. An elevator keeps bypassing your floor. Commonplace events such as these call for immediate releasing. If you fail to release on them, the stress they cause accumulates.

To benefit fully from Releasing, you should use the method on a daily basis and make it a regular part of your life. This can be done in a number of ways. You can release to help you cope with what comes up at the moment, to handle a difficulty that has *already* occurred, or to deal with an anticipated problem. Or you may want to use Releasing as a general "cleanup" procedure at the end of each day.

Automatic Releasing

As you become more experienced in Releasing, don't be surprised if you find yourself automatically releasing on situations as soon as they happen, or within a second or two afterwards. This may happen so spontaneously that you don't realize it's occurring. For example:

- Someone calls you on the phone with a disturbing request. As you hold the receiver in your hand and hear her out, you automatically think, "Could I let go of wanting to control her?" By the time it's your turn to speak, you will find that you can now handle the problem comfortably.

- A can opener doesn't work. As soon as you recognize that it's broken, you have *already* released to some extent on wanting to control it. This has happened without your even going through the process of thinking the Releasing phrase. You may simply find yourself deciding that it's not worth bothering about and you grab something else to eat.

- You fail to receive an eagerly awaited letter and wonder whether the person who was supposed to send it to you really cares about you. You automatically let go of wanting the approval of that person, and the incident fades.

With this almost subliminal kind of Releasing, you may have new insights and realize why the event really didn't merit excessive involvement in the first place. You will, in fact, probably notice reasonable thoughts of this sort occurring to you more often, now that you have learned to release. Because these thoughts seem so natural, their relationship to the Releasing process may go unnoticed. You will simply have acquired a Releasing attitude toward life, so that things which formerly caused you distress are now comfortably handled.

Usually, a number of situations will also occur each day for which you need to use the Releasing device consciously and deliberately. Generally, it takes only a second or two to release and is worth every bit of the small effort involved. For some of these occasions you will require unlocking tactics. You read about these troubleshooters in part 1 of this book and learned how others have used them in part 2. The methods are summarized in the "Table of Tactics" at the end of this book. When you can't readily release on a situation, turn to that table, run your eye down the list of tactics, and try various ones until you finally release. Certain tactics will probably become your favorites, and you will tend to use them much more than others. All the tactics may be useful to you at some time or place, however, so it is valuable to reread this list frequently.

You will also find it helpful to read part 1 of this book again or review selected portions of it from time to time. You may not have grasped certain points the first time you read about them because you were intent on learning the basic technique. These subtleties will mean much more to you after you have been practicing Releasing regularly. They can greatly improve the effectiveness of the method.

Releasing After the Fact

When you find yourself in an emotionally disturbing situation, your monitor can close down to a point where it may not occur to you to release—or you may not have the time to do so. In this case, it's useful to release as soon as possible *after* the fact. A distressing situation may require some unlocking tactics before it is completely neutralized, but the advantages of taking the time out to work on it right away can well outweigh the disadvantages. Since your monitor will be opened by the releasing, you may even feel *better* after releasing on the situation than you did before it happened! In a sense, we can look at troublesome incidents that occur during the day as supplying opportunities to release, chances to clear our systems of unnecessary emotional burdens.

Releasing in Advance

Some things that disturb us during the day are totally unexpected, but others can be anticipated. When we expect a certain event to be upsetting, our fear of the consequences can make it even worse when it finally does happen—the so-called "self-fulfilling-prophecy" effect. Anticipatory releasing can be invaluable in smoothing the way so that the "worst" doesn't happen.

To release in advance, rehearse the prospective situation in your mind and let go of wanting to change (control) those aspects of it that are bothering you. An effective way to release on an anticipated situation is to imagine the absolute *worst* that could happen—then release on *that*. If you release on your reactions to the worst possibility, what actually happens won't throw you.

The Releasing Review

On most days, many incidents occur that are frustrating but which we don't recognize at the *time* as particularly disturbing. Although they may slip by unnoticed, they can take a heavy toll by causing a residual buildup of stress. Fortunately, there is a way to counteract this problem—by conducting a "Releasing review" at the end of the day.

To do this, set aside a block of time, preferably as close as possible to the same hour each day. This is to be devoted specifically to your Releasing review. Some people prefer to schedule the review just before retiring, but you may like to conduct yours on your way home from work or at some other convenient time. Experiment, select the time that works efficiently for you, and then stick to it.

To do your Releasing review, sit quietly in a place where you're not likely to be interrupted and allow your thoughts to roam over the day's events. The aim is to catch as in a net those things which are still unresolved in your mind, the unfinished business of the day—and to release on each unresolved event as it comes up. Which events of the day still arouse resentment in you? Which make you anxious? Which are depressing?

You don't need to be systematic. Just relax and let thoughts come. Our minds seem to want to deal with our tensions if we just give them a time and place in which to do so. You will discover that one unresolved incident after another may surface during this quiet time. Some of these you may not even have perceived as being troublesome at the time they occurred. These are the subliminal irritations of the day.

As these leftover problems make themselves known, release on each in turn. Then let your mind go into idling gear once more. If further troublesome incidents come to mind, release on those, too.

Some people like to carry a Releasing notebook or an index card during the day to jot down events they would like to release on later. Then they handle these during their Releasing review. Whichever method you use—the Releasing notes or simply allowing your free flow of thoughts to bring the incidents up again—the Releasing review can be an important addition to your life. It can provide some of the same intrinsic satisfaction as cleaning up a desk piled high with papers. After the review, you are ready to move on to new things in your life. Many people have reported that the Releasing review is one of the most valuable experiences of their day.

Waiting-Time Releasing

There are often moments during the day when something is holding us up and we have to wait for the situation to be resolved. These are ready-made opportunities for releasing.

Imagine yourself waiting in line when you are in a hurry. It will be five or ten minutes until you can move up to the front. You could either champ at the bit or use this situation effectively to release. You might let go of wanting to speed up the line or spend the time releasing on difficulties that you experienced earlier in the day. This Releasing interval could give you a fresh start for the rest of your day.

Or imagine yourself phoning someone and the secretary who answers saying, "She's on the phone. Please wait." Before you can respond, "Have her call back," you find yourself on hold. This is a fine opportunity to release—letting go of wanting to change what just happened or the feelings generated by it. Or you might decide to spend that enforced waiting time releasing on other things on your mind.

Time spent waiting for traffic lights, elevators, buses, in

commuting or elsewhere can be devoted to releasing with double benefits. It removes the irritation from the delay, and it gives you a chance to catch up on your backlog of releasing.

A Releasing Partner

In Releasing workshops, we always end up by pairing each participant with a Releasing partner. The pair then holds daily telephone conversations about experiences with the technique. This is both a valuable practice and lots of fun.

To set up such a program, select a friend or relative who has learned Releasing and make plans to talk to him on the phone once each day at a prearranged time.

Whenever possible, Releasing conferences should be conducted over the telephone rather than in person. Personal encounters are apt to become informal occasions with a great many extraneous matters entering into the conversation. When a telephone call is made specifically for purposes of exchanging information on Releasing, both parties can agree in advance to stick to the point and exclude other topics of conversation, at least until the principal purpose of the call has been accomplished. If this is done, there is absolutely no reason why people living in the same household can't work together as partners.

Couples who have learned Releasing can agree to call each other at a set time for a Releasing conference. There is something enjoyable about being phoned by a person who is close to you for purposes of working on a constructive project. One former workshop participant reports that it has been a welcome addition to her life to know that her husband is going to phone her from his office at a particular hour each day, discuss his Releasing experiences with her, and help her with her own. This arrangement has brought the couple closer together.

During the conference, your Releasing partner may help you think up ways in which you might have released on a particular incident, or she can lead you through a release (provided, of course, that this is something you want her to do). One of the most valuable aspects of this mutual releasing is the fact that as one partner releases, the other partner also releases simultaneously. It's often easier to release on your partner's problems than your own (you're not so involved in them). This means that you get in a lot of "free" releasing each time you work together, a way to ease up your tensions even more. I know of one man who has been releasing on the phone regularly with his partner for a period of several years, and he reports that he does his best releasing this way. The two have every intention of continuing this practice indefinitely.

Releasing Gatherings

If several of your friends have learned Releasing, it can be constructive and fun to have periodic Releasing parties. At such gatherings, those present can take turns releasing out loud on a specific problem while other members of the group act as coaches. One member of the group may also elect to lead the person who is releasing through a release, with leadership rotating.

A major benefit of such gatherings is the vicarious releasing that those present experience as others go through releases. Even people who may speak little at the meeting, or who simply sit and watch, often benefit as much as do active members. A Releasing atmosphere can build to such an extent that one's own problems appear much easier to handle after such a session.

If you prefer to have an agenda for such a meeting, you can assign a specific theme to a particular meeting: releasing on work-related problems, releasing on parent-child problems, the use of the decision-making strategy, methods of releasing on physical discomfort; such themes as these can occupy a whole meeting, and the variations are endless.

The program can also include a general cleanup procedure at the end when the person who acts as leader asks the group, "Did anything happen this week that you would like to change? . . . Could you let go of wanting to change it? . . . Did anything else happen that you would like to change?" The other participants silently let go of wanting to change those events. Similarly, the leader could ask, "Did you meet anybody this week whose approval you wanted? . . . Could you let go of wanting their approval?"

I recommend Releasing gatherings as a way to increase the benefits you derive from the technique, and as thoroughly enjoyable social events. They are also a first-rate way of keeping you interested in Releasing. For many people, participating in a group has the advantage of keeping them regularly releasing.

Writing Down "R-Benefits"

It can be very useful to write down the gains you have made from Releasing before they fade from your mind. I call the benefits of Releasing "R-Benefits" for short. There are several ways you can record them.

You may want to keep a notebook or some index cards in your pocket to jot down information about your releases as they occur during the day. Or you may keep a journal at home in which you record your releases at the end of the day.

Below is a typical day's entry in an R-Benefits journal, written by a former workshop participant who uses the initial "R" to stand for "releasing."

Situation	Releasing	R-Benefits
Joe away from office early. Grouchy, a pain in the neck.	R on wanting to control his mood. R on wanting his approval.	Eased up. Could get on with preparing dinner. He was friendly later on. R-Benefit=*fight* avoided!
Kids late for supper. Kathy didn't arrive at all and didn't phone to tell me. Cooked too much steak.	R on my own anger. R on wanting to control Kathy.	Joe and I had a good meal together. I figured out a way to use the steak for a casserole tomorrow.

Situation	Releasing	R-Benefits
Blanche phoned to gripe about her husband Ted's "bad behavior." A bore. She wouldn't get off the phone. What does she want from me?	R on my anger. Put myself in Blanche's "shoes" and R on her wanting to control me.	Whole thing lifted. Was able to be quiet while she talked and let her know nicely that Ted has his side, too. Think she got the message, and it may have helped her.
Dishwasher jammed. Someone had dropped a spoon in the bottom, and it was caught in the machinery. Joe had gone out again, and I couldn't get the machine apart.	R on wanting to "rewrite history" and change the fact that the spoon was dropped there. R on wanting to to change the fact that Joe was not here to fix it. R on wanting to change the whole situation.	Felt fine. So what if it's stuck? I don't need dishes until tomorrow anyway.

General R-Benefits I've Been Noticing

- I don't get hassled about things going wrong the way I used to.
- Find myself humming a lot as I work. Unusual for me.
- Tasks seem simpler, and I do them more easily. Can clean up loose ends better when I release on them first. More done in less time.

A useful procedure is to follow your description of the specific R-Benefits for each day with a summary of the more general ones you're noticing in your life, as in the R-Benefits journal above. Many aspects of your life will change as a result of continued releasing, and your R-Benefits journal will be a valuable record of these changes. It is helpful to reread it occasionally to remind yourself of changes that have taken place.

Now we will turn to those practical steps which can make your Releasing practice even more effective.

Keep It Short

It's a good idea to keep the Releasing questions as short as possible. After the phrase, "Could I let go of wanting to change (control, have approval, etc.)," try not to add more than another five-to-ten words. Obviously, it's sometimes necessary to add another phrase (such as, "Can you just let it be?"), but this is for the times when you are locked in. For everyday releasing, you don't want to complicate matters. Too many words can be difficult to remember. Generally speaking, the shorter the Releasing question, the more punch it carries.

Use Shortcuts

Approval and control are such basic issues that one or both of these concepts will apply to almost any situation. To avoid the necessity of analyzing the situation, try releasing on *control* in general, or on *approval* in general.

For example, suppose you felt vaguely depressed but didn't know why. You might think to yourself or say out loud:

"Could I let go of wanting approval?"

Or:

"Could I let go of wanting to *control*?"

If either approval or control is involved (as they almost always are), this could bring about an immediate release. Strange as it may seem, releasing on the general concept (without even knowing what or whom you want to control or from whom you want approval) is often all you will need to do.

Releasing in this general fashion also has other advantages. When you release on control in general, your release may affect the entire control "network." A whole battery of related situations may then be simultaneously ticked off in your brain— release . . . release . . . release. You need not know what they are. You will feel the benefits. The same principle applies to approval. Releasing on approval in general can alter the entire approval network.

Releasing on control or approval in general *may work so well that it's not necessary to release any further.*

The ultimate shortcut, however, is to think to yourself the word "Release." If you are accustomed to releasing, this may be *all* you need to do!

Keep It Simple, Keep It Lively

When releasing, it's useful to keep your question to yourself as simple as possible. Everyday language is better than complicated language. The words you use should be those which mean the most to you. It's generally wise to stick to the basic phrasing as I have given it, but there is room within that format for much improvisation. Be creative!

You can also try varying your Releasing question from time to time so that occasionally it surprises you. Try not to use exactly the same phrasing all of the time. Surprise is a great help when releasing.

Reach Closure

An important principle of Releasing is to systematically follow each release through to its completion. Psychologists refer to this as obtaining closure. If you obtain closure when you release, you feel rewarded. In some respects, we are all like Oscar, the trained seal, in that when we get rewards for doing something, we are more apt to do that same thing again (see pages 177–8). Like the fish that Oscar enjoyed, even a partial release can be a great motivator. Be sure you get it each time.

By the same token, try not to release while thinking of half a dozen other things at the same time. If you do this, your mind wanders away from the Releasing process and you are apt not to finish the release. If you take releasing seriously, follow each release through to its completion and make sure you have obtained closure. This way, the method will become very powerful for you.

Be Specific

Releasing is most effective when you work with a specific situation. If, for example, you were to try to release on a "relationship," this could be too vague. But if you were to release on what upset you at the breakfast table this morning and let go of wanting to control *that*, it could have an impact on many aspects of your relationship with the person who shared your table.

Another advantage of being specific is that it enables you to check back more easily. It's a simple matter to go back over the scene at the breakfast table in your imagination and notice how it feels now after releasing. It's not nearly so simple to review an entire relationship in your mind and see how *that* feels now. Being specific in your releasing and using concrete situations is actually a way of using the divide-and-conquer strategy effectively.

Release on the Easiest First

When you need to release on several aspects of a situation, it is usually wise to release first on the one that seems easiest. This gets the ball rolling. Sometimes releasing on the easiest is all you need to do to release on the whole situation—the other parts of the situation may take care of themselves because a release network has been ticked off.

When Heavily Locked In

If you have tried all the usual unlocking tactics but still find a particular situation overwhelming, a good next move is to think to yourself or say out loud:

"Could I let go of wanting to change the feeling of being overwhelmed?"

This can open your monitor so the Releasing process starts again.

Another option is to phone a friend who is experienced in Releasing (perhaps your Releasing partner) and talk about the situation. An objective opinion can be a great help. If you have no one to discuss it with (or don't want to share this particular problem), then try releasing out loud to yourself. The sound of your own voice going through the Releasing process may shock you out of your sense of helplessness.

Another useful strategy for dealing with overwhelming situations is to review your past R-Benefits, particularly the biggies—the dramatic successes where you were able to release on very difficult situations. When you read about situations on which you have released in the past, you are likely to feel the wheels starting to turn again, and you will begin releasing once more.

If all else fails, then release on *wanting to release*. This takes the pressure off, opens your monitor, and may in itself lead to a release.

When You Don't Want to Release

There may be times when you feel so strongly about a situation that you resist the idea of releasing at all, even though you realize it would be beneficial to do so. When this happens, if you still want to get the benefits of a release:

- Release on "not wanting to release."
- Write down the situation, and then *keep* on resisting all you

want. Your notes will serve as a reminder so that you can release on this matter later.

* Absolutely forbid yourself to release! (The forbidding tactic in chapter 5.)

Thinking in Circles

Shakespeare describes Hamlet as being hampered by a character trait that prevented him from taking action, ". . . some craven scruple of thinking too precisely on the event."

If you find yourself "thinking too precisely on the event":

* Identify the feeling involved and release on that, ignoring reasons, arguments, or thoughts. Feeling is at the core of what is happening to you, anyway.
* Release on wanting to change the fact that you "think too much." A release is a release. It's always valuable, however you obtain it.
* Release on *ten things* completely irrelevant to the issue you are concerned with. When your monitor has opened up, all problems are viewed differently.

When You're Uncertain

Doubts about Releasing are more apt to plague some people than others. If you're uncertain about whether or not you have released on a situation, try the following:

* Release on wanting to know whether you've released.
* Release on wanting to change your confusion about releasing (or accept 1 percent of your confusion).
* Reread your R-Benefits journal.
* Keep on releasing even if you don't know where it's taking you. Eventually, you will see light at the end of the tunnel.

When You're Dissatisfied

All of us occasionally try releases which don't seem to work. If this happens to you, let go of wanting to control the results. Releasing takes place in its own way. When you let it have free rein, it works.

If You're Discouraged

There are times when any self-development program, whether it involves exercise, diet, or a new skill, can reach a temporary stalemate. At such times, participants may become discouraged and drop the program.

You might run into this sort of program with Releasing, too. This is particularly apt to happen if you are extremely busy and haven't remembered to do much releasing, or have encountered a number of difficult problems so that your monitor has closed down. The problem now is to get started again. Here are some things that can help.

- Reread your R-Benefits. Past successes are powerful persuaders.
- Select a time in which you will release on everything that you think about or experience during that time. If you do this, you will probably find that something interesting happens. It is hard to remain disenchanted with a process that works.
- Check on whether you have been getting closure on your releases. If you have been somewhat offhand about Releasing, select a simple (not intense) situation to release on and carry the process through to *at least* a partial release. Then remind yourself to reach closure every time you release in the future.

Remembering to Release

When your monitor shuts down, you may forget to release. Here are some solutions that former workshop members report for this problem:

- Tack up Releasing reminders where you can see them. You might fasten one up on the refrigerator door or the bathroom mirror, or put one by your bedside. Or you may want to put one on a bulletin board, your desk, or in some other noticeable spot. The reminder can contain a little note, quote, or "wise saying" which will remind you to release.
- Place a representation of a person or animal which you dub your "Releasing statue" in a prominent place in your home. You will know what it signifies. Every time you look at it, it will remind you to release.
- If you have a daily appointment book, write the word "RELEASE" in large letters across the top of every page for the rest of the year, and then circle these words in red. Whenever you look at your appointment book, the first think you see will be the word "RELEASE"—a powerful reminder.
- Place a sticker with an "R" written on it on the side of your office or home telephone that *faces* you.
- Leave a copy of this book around where you can see it easily. It is an automatic reminder to release.
- Carry a copy of the Releasing Card at the back of this book with you during the day. It serves as an excellent reminder to release as well as supplying an at-a-glance summary of the major unlocking tactics.
- Do a Releasing review daily. This will act as insurance against accumulating problems that have not been released on.

Seeking Out Releases

If you seek as many opportunities as possible to release, you will move ahead faster in your program. One way to so this is to consider each frustration that occurs during the day as not only an annoyance but an opportunity. The greater the frustration, the more releasing you will have to do in order to neutralize it, and the greater the payoff will be for the remainder of your day.

When you get into the habit of recognizing the opportunities for releasing that occur in frustrating situations, frustrations themselves, when they occur, may start *the Releasing process.*

Or you can make up your mind that each time the phone rings on a particular day, you will release before saying hello, letting go of wanting to control the outcome of the phone call. This is excellent practice and greases the wheels of the Releasing process, so that if a difficult event occurs later on, you are likely to release on it automatically with little or no difficulty.

When You Want Someone Else to Release

Those who have learned Releasing often observe other people in situations where Releasing could be of benefit to them. If the others know how to release, the temptation may be great to suggest to them that they *release* on their problem.

Unless we approach this task with a totally released attitude on our own part, however, such suggestions are apt to backfire. They will certainly do so if we make a suggestion of this sort when we are having an argument with another person.

If a person who is annoyed with us says, "You'd better release!" this is not likely to make us feel more like releasing. In fact, we may now be less apt to want to release than before the suggestion was made!

Releasing can't be used to control. If you try to use it in this way, it makes matters worse instead of better.

If you want to remind someone to release who seems to have forgotten about using the technique, the appropriate thing to do is to release first on wanting to control *whether or not that other person releases*. If you do this before you speak up, this removes the issue of control from the transaction. When you now make the suggestion that the other person release, you will be giving her a free choice. She will sense this, and offering to lead her through a release at this point may now be gratefully received.

If necessary, you might also release several more times on your need to control the situation while you are discussing the question of releasing with her. This will help you not to tell her she *should* release—a futile maneuver.

An example is worth a thousand words. At this point, you will be a good example of Releasing.

Now that you have used Releasing to handle problems, you are ready to consider a revolutionary aspect of this technique—its ability to promote a new kind of *awareness*. The following chapter deals with this possibility.

Chapter 19

BEYOND THE
FRONTIERS

So far, you have used Releasing to cope with problems. There are other benefits to be derived from the technique, however. Releasing can be used to help you increase your sensitivity, explore new inner and outer frontiers, and expand your awareness. Here are some ways.

Releasing on "Everything"

One variation on the technique which you may want to try is to release systematically, for a stated period of time, on *each* activity you perform or on each thing that happens, no matter how insignificant. For example, you might let go consecutively of wanting to control everything that occurs during a particular half-hour. This might include the fact that the telephone is ringing, the way you handle the receiver, who is on the other end of the line, your dinner, each food that is served, someone else's behavior, an appliance that isn't working, the way a book opens as you lift it up, the way the book reads. And another time you might let go of wanting to control how you brush your teeth, how your mattress feels or whether you fall asleep soon. The goal is to let go of wanting to control all events that occur during the span of time you have put aside.

The purpose of this exercise is to change your perspective. We can get so caught up in planning that we limit awareness of our own activities to what we want to get done and how the activity in question fits into our plans. Because of this, we often retain only a dim awareness of the activity itself. We do not realize that each time we pick up a pencil to write, each time we put on our shoes, each time we take a bit of food, a unique event is occurring. It has not happened before and will not happen again in exactly the same way. When we try to control an event by making it part of a planned agenda, we sacrifice its special quality.

When you practice releasing on all things that occur in a given time period, you may discover that almost everything you have been doing up until now has been overcontrolled and therefore hampered. When you release on wanting to control what you do, you find a new harmony in your movements and your interactions with things and people. This sense of harmony can enormously increase your enjoyment. The blinders will have been removed.

A member of a former workshop who has used this method reports that she now releases on everything that occurs every time she drives her car. While she is driving, she regularly asks herself whether she can let go of wanting to control the brake . . . the directional signal . . . the steering wheel . . . the accelerator . . . the car ahead of her . . . the red lights . . . the road, and so on with everything in sight. Since she has been doing this, she has realized how much she used to struggle to maintain control of these routine actions. She feels she must have been "fighting the car" the whole time she was driving it.

Releasing while driving has also brought to her a new awareness of the other cars on the road, and what she calls a "gentler" way of thinking about other motorists. Paradoxically, it has also made her almost impervious to rudeness or attempts to control *her* on the part of other motorists. An impatient driver honking a horn behind her, when she herself is driving at a reasonable speed and not violating any traffic regulations, no longer makes her feel nervous, uneasy, or retaliative. It is simply irrelevant.

When we let go of wanting to control, we can no longer be controlled.

Releasing ourselves from wanting to control the exigencies of life also acts as a relaxation technique. Excess muscle tension comes from fighting to make our own actions turn out the way we want them to, or the outside world to behave in a certain way. As we release this struggle (even in small ways), we feel the tension draining away.

The ease that follows releasing can also bring a surge of energy. Each time we release on something (large or small), we return a quantum of energy to what might be called our "central fund of energy." This stored energy can then be used by our systems for inner growth, allowing us to become more inventive, effective, loving, and joyous. It may also be involved in physical healing.

With every new release, the gradual accumulation of energy in our "central fund" makes it that much easier to tackle the next problem. The result is that as we continue to release over time, little by little the balance begins to shift to the positive side of the ledger, and life seems easier.

Repetitive Releasing

A variation of the technique I have just described is to engage in a routine activity and while carrying out this routine to release on wanting to control each single action or each separate object involved in it.

For example, imagine yourself washing dishes in your sink. As you pick up the first dish, you ask yourself, "Could I let go of wanting to control this dish (cup, saucer, etc.)?" You then repeat this same question to yourself as you pick up each consecutive dish. This process continues until you find yourself releasing automatically on each piece of dinnerware, or until you have finished the sinkful of dishes. When you release in this manner on routine activities, even if they are customarily monotonous or irritating, they can become peaceful and comforting.

Recently, I released in this way while using an office copier. When I did so, each sheet of paper became of interest. It had its own feel, its special way of responding to my touch, its individual way of collapsing and flattening onto the copyplate.

When I collated the sheets, I released again on wanting to control each single piece of paper. To my surprise, my fingers were then more delicately capable of sensing the edges of the paper. The whole process was easier.

When we respect the objects we work with, they become easier to work with.

Repetitive Releasing can be applied at some point during almost every day. You can release on each nail you drive into a board, each tennis stroke, each golf swing, every third swimming stroke, every other stride when you're walking . . . the list is endless.

Releasing on Major Categories

While it is possible to benefit from releasing on very small details of our lives, we can also release productively on major categories of our experience. Here are some ways.

Releasing on Sports

Aside from releasing on wanting to control each individual component of a sports activity, there are ways to release on sports or physical exercise in general which can make these experiences more meaningful to us. To do this, before commencing your practice or game, think to yourself, or say out loud:

"Could I let go of wanting to_____?"

(Insert appropriate word or phrase)

List of Possible Words or Phrases

WIN

LOOK GOOD

HOLD UP

DO IT RIGHT

SCORE

GO FURTHER (DO BETTER) THAN YESTERDAY

CONTROL WHETHER I GOOF

CONTROL WHETHER I STRIKE OUT, ETC.

(Fill in blanks with categories meaningful to you.)

_____   _____

_____   _____

_____   _____

_____   _____

Releasing on Creativity

Creativity requires a free flow of ideas and a lack of self-consciousness which can be substantially increased by releasing on wanting to control the creative activity. Workshop participants report excellent results from releasing just before, or while engaged in, painting, writing, playing a musical instrument, or pursuing some other form of creative endeavor.

To release on your creativity, think to yourself, or say out loud:

"Could I let go of wanting to control_____?"

List of Possible Categories

THE LINES

THE COLORS

THE PAINT

THE BRUSH

THE WORDS

THE TYPEWRITER

THE SENTENCES

MY IDEAS

HOW IT SOUNDS

HOW IT LOOKS

THE PIANO KEYS

MY FINGERS

MY RIGHT HAND

MY LEFT HAND

THE TONES

MY SPEED

HOW I DO

HOW "THEY" LIKE IT

_____

_____

_____

Releasing on Appreciation

Releasing can also be used to enhance your appreciation of such passive activities as listening to music, going to a museum or theater, or watching a sports event. To release on these activities, think to yourself, or say out loud:

"Could I let go of wanting to control_____?"

List of Possible Categories

THE MUSIC

THE NOTES

THE COLORS IN THAT PAINTING (release on each individual color)

THE WAY THE LIGHT FALLS ON IT

THE WAY IT'S DISPLAYED

THIS ACTOR (ACTRESS)

THE PLAY

MY FEELINGS

WHAT OTHERS WILL THINK OF MY TASTE

THE AUDIENCE

THE BALL TEAM

EACH PLAYER

WHO WINS (Remember that you don't have to give up your *goal* of desiring one or the other team to win!)

_____

_____

_____

_____

Releasing on Attitudes

Releasing can be used to alter basic attitudes as well as specific responses. For this purpose, the ordinary Releasing phrases are bypassed and you go directly to the general topic, using words that speak directly to you.

Some words may be helpful for your own releasing but will have little meaning to anyone else. But there are words that are appropriate for almost everyone. To give you an idea of the possibilities, I have collected phrases which have been suggested by past members of Releasing workshops. Most people prefer to use one of four basic formats. I will present each of these in turn, with a list of categories that may be useful for you.

**Format 1. "Could I let go of wanting
(him/her/them) to be_____?"**

(adjective describing desired quality)

(Use a positive word or phrase that describes what you *want* of the person, not what you *don't* want.)

List of useful words or phrases:

SENSIBLE	COURAGEOUS
CONSIDERATE	ATTRACTIVE
AGREEABLE	FUN
FAIR	WELL
RESPONSIVE	ENERGETIC
RESPONSIBLE	CREATIVE
SUPPORTIVE	ON TIME
REASONABLE	SANE
UNDERSTANDING	DIFFERENT (from the way they are)
HONEST	_____
COOPERATIVE	_____
INTELLIGENT	_____
AMBITIOUS	_____

- -

Format 2. "Could I let go of wanting (him/her/them) to_____**?"**

(word or phrase describing desired action)

List of useful words or phrases:

AGREE	UNDERSTAND	PAY ATTENTION
RESPOND	COOPERATE	LOVE ME
OBEY ME	TELL THE TRUTH	_____

PRAISE ME	BE LIKE ME	_____
LISTEN	BE QUIET	_____
RESPECT ME	ENJOY THEMSELVES	_____

- -

Format 3. "Could I let go of wanting
_____?"
(word or phrase referring to object or quality desired)

List of useful words or phrases:

LOVE	A HUSBAND	MORE TIME
SECURITY	A WIFE	HAPPINESS
REVENGE	A LOVER	RELATIONSHIP TO WORK
WEALTH	A CHILD	GOOD HEALTH
SUCCESS	ACCLAIM	_____
PRAISE	YOUTH	_____
TO WIN	THINGS TO BE EASY	_____

- -

Format 4. "Could I let go of wanting
to be_____?"
(adjective referring to yourself)

List of useful words or phrases:

PERFECT	YOUNGER
REASONABLE	DIFFERENT (than I am)
LIKED	SPECIAL

LOVED	THE BEST
UNDERSTOOD	ON TIME
HAPPY	UNIQUE
RIGHT	TALENTED
RICH	POWERFUL
BRILLIANT	APPRECIATED
SUCCESSFUL	_____
ADMIRED	_____
THIN	_____
BEAUTIFUL (HANDSOME)	_____

Some people like to set aside a special time each day during which to release on attitudes. You can use the above lists or make up your own. When you do this, release on only a few categories each day. Remember that you're not necessarily letting go of the goal of achieving some of these things. Your purpose is only to let go of your excessive striving.

Since releasing on attitudes may represent a fundamental challenge to your ordinary ways of thinking, you may at first have to use unlocking tactics. After you have released on several attitudes, you will begin to recognize that even the most fundamental categories can easily be released on. This can lift a weight from your shoulders.

Beyond the Frontiers

Surprising as this may seem, Releasing can be used to enhance life experiences which are *already* positive and satisfying, making that which is pleasant even more so. This occurs because a fulfilling event rarely affords undiluted pleasure. It usually contains hidden elements which serve to contaminate the joy— feelings such as doubt, anxiety, or guilt. When we release on a pleasurable event, we shed those unwanted aspects of the situation *without even knowing what they are*. What is left is the kernel, the positive experience. Releasing on the positive is one of the most deeply satisfying moves that we can make when we are *already happy*. There are several ways we can do this.

Releasing on Pleasant Events

A practical way to begin releasing on the positive aspects of your life is to set aside a stretch of time, say a morning or afternoon, during which you make a point of noticing *everything* positive that happens to you. Each time during the Releasing session that you identify a positive event, think to yourself, or say out loud:

"Could I let go of wanting to control (the pleasant event)?"

This technique can lead to important insights. Most of us spend too much time trying to control, manage, and otherwise manipulate everything that is happening to us—even good things. This manipulation can take the form of calculating how we can maintain the good experience, increase it, or repeat it. It can also take the form of worrying about losing the good experience and trying to think of ways to protect ourselves against this. All of these control maneuvers detract from the beauty of the moment, and from the excitement and fulfillment of whatever is "going right."

To apply Releasing to positive situations, release at random on good events that occur throughout the day. For example:

- A delightful letter arrives in the mail. Let go of wanting to change the fact that the letter arrived. (*It makes no difference that you didn't want to change this to* begin *with. Just release! What happens may surprise you.*)
- Someone greets you with a radiant smile. Let go of wanting to change the fact that he has greeted you so warmly!
- After many tries, you finally solve a pressing problem. Let go of wanting to change the fact that you *solved* it.

Strange as this may sound, when you let go of wanting to

change a positive experience, it enters your consciousness in a new way. A moment of happiness has been allowed to exist without being part of any hidden agenda. You have released it, and, like a soap bubble floating upwards in the sunlight— spinning gently and reflecting the myriad colors of the rainbow—this moment of happiness will remain as long as it wants to remain and, during its brief existence, will be all-absorbing.

A former member of a Releasing workshop tried this after he heard the good news that his daughter was coming home from college for an unexpected vacation. She worked in a distant city. When he let go of wanting to *change* the fact that she would be coming home ("unreasonable" as such a maneuver was, since he was delighted with this idea), he found himself now more confident that she actually *would* get home. The anticipated visit seemed more real. His day was now a happier one.

Releasing on Events That Bring Relief

We often worry about things that don't materialize. We may fear that an abdominal pain is going to require surgery—it turns out to be a simple reaction to some food we've eaten. We may be afraid we won't be able to pay an unexpected bill—we discover that with some juggling of resources we will manage quite nicely. We may worry about a relationship—we contact the party involved and find that the problem can easily be straightened out.

As someone once commented, "Ninety-five percent of the crises in our lives never happen!" The worst eventualities are usually handled or averted. We therefore have opportunities for relief each day of our lives. Unfortunately, however, most of us fail to take advantage of these opportunities. We tend to cling to the original problem, as though it had not been solved at all. Releasing on events that have *already been solved* can contribute greatly to our sense of well-being and relaxation.

A former workshop participant used this tactic when a classmate of her daughter's contracted a serious illness. Her own child was perfectly healthy, but the news had ruined her day. She was worried about the possibility of her daughter contracting the illness. The fact remained, however, that at present her daughter was in fine shape.

To cope with the problem, this woman decided to release on the "good" in the situation. She did this by asking herself if she could let go of wanting to *change* the fact that her daughter was, at present, happy and energetic. Strange as this seemed (it *is* an illogical maneuver), when she released in this manner, if felt as though a load had been taken off her shoulders. She still planned to have her daughter checked by the pediatrician, but now she was picturing the child as she had looked that morning, "her usual bouncy self." She had almost talked herself into seeing her child as pale and sickly, when she hadn't been that way at all. As she released on wanting to *change* the thought that her daughter was healthy, she allowed herself to fully *accept* the fact of the child's present good health!

There are many situations in which we can use this method of Releasing. . . . Could we let go of wanting to change the fact that we *weren't* injured when our car skidded? That we still have some money in the bank? That we weren't fired? That an angry opponent *didn't* win his point? Relieving thoughts can be much more useful when we release on wanting to *change* the relief!

To release on situations of relief, you may want to set aside a time to think of problems which have recently been resolved or catastrophes that have not materialized. Consciously seek out areas of "relief." Then release on wanting to *change* the relieving outcome. You may be surprised at the benefits this can bring.

Releasing on Another Person

Releasing on another person's attributes can greatly enhance your relationship with that person. To do this, set aside a period of time to think quietly about someone. Try to remember everything you can about this person—appearance, typical behavior, special qualities. Then start releasing on these memories. You can start anywhere; then let go of wanting to change attribute after attribute, behavior after behavior. Include positive traits, neutral traits, and negative ones, releasing on all of them.

When one workshop participant released on the important man in her life, she let go of wanting to change the way he continued to read the newspaper while she was talking, the particular sound of his cough (different from anyone else's), the way his eyes squinted in the sunlight, the way he combed his hair, the way he got lost in watching TV, the way he moved with the music when he danced, the way he would suddenly laugh, the special tone of voice he used when he criticized her, the way his eyes would light up in humor, the way he piled papers on the dining-room table, how he was "always" late for appointments, the way he sang when doing carpentry, the way he made love, the way he talked to the dog, the way he looked when he emerged dripping from swimming, the way he cooked a hurried breakfast, the way he raged about the future of the world, the way he played the same piece on the mandolin over and over again. . . .

A list such as this can go on for as long as you feel it is productive. The aim is to release repeatedly on wanting to change each and every detail of the other person. When you are finished with a Person-Releasing session, you will have learned some new things about your relationship with this other person. You may decide to allow him his own personal space in a way that you hadn't before. This may result in your feeling less pressured by him, too.

Releasing is a two-way street. It affects both parties. When you release on someone, you are released. When he releases on you, he is released.

Releasing on Wanting to "Hold On" to Your Good Fortune

One of the most productive ways to release on the positive is to release when you're concerned about losing gains you have already achieved, or having good things which are happening in your life come to an end.

Suppose you are feeling at ease, free of burdens and buoyant. Suddenly the thought crosses your mind, "When is this great feeling going to end?" When this happens, a useful move is to release on wanting to *hold on to* your benefits. To do this, think to yourself, or say out loud:

"Could I let go of wanting to *maintain* this good feeling (time, happening, etc.)?"

By letting go of wanting to maintain it, you allow yourself to retain contact with the good feeling (person, happening, etc.) even longer.

After you have released, you can also let go of wanting to maintain your Releasing benefits. If you do, you are likely to retain *them* much longer.

The following scene is typical of what can happen when you release on wanting to "hold on."

You are a runner. You jog up a hill in the cool, crisp autumn air. Somewhere near the summit there is an open space, rolling pasture-land beneath you, and woods, and silence. You feel an incredible rightness about your day. This good feeling is tinged with sadness, however, as you recognize that your vacation is drawing to a close, that the beauty of the day, the air, the forest, you, and your tingling body will fade and become past history. You release on wanting to maintain the feeling of rightness. Now it belongs to you.

Most of the time we are future-bound creatures. Because of this, we are continuously trying to force present moments to become future moments.

"If only my baby would be just this age forever."

"If only this love could last."

"If only today would never end."

"If only I could hold on to this wonderful mood."

The things that you fear ending and changing and dissolving will, of course, eventually end and change and dissolve. When you let go of clinging to them, however, the present, at least, *is* yours.

When we relinquish the moment, that moment belongs to us

To become closer to the loveliest things in life, you only need to let go of struggling to retain them.

Let go of wanting to hold on to that incredible passage of music. Let go of wanting to hold on to the touch of that beloved person. Let go of wanting to hold on to the vigor of your body stretched to its limit. Let go of wanting to hold on to the last day of summer.

Let go of holding on to all these things, and they are yours.

Releasing and Meditation

Modern meditation is a simple mental technique used to cope with stress and enhance personal fulfillment. When practicing it, a person sits quietly and pays close attention to a single source of stimulation. The object of this attention may be a sound repeated mentally, the meditator's own breathing, a candle flame, or the rustling of wind in the trees—or it may be any one of a number of other appropriate centers of focus; the object used depends upon the particular system of meditation being followed. When the meditator's attention wanders, he/she brings it back to the center of focus. The aim of this repetitive task is to quiet the "inner chatter" of thoughts, allowing the body and mind to achieve a state of profound rest.

There is a subtle relationship between Releasing and meditation. Each of these practices helps us to feel less urgent, more open, and more responsive to our own needs and those of others. Your Releasing program may therefore be even more productive if combined with the regular practice of meditation.

Many people report that when they meditate just before releasing on a difficult situation, their subsequent releasing goes more smoothly. If you plan to do some sustained releasing, meditating for five minutes before commencing to release can be excellent preparation.

This facilitation seems to work in both directions. Many of us who have learned Releasing have noticed that our meditation sessions are greatly enhanced by the spontaneous releasing that tends to occur *during* meditation. Extraneous thoughts are present during all forms of meditation, and these thoughts often bring to the surface problems which then appear to be handled in some manner by the meditative process. When these problems arise during meditation, they tend to be released on automatically, so that the quiet of the meditative state is restored once more.

Some forms of meditation make use of a "mantra," a mentally repeated sound designed to have a soothing effect. If you practice mantra meditation, you might want to try thinking of your mantra once *as you release*. One workshop participant reported finding it helpful to take a deep breath, then to let it out and think his mantra to himself *at the same time as he was releasing*. Doing this deepened the release. This way of using a mantra is similar to the advice of connecting the feeling of releasing to a touch on the skin, then using this anchor to recall the releasing mood.

If you practice some form of meditation, you may already be experiencing ways that releasing and meditation complement each other. If you are not a meditator, you may want to learn a modern form of meditation to enhance the Releasing process. If so, you might consider learning Clinically Standardized Meditation (CSM), which I teach on audio cassettes in the *Learn to Meditate Kit*.* I originally developed this modern form of meditation to fill the need for a simple, scientifically based system of meditation that involves no mystery or secret rituals and fits in easily with contemporary lifestyles. CSM has now been successfully used by organizations, medical centers and individuals in many different countries to reduce stress and improve quality of living.

It adjusts flexibly to suit each person's needs and can be practiced almost anywhere—on a train, bus, plane, as a passenger in a car, while waiting in an airport or a doctor's office—any time you have a few minutes that might otherwise be "wasted." With this method, after the first instruction session, you are already meditating on your own. By the end of one week, you will have completely mastered the technique. CSM works excellently with Releasing and many people I have worked with have combined the two approaches, using Releasing for handling specific situations and meditation to

---

* P. Carrington, *Learn to Meditate Kit* (Shaftesbury: Element Books, 1998).

ensure lowered tension throughout the entire day. You will find specific methods for combining Releasing with meditation in Appendix E.

The Meditative Mood and Releasing

In addition to its use along with formal meditation, Releasing can evoke what I call the "meditative mood," a state of mind characterized by gently drifting thoughts and a deep sense of calm. Such a mood has therapeutic properties and can affect your health and well-being positively on a number of levels.*

To use Releasing to evoke the meditative mood, sit quietly in a place where you are not likely to be disturbed and select some simple object in your vicinity to look at. The object need not be beautiful or inspiring. It need not even be particularly pleasant; anything will do—a pillow, a clock, a telephone, a scrap of paper, a pencil, a jar of paper clips, some flowers, a lamp—whatever your eye lights upon.

When you have selected the object, let go of wanting to "change" it. You don't need to *consciously* feel that you want to change it to do this. We spend so much time unconsciously wanting to change everything around us that letting go of our drive to control automatically works to alter our attitudes.

When you have released, check on how the object looks to you. You may be surprised at what has happened. As you release on object after object in your surroundings, you will discover that there is a very different world directly within your reach. You may now notice that there is a special character in each single thing that exists. It is only after you have let go of wanting to change a particular thing that you can really perceive its nature.

We can only be fully conscious of that which we don't attempt to control. When we attempt to control, we are mainly conscious of our controllingness.

* For detailed description of the benefits of meditation, see P. Carrington, *The Book of Meditation* (Shaftesbury: Element Books, 1998).

When we release on wanting to change the objects around us, the sense of wonder which makes life so fascinating for the young child is restored. Setting aside periods of time for releasing on things in our immediate environment restores a refreshing simplicity to our relationships with all things which influence our lives. After this positive kind of Releasing, when you run into the inevitable problems of the day, you will be able to release more easily on these, too. In comparison to the harmony you experienced with the world around you when you released, the "out-of-synch" nature of man-made disturbances may seem irrelevant.

Releasing can open the door to a wider and more promising perspective. It is a means of promoting the positive in your life, as well as helping you handle life's difficulties. Now the method is yours to use as you wish. I hope that your experience with it is rich and satisfying.

APPENDICES

To set up a RELEASING CHART, take a blank sheet of paper and copy the format below. The chart consists of two columns, the left column wider than the right. Above the left column is the heading, "Desired Goals." Above the right column, the heading, "Feelings."

RELEASING CHART

DESIRED GOALS	FEELINGS

Suppose that you are awaiting some good news but have not yet heard from the person involved and are beginning to feel impatient and anxious. If you were to fill in your RELEASING CHART for this, it might look like this:

DESIRED GOALS	FEELINGS
1. To hear the news (F)	Impatience
2. To have your wish to hear respected by the other person (F)	Anxiety

You will notice that two separate goals are written on your chart. We often have more than one result that we'd like to get out of a situation. When this happens, write down each of your desired goals, one under the other.

You will also notice an (F) written after each goal. This stands for "Future." The goals we need to release on may be located either in the past or in the future. "Past" goals are indicated on the chart by a (P), future goals by an (F). Indicate where "in time" the goal is located by writing either an (F) or a (P) after it.

In the right-hand column list your feelings about the situation. This helps you identify the feelings involved so you can release on them.

As an example of a goal located in the past, suppose you intended to make an important phone call earlier today but forgot to do so. It's now too late to call the person in question because they have left town. As you realize your oversight, you're annoyed at yourself and somewhat anxious about the consequences. Your RELEASING CHART for this situation might look like this:

DESIRED GOALS	FEELINGS
1. To have remembered to phone (so and so) (P)	Annoyance
	Anxiety

You'll notice that the desired goal, as written, states what you would have liked to have *had happen*. It doesn't suggest any practical plans for the future, such as obtaining the person's address or where they're traveling so you can get in touch with them. Such considerations become important only after you have been able to release on the situation (otherwise, you probably wouldn't have needed to release on it in the first place). What you list under "desired goals" is a statement which expresses your *preoccupations*—the *wanting* which takes over your mind and closes off practical alternatives.

Your RELEASING CHART gives you information on whether your goals are located in the future or in the past, keeps track of the different "layers" of Releasing, and serves as a guide for releasing on your feelings. It can be very useful to make up a chart whenever you find yourself having difficulty releasing.

Reminder: Don't release to try to control other people.

Also, it's best to release on goals for the future that seem *realistic* to you.

Realizing that you can hold on to your intention while letting go of your wish is in itself a release!

APPENDIX B

Some people *tell* themselves to "let go" when posing the Releasing question to themselves, rather than asking, "*Could* I let go?" If they say this to themselves as an easy, casual, reassuring statement, that's fine. But if they think the phrase "let go" in a demanding inner tone, it won't work. If you do this, notice how your inner voice *sounds* to you. If the tone is not demanding but friendly, then this strategy will work because it's a gentle way of reminding yourself to release. If not, go back to using the question, "Could I let go?"

APPENDIX C

When thinking the Releasing question, some people phrase it to themselves as if they were talking to another person. Instead of thinking, "Could *I* let go of such-and-such?" they say to themselves, "Could *you* let go of such-and-such?"

If you do this and it works for you, fine. Releasing is a process which you can adapt to fit your own needs. All you need to do is adhere to the basic principles of phrasing which you have learned—and take it from there.

APPENDIX D

Physical Representations of Releasing

When you demonstrate to yourself that you can "let go" easily on a *physical* level, a mental release often follows with ease no matter how blocked your Releasing process may have been just a minute before.

When heavily "locked in" and unable to release, or simply to assist the process along if you are trying to release on a complex problem, or for use as an alternate unlocking tactic, try the following:

Shoulder Breaths

Shoulder breaths are an excellent physical equivalent to the mental Releasing process. Some people use this exercise regularly along with their Releasing practice. Others reserve it for especially difficult circumstances.

Instructions:

1 With your eyes open and gazing quietly at nowhere in particular, take a breath and, as you exhale, just drop your shoulders a little further away from your ears than they were before.

2 Now take three more of these comfortable breaths at your own pace, and with each exhale, drop your shoulders still further away from your ears. It is surprising how your

shoulders seem to keep dropping more and more; allow them to do this.

3 Each time you drop your shoulders mentally repeat the words "let go" to yourself.

4 After you have done this exercise three times, ask yourself your original Releasing question once again—the question you found it difficult to release on. This simple exercise usually "greases the wheels" so that a full release follows easily and naturally even if before it was difficult.

5 If three breaths are not enough to relax you fully, keep on with this exercise, continuing to let your shoulders drop with each out-breath.

The shoulder breaths are particularly valuable because no one will notice that you are doing them. You can readily use them to assist a release when in the presence of others.

Diaphragmatic Breathing

Sit, stand or lie down comfortably and place one hand on your abdomen just below your navel. Place the other hand on the center of your upper chest.

Now pretend that you are *breathing from your belly*. Draw your breath in slowly and, as you do so, feel your belly expanding with each breath you take. Your upper chest should be relatively still as you breathe; it is not the part that is supposed to be doing the main work so that the hand that is placed there should barely move.

Let yourself enjoy the nourishment of these full, deep "belly" breaths. Imagine that you are inhaling a lovely natural scent such as the smell of a pine forest, or of new mown grass, or of lovely flowers, or of mountains, or the sea. Draw this imagined scent deeply into your lungs and fully relish it.

As you exhale fully and comfortably, the hand on your belly will move inward toward your body.

Each time you inhale you may want to repeat mentally to yourself the words "take in" or "create," and each time you exhale mentally repeat to yourself the words "let go." Some people prefer to think "let go" on the out breath, and that is all. Notice how easy it is to let your breath go out of your body after you have experienced the satisfaction of taking it in so fully.

What comes—goes—and then comes again. This is a natural process.

You can continue to breathe with diaphragmatic breathing easily and comfortably for several minutes, or you can stop any time. This exercise by itself can restore a surprising perspective and give you renewed energy and a sense of deep calm.

Complete the exercise by once again asking yourself the Releasing question that caused you difficulty. You may now be able to release fully and comfortably on it.

APPENDIX E

COMBINING MEDITATION WITH RELEASING

There are several ways to combine meditation with your Releasing practice:

1 Before releasing on a difficult problem, meditate following your accustomed routine for meditation.* Don't try to deal with the problem at hand or release on it during meditation— just let the process take you where it will. When you have finished your meditation, in an easy, off-hand manner, simply pose the difficult Releasing question to yourself once again. You will now be much more likely to release on it.

2 *After* having released successfully on a difficult problem, follow this successful release with an immediate meditation session. Meditating can remove the last remnants of a problem for you and allow your release to become permanent.

3 When you find yourself heavily locked in to a problem and unable to release on it, stop trying to release and do a two to three minute mini-meditation instead.* After you have completed your mini-meditation, again ask yourself the Releasing question you found difficult. A mini-meditation by itself, with nothing else added, can often serve as an effective unlocking tactic.

* If you do not know how to meditate, or for instruction in mini-meditations, see description in P. Carrington, *The Book of Meditation* (Shaftesbury: Element Books, 1998) or instruction on audio tapes in the *Learn to Meditate Kit* (Shaftesbury: Element Books, 1998).

APPENDIX F

FOR THOSE TAKING PRESCRIBED MEDICATION

One of the frequent benefits of the Releasing technique is the reduction of stress. It is, therefore, wise to observe some sensible precautions that apply when you undertake any program that successfully reduces stress.

Certain physical conditions for which a required dosage of medicine may have been prescribed sometimes require a reduction of drug dosage during such a program. If you are currently suffering from a physical illness which requires medication, it is advisable to have your physician monitor your physical state after you have learned how to release. Those taking medication to reduce high blood pressure, for example, may find that they require a lower dosage of medicine as a result of Releasing, and some people suffering from diabetes may require a lesser dosage of insulin. In like manner, requirements for antianxiety (tranquilizing) or antidepressive medicines may be lowered due to Releasing. Releasing may permit a lower treatment dosage with respect to other regular medications as well and occasionally permits the discontinuance of drug therapy altogether. Your physician is the one who must make this judgment, however. It is, therefore, advisable that you report to your physician any change in symptoms which you have noticed since you started releasing.

FOR THOSE REQUIRING PSYCHOTHERAPY

While Releasing can be highly effective in reducing emotional stress, it is *not* a form of psychotherapy. If you suffer from disturbing psychiatric symptoms such as depression, phobias, drug dependence, or others, you should consult a qualified professional in the mental-health field—a psychiatrist, psychologist, or other mental-health practitioner—and be guided by them. Releasing can be an excellent *adjunct* to psychotherapy, however, and you might want to lend this book to your mental-health practitioner so that he/she can help you make use of releasing to further your treatment.

TABLE OF TACTICS

WHAT TO DO IF YOU CAN'T READILY RELEASE

1   Recall the sensation of Releasing (or use your Releasing signal).
2   Let go of only 1 percent or 2 percent of wanting to change the situation (or *accept* 1 percent of the situation).
3   Let of of the *wanting* for only one or two seconds—then take it back (if you wish).
4   Let go of the *feeling* of wanting ("just the *feeling*").
5   Release on unimportant details, then return to the total situation (if you haven't already released on it automatically).
6   Locate the *feelings* involved in the situation and release on them first.
7   Handle a troublesome feeling by asking yourself to let go of wanting to change the feeling—just let it "be" without justifying it.
Or else:
Simply *let go* of the feeling.
8   Exaggerate (hold on to wanting to change—keep on wanting to change—increase your wanting to change).
9   *Forbid* yourself to release.
10   Ask yourself whether the situation has to do with wanting approval or control—then let go directly of wanting approval or wanting to control. (If it's approval, find out whether your own or others', then release on that. Also see additional approval-unlocking tactics in chapter 8.)

11 Check whether or not you are remembering that you can hold on to your intention while still releasing. If not:
   a Precede your Releasing question by thinking to yourself, "It would be useful (nice, etc.) to have such and such happen, but . . ."
   b Write on a card, "I can *hold on* to my reasonable goal of_____." Look at card as you release on the *wanting*.
12 Identify the *general* categories involved (revenge, love, justice, etc.) and let go of wanting them.
13 Change wording of your question to yourself as follows:
   a Use word *change* instead of *control* (or vice versa).
   b If approval is the problem, ask yourself if you can let go of wanting to *control* so-and-so's approval or if you can "accept the loss of 1 percent of his/her approval."
   c If you can't conceive of not wanting a condition to change, ask yourself if you can let go of "mentally pushing" for the change—or if you can accept only 1 percent of the condition.
14 Release on something entirely different which is much less important to you—or several such things—then return to your original problem.
15 Do something entirely different—exercise, etc. Then return to releasing on your problem.
16 Release on wanting to *release*.
17 If the situation is in the past, let go of wanting to "rewrite the past."
18 If the situation is anticipated, release on the *worst* that you fear happening.
19 Use a form of physical exercise that tangibly demonstrates your ability to release (see Appendix D), then ask yourself once again your "locked" Releasing question.

FOR SPECIAL SITUATIONS

Arguments

1 Release on wanting to change (control) opponent's behavior.
2 Release on unimportant details of opponent (appearance, etc.).

3   Release on wanting to protect yourself (but hold on to intention of staying safe).
4   Release on the emotions created by the argument (anger, fear, etc.).
5   Release on wanting opponent's approval (or your own).
6   Release on wanting opponent to be "fair" ("rational," etc.).
7   Pretend you are opponent; then release on wanting to control your own behavior—from their vantage point.

Pain

1   Let go of wanting to change the pain.
2   Release on wanting to change the emotions (fear, anger, depression, etc.) that accompany the pain.
3   "Flow with" the pain wordlessly.
4   Mentally divide the pain and release on each segment of it.
5   Locate bodily sensations distant from the site of pain, and release on wanting to change them.

Illness

1   Release on each aspect of illness.
2   Release on *struggling* to change illness.
3   Release on *mentally pushing* to change illness.
4   Ask yourself if you can "accept" the illness (or 1 percent of it).
5   Release on wanting to be a "perfect" nurse, helper, etc.

Death

1   Release on wanting to change the feeling of *helplessness*.
2   Ask yourself if you can "accept" that this person died (will die) or accept only 1 percent of this reality.
3   Release on needing to "understand."

SPECIAL STATES

1 *Confused by Releasing.*
   Release on wanting to change confusion (uncertainty), etc.
2 *Overwhelmed by Strong Feelings.*
   Release on wanting to change feeling of being overwhelmed.
3 *Not Wanting to Release*
   a Release on wanting to change the fact that you don't want to release.
   b Write down troubling situation and release on it *later*.
   c Forbid yourself to release.
4 *Thinking So Much About a Situation That You Can't Release on It.*
   a Release on the emotions involved instead.
   b Release on wanting to change the fact that you're thinking so much.
   c Release on *ten* things irrelevant to the issue at hand.
5 *Uncertain Whether You Have Released.*
   a Release on wanting to control whether you have released.
   b Keep on releasing anyway.
   c Reread your R-Benefits journal.
6 *Discouraged About Process*
   a Check whether you have recently been obtaining closure on your releases. Have you been devoting serious attention to releasing?
   b Release on *everything* that happens for a stated period of time, whether or not you *want* to change it.
   c Reread your R-Benefits journal.

Always remember to check to see how the situation seems to you after releasing. Has there been any change in perspective? Are there any residual problems that still need to be released on? If so, release.

RESOURCES

1 Readers may obtain two audio cassette tapes where Dr. Carrington demonstrates the tone of voice and approach she finds particularly effective for Releasing. On the tapes she leads the listener through demonstrations of the unlocking tactics, releasing on unwanted emotions, and several new approaches to Releasing. For information on Releasing tapes, contact the sources listed below.

2 Readers interested in learning a modern form of meditation to use together with their Releasing practice may obtain a course in Dr. Carrington's method, "Clinically Standardized Meditation" (CSM), taught through four audio cassettes and a step-by-step manual in the *Learn to Meditate Kit* (Shaftesbury: Element Books, 1998). You may read about all aspects of meditation and learn many unusual facts from her book *The Book of Meditation* (Shaftesbury: Element Books, 1998). Both are obtainable from your local bookstore or may be ordered from the sources listed below.

Audio cassettes and books by Patricia Carrington, Ph.D.
To obtain information on the Releasing cassettes described above, or Dr. Carrington's other training materials, contact the following centers in the United States or the United Kingdom:

Pace Educational Systems, Inc.
61 Kingsley Road
Kendall Park
NJ 08824
USA
Toll-free Tel: 1 800 297 9897
Fax: 732 297 0778
E-Mail: Carring101@aol.com

Learning for Life Ltd
The Coach House
Chinewood Manor
32 Manor Road
Bournemouth BH1 3EZ
UK
Tel/Fax: 01202 390008

CARRY A PHOTOCOPY OF THIS IN YOUR POCKET OR
PURSE AS A REMINDER TO RELEASE

RELEASING CARD
(R stands for *Releasing*)

- Recall sensation of R in past (or use Releasing signal)
- Let go of *feeling* of wanting to change—hold on to intention.
- 1 percent solution (let go of only 1 percent or "accept" 1 percent)
- "Suspend" tactic (let go for only two seconds)
- Divide-the-divide (R on small details of situation)
- Approval or control?
- Exaggeration effect
- Forbidding Tactic
- Qualifying phrase ("It would be nice to have, *but . . .*")
- R on *feeling* involved (let feeling, "be," or just let go of feeling)
- R on general category involved (revenge, love, justice, etc.)
- R on "mentally pushing"
- R on something else that can be released easily
- Take a break, then come back
- R on wanting to *release*
- R on wanting to "rewrite history"
- R on your worst fears
- Use physical exercises to demonstrate R (Appendix D)
- Do a mini-meditation

(fold)

To release in an argument:
a. R on opponent's:
   i   behavior
   ii approval
   iii "fairness"
b. R on details about him or her
c. R on wanting to protect yourself.
d. R on your feelings
e. change places with opponent; R on your own behavior

To release on pain, illness, etc.:
a. R on wanting to change the pain
b. R on wanting to change your feelings
c. "flow with" pain wordlessly
d. mentally divide pain—release on each segment
e. dispersal tactic—locate sensations distant from site of pain and release on them
f. R on mentally pushing to change illness, etc.
g. ask yourself if you can "accept" situation (or 1 percent of it)
h. R on wanting to be "perfect" nurse, helper, etc.
i. R on feeling of helplessness
j. R on need to "understand"

INDEX